INTERVIEWS WITH ICONS

Flashing on the Sixties

LISA LAW

LUMEN BOOKS

SANTA FE, NEW MEXICO

Lumen, Inc.
40 Camino Cielo
Santa Fe, New Mexico 87501
www.lumenbooks.org
ISBN 0-930829-44-1
Library of Congress Catalog Card Number 99 75420
Interviews with Icons © 2000 Lumen, Inc.
Text and photographs © 2000 Lisa Law
Photograph of Lisa Law (page 285) © 2000 Pilar Law
Photographs printed by Isgo Lepejian, Custom Lab
2411 West Magnolia Blvd., Burbank, CA 91506
Book printed by Thomson-Shore, Inc.,
7300 West Joy Road, Dexter, MI 48130-9701
Cover & Book Design: Dennis Dollens

INTERVIEWS WITH ICONS
Flashing on the Sixties

This book is
dedicated to
John Paul DeJoria,
for his unending
support and enthusi-
asm and for keeping
the spirit of the 60s
alive
in everything he
does.
Thank you, JP, for
being so far out.

Interviews with Icons

Preface

You are about to take a trip to a time and place in the human race when reality was defined corporately, politics was waged militarily, and consciousness was leapt quantumly. Welcome to the 60s. Your guides—the people who made it happen: the poets, artists, actors, musicians, comedians, philosophers, and vets who knew most intensely the pleasures of losing inno-cence, the agonies of waging war, and the joys of growing awareness and expressing commitment. Their memories make the 60s live again. Contrary to Wavy Gravy's oft-quoted dictum, "Anyone who remembers the 60s wasn't there," these people remember. Even Wavy.

For those readers who missed those expansive times, introductions may be in order. The late Allen Ginsberg is America's most popular and influential poet, while his cousin, Dr. Oscar Janiger, remains a guiding spirit of enlightenment. Dr. Janiger is the psychiatrist who, between 1958 and 1960, conducted a series of groundbreaking and mindbending experiments in which he administered LSD-25 to such creative luminaries as Cary Grant, Henry Miller, Anaïs Nin, André Previn, and Lord Buckley—with astonishing results. Not a part of those experiments but equally trippy, Wavy Gravy is a comedian/humanitarian/Hog Farm Commune founder, Ben & Jerry's ice-cream flavor, and one-time MC of the Woodstock Festival. Jahanara Romney, his wife, is a founding member of the Hog Farm Commune, director of Camp Winnarainbow, and was co-coordinator of food services for Woodstock. Peter Coyote is a well-dug actor now, but back then he did the Digging. Dennis Hopper and Peter Fonda are household names who taught America how to ride a bike. Ram Dass and Timothy Leary were Harvard professors who touched the sky and went on to become sky pilots. Paul Krassner is an author/comedian/satirist/activist whose maga-zine-turned-newsletter, *The Realist*, continues to put pop culture in its place, while Mountain Girl saw the 60s as Jerry Garcia's old lady. Ron Thelin opened our minds when he opened the doors to his Psychedelic Shop in the Haight-Ashbury. Ben Friedman is a survivor from San Francisco's Fillmore era, and Carol Hinton, Rick Klein, as well as Steve and Ina Mae Gaskin are survivors from the communes. Graham Nash, with friends Crosby & Stills, continues to make timeless music with the same exquisite harmonies they introduced at Woodstock. Vietnam vet Craig Preston blew his mind out in a war and now lives in Golden Gate Park, with hundreds of other vets. Tony Price turns nuclear bomb parts into beautiful sculptures for a newclear age free of nuclear threats. Taj Mahal, Mickey Hart, and Johnny Rivers remain unique American artists, while Simone Ellis, Carl Gottlieb, and Viola Spolin remind us to laugh and look inward. Finally, Pilar Law provides a bridge for the 60s into the 90s with her remarkable insights.

Listen to their voices. They speak for their age—the 20th century's age of reason—that very far-out time when a rut became a groove.

Tom Pope

Foreword

Ever since I was a child, I have believed in magic. To this day I still use a magic wand and also make them for children I know. Children seem to understand magic more than adults do, and by making them magic wands I give them a little more power. They usually toddle off, waving their wands at their parents or at their fish or dog. It's a beautiful sight.

After my first book, *Flashing on the Sixties*, was published, which was a magical event in itself, I was persuaded to go a step further and film a documentary of the 60s. I had shot a one-hour silent film of the Woodstock Festival in 1969 and a few other small pieces, but I usually stuck to my 35 mm cameras for catching special moments in my life. Being a Pisces, I am easily persuaded to do things at the drop of a hat. Sometimes I don't even think first. I jump right into it head first. One would think that the older one gets the more cautious one becomes, but that doesn't apply to me, or at least not yet. Maybe when I reach sixty-four.

My intent, with my film, was to record stories from the same people who were in my book, many of them icons and movers and shakers. I let them know that the film would be a vehicle for them to share with others their thoughts, dreams, and remembrances, and how these all fit into the history of our generation. I have found that most people love telling their stories—they just don't have anyone to tell them to. Everyone was delighted to take part.

As luck would have it, I had a little extra money and started filming right away with a small crew. This was in 1989. We were getting some good interviews with Taj Mahal, Ram Dass, Dennis Hopper, Graham Nash, David Crosby, and Allen Ginsberg when I ran out of money. This is where the big magic came in. I don't know if it was good karma or good luck, or maybe both, when my dear friends Jack Mahoney and Louise Scott gave my proposal to John Paul DeJoria.

I had never met John Paul, but I had been using his hair products (Paul Mitchell) for years and loved them. He had made it big in the cosmetics industry, starting at the bottom and going to the top. He is a very determined man and goes after things with great gusto. The first time I talked to JP he said, "If I were to do a movie about the 60s, I would do it just like you are, and Jack says you are a nice person, so I'm going to invest in your movie. I'm going away for the holidays, so come and get it."

I had learned a few years before that if you ask for what you want you will undoubtedly get it. He gave me just what I needed, and the next year was a great learning experience. John Paul and I still do many projects together.

With my friends' help in writing, filming, producing, and editing, we were able to get some truly fine interviews down on celluloid. What was fun about making *Flashing on the Sixties* was weaving those different opinions and images together to make a cohesive document.

I went on with my life for ten years, raising my children, doing exhibitions, giving lectures, selling photographs, shooting concerts, raising money for Native American causes, driving aid to El Salvador, helping to start a telecommunications company, then buying some land with my kids, taking care of my mom, and building a house. And then I realized we were about to hit the year 2000 and the millennium. Our friends were disincarnating at a rapid rate—Tim Leary, Allen Ginsberg, William Burroughs, Jerry Garcia, Bill Graham, Ron Thelin. They were gone. I could never talk to them again. No more sitting around chewing the fat, listening to great poetry readings and dissertations.

I suddenly got the urge to share again all the interviews from ten years before, and what I was short on, I figured I could get. I called my dear and trusty friend Tom Pope, who had edited the *Flashing on the Sixties* book with me. We spent a year trading off floppy disks and e-mailing each other until we had honed all the interviews from the film, called a few friends for some final questions, and got one last interview with Simone Ellis, a great writer and poet and historian herself. She was very happy to be included in the text.

It was more magic and a touch of karma that brought me together with Ronald Christ and Lumen, Inc. I gave Ronald my manuscript on our first meeting. He said he picked it up that night and didn't put it down till he was finished. That is a good sign, a really good sign. And now we want to share it with you.

INTERVIEWS WITH ICONS

VIOLA SPOLIN

*Viola Spolin was the mother of Improvisational Theater. When
I was six, I studied under her at the Young Actors Company in
Hollywood and got some of my first lessons in self-reliance
and self-esteem. I asked her, after I had acted in* Once upon a
Clothesline, *"Was I good?"*
*"You had good point of concentration and stage presence,"
she said.*
"But was I good?" I repeated.
"You had focus, and you shared your voice."
"But was I good?" I insisted.
"Yes, you were good," she said with a big smile.
*In 1989 I asked Viola if she would allow me to tape what she
felt captured the soul of the 60s in a couple of sentences. She
was suffering from a series of strokes but was able, with the
encouragement of her husband, Kolmus, to recite for me these
wonderful lines. That was the last time she was to be in front
of a camera.*

Do not consider present time as clock time, but rather as a
timeless moment when all are mutually engaged in experienc-

ing an experience, the outcome of which is yet unknown. You're right there. You're connected and you don't know what's going to happen and that's where the excitement is and that's where the spontaneity is and that's where the vitality is and that's where the joy is and that's what happiness is and that's the everlasting, never-ending spiral.[1]

1. Viola Spolin. *Improvisations for the Theater*. Evanston: Northwestern University Press. 1963.

ALLEN GINSBERG & OSCAR JANIGER

When my crew and I went to interview Oscar Janiger at his home in Santa Monica, California in 1989, his cousin Allen Ginsberg was visiting. It was perfect having the two of them together to bounce ideas off each other. Both were pioneers of the psychedelic era: Oscar doing studies in mind-altering drugs, and Allen writing mind-altering poetry.

Allen: Was your first LSD trip more a reconfirmation of experiences you'd already intuited, or your first entry into that area?

Oscar: Well, the first experiences that I had—the only frame-work they would fit into, unfortunately—was a psychopatho-logical one. In other words, I thought that these trips I had made as a child, well, I thought I was crazy then.

Allen: So you had other visions of reality as a child, and you

---

Oscar Janiger (*right*) holds pictures representing an experiment that was done by a series of artists between 1955 and 1962. The picture on the left shows the artist's painting of a doll prior to taking LSD, and the one on the right his painting of the same subject during the LSD experience.

weren't able to relate them or absorb them into your everyday working practical consciousness.

Oscar: I kept them at the limits of myself, because I thought they represented some abnormality.

Allen: In hindsight now, what do you think of your earliest experiences without drugs?

Oscar: Well, I think that whatever membrane separated me from this other space was more permeable, and I was getting these messages and very often looking at the world in these altered ways—beautifully and illuminatedly—and I began to think: if I had had modest guidance, I could have dealt with that and perhaps moved it right through my entire life experience.

Allen: That's interesting. I had a similar natural experience of mind-manifesting awareness or vestation or a sense of the vastness of the universe or a sense of the ancient kinship, and I had no terminology or institutional structure in which to place it or interpret it or of knowing any way to interpret it. So I thought it was a hallucinatory or freakish thing or the opposite, a divine and selected experience. I had to either think of it in terms of psychopathology or mystical experience, rather than simple, ordinary mind—an incident in ordinary mind that was uncommon. So it wasn't until checking out peyote in 1951 and then mescaline and LSD later that I was able to return to that kind of experience and reconstitute or approximate it. But I thought the natural experience was more ample, actually. Is that your experience?

Oscar: Yes, that's my experience too.

Allen: It's a catalyst to approximating a break out of quotidian, limited scope.

Lisa: How important is it for us to reach the other world?

Allen: Well, when you call it "the other world," it makes it sound much too mystical. It's this world, except a world that's not often seen because you're not taking the time to notice it.

You could probably also reach some approximation of that kind of opening of mind through meditation. Not so abruptly and not so interestingly or so sensationally, but, with meditation, over the longrun you could develop a sense of the vast and a sense of kinship. I don't think the LSD experience is that otherworldly or unnatural. It may seem so because it's such an abrupt transition, but a slow training could bring something similar. Not exactly the same thing. It's pretty spectacular.

Lisa: Remember how LSD came into the 60s, its effects on the culture?

Oscar: Well, the complications of what caused the 60s, the social/cultural factors behind the 60s, is very complex. And I can only say that the ingredient of the consciousness-changing drugs found a sort of ready partnership with whichever of those forces were beginning to burgeon and bring on the social and cultural changes. There was a point of interdigitation between those two forces, and in the end they became sort of a mesh. So much so that it would be hard to say what influence one thing had on the other.

Lisa: If the times were not what they were, LSD would not have had its interdigitating effect, and if LSD hadn't been there, then the social change wouldn't have taken that direction. Can we say that?

Oscar: Yes, you certainly can.

Lisa: A wedding between forces brought on a quantitative leap into a change.

Oscar: That famous quantitative leap, which has been leapt so many times in rhetoric. All of the factors that went into making for the social/cultural changes that are characterized by the phenomenon of the 60s were on the rise, and, roughly around that time, there was the advent of the use of these drugs. So it seems that they met and made a ready partnership at that point. And much of the coloration of the 60s was due to the art of the drug activity. And the reverse: the way in which the drugs were employed and found their special destinies was also part of the substrata of the cultural changes as well.

Allen: But were there specific cultural changes you had in mind?

Oscar: Well, that people were breaking loose from the shackles of the 50s, and the social/cultural cycle was now moving to a more liberated frame of mind; and that the oppressive sexual restrictions were now loosening. The Wolfenden Report came out and was very important. It was clear that we wanted to be out of the constraints of the repression of the 50s, and I think that was one of the forces. Another—or two or three—I'll leave to the social historians. I'm not that adept at that, but I know it was on that soil that the consciousness-altering drugs fell. And they germinated in that soil and gave point and direction to the way this ferment went on.

Allen: I would add to that background, natural evolutionary or biological or historical development that initiated a new consciousness, in any case, without the psychedelics—a consciousness of this being a fresh planet or of our being on spaceship earth or that we were in the midst of a universe, of a vast universe, and I think that was catalyzed maybe two decades earlier by the explosion of the bomb, the splitting of matter, just at the time that Albert Hoffman was discovering LSD. It is interesting that the splitting of the atom and the opening of the mind occurred in the evolutionary moment simultaneously and as opposites: one to threaten and destroy the world if human aggression went that way, the other to explore the nature of the mind itself and open up a new space in the mind; one closing off the space of historical existence by threatening the planet with extinction, the other opening up a way of examining our consciousness and examining our own aggression and maybe reaching more kinship between inside and outside that would dissolve the territorial aggression of protecting the self with a great defensive anger—finally.

So I think the bomb made it obvious that the world was threatened and that it was one world and one world of interrelated consciousness. By the time the 60s had come along, there was an awareness of the ecological threat, not only of the bomb but also the ecological threat to the planet. I think Rachel Carson's *The Sea around Us* was published in the late 40s, and people were beginning to pick up on the fact that we could extinct the earth.

So I would say that the sexual revolution was preceded by a kind of opening of spirit, or spiritual liberation, which led to liberation of the word in the late 50s, which then led to liberation of communication and then black lib, sexual lib, women's lib, gay lib, old folks lib, indigent lib, animal liberation, liberation of earth from hyper-industrialization. Those were the evolutionary or social grounds into which the seed of a catalyst like LSD was dropped, and so, immediately, a lot of people were able to potentiate or share a new and almost microscopic awareness of the environment and the threat to the environment. I would say that LSD was almost like a foam—like the literature was, or even as the 60s were—like froth or foam on a larger biological wave of self-preservation at a time of threat to the entire ecosystem of the planet. Maybe that's too large a scope, but those were the preoccupations of the people who took acid: a sudden realization of the integral nature of the planet, of the whole earth. The Whole Earth sense.

Oscar: And such was my thing. But I'd like to shift briefly to another, I think, important emphasis, and that is biological. The new work going on, the chemistry of the mind, for example, began. Work in which we were re-evaluating the effects of mescaline, for example. And we were beginning a whole new idea in psychology-of-consciousness research, which is to say that we began to see ourselves as an instrument that measures everything and all reality, and this was also reinforced by the new ideas in physics, so that we were the measure of all things, and our perceptions began to come under closer scrutiny, and those perceptions, we found, could be altered. The notion that consciousness is not a static phenomenon, but one that is in constant flux, began to give rise to the modern idea of so-called psychological-consciousness theory. So I'd like to say that was another very important leg of the chair that we were looking at.

Allen: What aspect of physics is it that says that scientific data is not data until there is an observer or a subject reacting with it?

Oscar: Well, the Heisenberg Uncertainty Principle would fit

there, and Einstein's notion of the . . .

Allen: The measuring instrument determines the appearance of the phenomenal world.

Oscar: The whole notion of relativity draws from that.

Allen: And that seemed to fit in very much with the subjective experience of acid, that . . .

Oscar: . . . that reality itself may be relative.

Allen: I once asked Dr. Hoffman what he had learned from LSD, and he said that there are many different realities. And then I said, "Well, how many times did you take LSD?" and he said, "Oh, maybe eight times." And I said, "So few times?" And he said, "Well, how many times do I need to get the same experience? I already got the idea." His main perception was the relativity of what reality is supposed to be, depending on the observer, I guess. I think that was one of the big insights, that we are part of the universe, an active part of the universe that influences how our world and how our ecosystem and how the environment moves, that we interchange and inter-react with the environment, and we have a decisive role in it, so that the environment becomes part of ourselves. That was what you referred to in the breakdown between subject and object.

Oscar: It made a good deal of difference in a number of quarters, notably in my field, where there was a much greater tolerance for ambiguities of consciousness. For example, the thing that happened to Allen and me—the judgments that were imposed on us—were reflections of what we heard around us: that you were crazy, queer, weird, and the like. And "weird" and "crazy" in my time changed from pejorative terms to kind of affectionate terms . . . if somebody was weird, they were fun. That to me tells a very big story.

Allen: Like "freak," the word "freak" . . .

Oscar: . . . became suddenly something that was tolerant and tolerable . . .

Allen: . . . humorous . . .

Oscar: . . . and it relieved them of all the problems that you found in people who for various degrees of eccentricity suffered a great deal, as a consequence, from their self-approbation and also their expectations of what others would think of them.

Allen: So there was a shift toward self-empowerment of people who felt that they were pushed outside of the normal, human social realm.

Oscar: That kind of experience, in primitive cultures, happens all the time. You know, like Bellow's Henderson, the Rain King.

Allen: There always was, in primitive cultures, some form of visionquest, where you isolated yourself from the community, went up on the mountain, learned your own song or were spoken to by the animal spirits or had some contact with nature. We didn't have that in American culture, except for the sort of destructive thing that you might have seen with the Jimmy Dean movies—kids playing chicken with automobiles, challenging death.

Oscar: There's an interesting exception to that in the great feasts—the Mardi Gras and those things which I call "social dreaming"— shifts in attitude that are extremely basic.

Allen: So I was pointing out that your notion of liberation of . . .

Oscar: . . . I called it "social dreaming."

Allen: So, Dr. Janiger was saying that the institutionalization of social dreaming found political form in the mid 60s with the political slogan, "All power to the imagination," which meant breaking out of the bounds of the rational, chauvinistic sense of identity and opening up the imagination to what we really were and what the universe was and what our role in the universe was—to a more expansive and more experimental set of worlds and set of realities. All power to the imagination, meaning: how do we get out of the Cold War without blowing up the earth? How do we get out of overpopulation? How do we get out of the boredom of television? How does the individual imagination get liberated and self-empowered? And then, how do you bring it down to earth, and one of Kerouac's answers to that was, "Walking on water wasn't built in a day." Those are two good slogans from the 60s—"All power to the imagination," which is political, like "All power to the people," and "Walking on water wasn't built in a day."

Lisa: What were the people who went back to the land trying to prove?

Allen: Did you know many people like that?

Oscar: I knew some, but probably you have more acquaintances.

Allen: Well, the primary thing was the realization of the ecological fix. The primary reason for going back to the land and re-inhabiting the country was the realization of the ecological fix that we were in: that small-scale, appropriate technology, organic gardening, and some 19th-century technologies, like windmills and hydraulic rams and whatnot, were, in the long run, as conservation, much more healthy and sensible than large-scale agribusiness, which leads to, in a half century, desertification and the despoiling and exhaustion of the aquifer below the surface of the earth and the pollution of the rivers and the lakes due to large-scale industrial-farming wastes. The use of nitrates and fertilizers—large-scale agribusiness fertilization—was seen as a kind of shooting speed into the veins of the land, and it finally turns the land into a kind of blotting paper, but destroys all the microorganisms—the worms, organic life that makes soil fertile. So that was a part of it.

    Second, the overpopulation of the cities and the need to get out from the noise and the crime and the dope and the hyperactive business mentality of the cities and return to some healthy observation of nature, like the seasons, to see stars, the moon, sun, passage of seasons, and the natural growth and flowering of plants. Like in the suburbs, as Oscar has—he has a whole garden in which he has very selective flowers that bloom in each different season, and he knows the cycle. It's our natural inclination to keep track of the clock of nature, so to speak, rather than to lose sight of it in the middle of the megalopolitan wastelands, so it's getting back really to our own roots as they say—literally, *roots*. That's part of it.

Third was a desire for privacy, I think. The other was a realization that a police state might come down with a hyper-mechanization of the absolute state caused by the absolute nature of the bomb, that the extreme, deathly nature of the bomb would force a surveillance state, because any terrorist can make a bomb, so pretty soon the state has to inspect everybody's tipi.

That was one. Wanting to get out from under the oncoming surveillance society.

Another was a desire to smoke dope in private and peace and raise your own marijuana as a small-scale, cash crop to save the family farm. The old Norman Rockwell Christmas dinner family farm, which would be disappearing under the pressure of agribusiness, might have been saved had the government allowed a free market of a small-scale cash crop of cannabis.

And there was a desire for communes, new kinds of experiments with the family structure, and peace and quiet in the rural areas. And just a desire to run naked in the woods, I think, was part of it; to get back to nature, as Walt Whitman wanted to when he wrote about how great it felt to feel the breezes in the air on his naked skin. Which everybody likes. And organic food and also a desire to try psychedelics in a comfortable home environment out in nature rather than in the clanking city full of electronics. I think that was a very big catalyst. LSD was probably a great catalyst of the return to the land, for all these organic reasons—food and whatnot—but also for a place to experience the psychedelic expansion of mind or mind manifestation: leaves, trees, flowers, deer and raccoon, and mountains and rolling hills. It was probably a great reason which fit in very well with the realization that earth was threatened by human excrement, by the lack of recycling, by garbage. LSD made people much more sensitive to the garbage problem, the poison-garbage problem, the plastic-garbage problem—in fact, the notion of plastic itself. Plastic universe, plastic thought. Plastic television imagery, I think, rises out of that LSD culture of the 60s. The realization of the inimical nature of plastic: that in itself it is not organic. There's something wrong with dredging up the carbonized, pressured detritus of dead bodies, of organic wastes, and spewing it out in the atmosphere in funny little odd homunculus dolls made out of plastic.

Oscar: Also a very important aspect is the acceptance of intermediate images instead of direct experience, and that's very well expressed in the joke where a man sees a woman coming down the street with a very attractive child and says, "Well, that's a beautiful little girl you have there." And she says, "Oh that's nothing, mister, you should see her photographs." That really goes to the heart of the matter in many cases, where you substitute all of this intermediate experience for direct experience, and LSD provides one of the opportunities for direct, intrinsic experience.

Lisa: What do you think Woodstock's effect was on the nation?

Allen: I was just thinking of that. The deep thing, both with acid and the Be-Ins and with Woodstock, was some kind of faith in the sacred nature of human soul or human spirit and the sacred nature of the phenomenal world—that we were basically good and intelligent. The human race was basically good, intelligent, capable of vulnerability and appreciation, of pain and suffering, and willing to try to relieve the pain and suffering of others. A kind of universal bodhisattva impulse of wanting to be of help rather than inflicting more pain, more damage, more garbage. So both the Be-In in San Francisco and Woodstock were triumphs of masses of people being able to assemble and live with each other and help each other for a short period of time without violence and without animosity and without deliberate aggression and infliction of wounds, illness, knife fights, atom bombs. And that was what they were notorious for.

The kitchen yoga cleanup after the Be-In in San Francisco in 1967, where we left the park in better shape than before we came in, is an example, and so is the mutual sharing of acid, sharing of food, sharing of tenderness at Woodstock. The prevailing theory of the 50s, and later under the Reagan years, was a more Darwinian notion: survival-of-the-fittest, dog-eat-dog, cutthroat competition and rivalry as the main commercial and social relationship between human beings. Whereas the Buddhist view and, I think, ultimately the Western Christian view as well, is that there is some innate intelligence and awareness of pain and empathy in human beings, both to their own selves and to others and to nature, that in favorable conditions can be brought out. Or the opposite take, which supplements it, is what Burroughs says: "Human beings can't be expected to act like human beings under inhuman circumstances. You don't threaten them with a bomb or starvation or police or concentration camps. Naturally they'll not be able to act normally." But unobstructed human behavior, unobstructed by neurosis or a police state or compulsion, generally would be friendly. Why not? There is the alternative police-state view that everybody is unfriendly and that you can't give acid out because people are too evil and that they'll kill each other and kill themselves.

Lisa: What was a Beatnik?

Allen: "Beatnik" was a newspaper term, invented by a newspaper columnist, to convey the idea of those poets or literary people in San Francisco in the late 50s who were so far out of this world they were like Sputnik. It was a combination of Sputnik, the Russians' rocket, and the Beat Generation—so, Beatnik. It was a way of stereotyping. The inventor of that phrase was Herb Caen, the gossip columnist. Then the question was: would a generation of more sensitive people—or people who were beginning to get sensitive to the environment, the ecology, the bomb, their own self-empowerment, to psychedelia, to poetry, to a breakthrough in poetry as well as mind—were they going to sit around and fight over the use of the term or give it value by enriching it with their intelligence and their artworks? I think the general idea was to transform the word, make it a valued word in the long run. Might take a couple of generations.

Lisa: What's a hippie?

Allen: That's 60s.

Oscar: I don't know the origin of that word, I have no idea.

Allen: A "hipi" in the Wolloff language, which was adopted by black American musicians, means musician. If you look in Robert Thompson's book on African rituals, a hipi is a Flash of the Spirit. He traces the word back to musicians. A hipi was somebody who was in on, or knowledgeable, and had been initiated into, sacred rituals. I think it's something in that direction.

Lisa: We're going to do this list now. It's free association. If it turns you on, do it.

Allen: OK.

Lisa: Kennedy.

Allen: Shot in the head by the CIA while it was on an acid trip trying to turn psychedelia into a war weapon.

Lisa: Kerouac.

Allen: Sat down at midnight and wrote sound sketches of all the phenomenal noises of the universe outside of his porch in Ozone Park, Long Island . . . listening to the vowels come up through his throat.

Lisa: The 50s.

Allen: Well, there's a certain amount of hot-dog cha-cha in Eisenhower reading *Lady Chatterly's Lover* at his desk, given to him by Postmaster General Arthur Sommerfield, who had underlined the dirty words. And Eisenhower said, "We can't have this. Terrible." Meanwhile, Dulles refused to shake hands with Ho Chi Min at the Geneva Conference, and that led to the Vietnam War. Dulles thought Communism was a monolith and didn't realize that the Vietnamese and the Chinese were fighting already.

Lisa: Pot.

Allen: Well, as my father said, "You always want to have lots of pot in every chicken."

Lisa: Jazz.

Allen: Was a spontaneous speech of musicians through their
birdlike saxophones, imitating what they heard on the street
corner, which Kerouac then transformed back to the cadences
and rhythms and babbles from your spontaneous tongue.

Lisa: Dylan.

Allen: Dylan was a great prophet, rose up in the West to be
one of the greatest blues singers of all time—and talk about
"The motorcycle black madonna / Two-wheeled gypsy queen /
And her silver-studded phantom cause / The gray flannel
dwarf to scream."

Lisa: The Beatles.

Allen: The Beatles started this opening up the top of the skull
by a kind of high-masculine woodle that brought out all the
feminine nature—as the blacks had already done in the blues,
as Screamin' Jay Hawkins had—the exhibition of intelligent
sensibility with a falsetto. My sentences are getting too long.

Lisa: No, this is fun. It's working just like I want it to. The
Beatles . . .

Allen: The Beatles bonded their comradeship in a high
feminine woodle, acknowledging the feminine principle in
themselves with "I wanna hold your hand, Yeaaaaah." So it
was sound that came off the top of the skull and turned all men
on to their own softness and gentility and delicacy of mind.

Lisa: Emmett Grogan.

Allen: Emmett Grogan was a funny kind of macho long-hair
who wanted to give away everything for free, but also was
contending for superiority and leadership too, while he was
saying, "Don't follow leaders." But he was a good conspiracy
artist, actually. He realized that the Israelis had stolen a lot of
plutonium to make their own bombs, and he also realized that
the CIA had delivered a pound of heroin to him to destroy the
Diggers, of which he was one of the leaders.

Lisa: Vietnam.

Allen: Vietnam was like a great big mistake, because we thought that if we put the Christians in there they would fight the Commies, not realizing we should have given a couple of billion dollars to Ho Chi Min to fight China if that's what we wanted.

Lisa: Hell's Angels.

Allen: Hell's Angels . . . Well, they needed wings, they didn't have quite a large enough wingspread, so they could never get on the stage of Radio City and make music.

Lisa: Corso.

Allen: Gregory Corso—pure velvet, poet's poet. John Keats's return, fried shoes and aluminum electricities.

Lisa: My Lai.

Allen: My Lai Incident. Well, yes, we had to kill the entire town in order to save it from itself.

Lisa: Tim Leary.

Allen: Timothy Leary's a good football coach for kicking the psychedelic or consciousness ball around the field and leading the team onward, but I think probably you need a referee too.

Lisa: Nancy Reagan.

Allen: Nancy Reagan discovered Noriega only yesterday, and so her anti-dope, just-say-no business is a hype really. She's addicted to power.

Lisa: John Lennon.

Allen: Lennon was an excellent revolutionary musician who applied his own personal breath-spirit to redeeming the black-race blues and making it popular among the Chinamen.

Lisa: The Tao.

Allen: The Tao is an unraveling pivot, and if you sit on it you can watch your breath.

Lisa: The 60s were . . .

Allen: The 60s were . . .

> *The 60s were*
>> *an explosion of penguins into*
>> *the tropical atmosphere of belly button.*
> *The 60s were*
>> *ecology realized in your backyard garden*
>> *watching a worm turn.*
> *The 60s were*
>> *the breakthrough from the heavy metal crust*
>> *of hyper-industrialized civilization*
>> *back to the garden of Eden,*
>> *with Michael and the sword*
>> *or Gabriel*
>> *or somebody*
>> *trying to tell you to get in there*
>> *and get out,*
>> *but whatever you're going to do,*
>> *don't destroy the entire world.*
>> *Or maybe take a note from the serpent*
>> *and eat the apple of knowledge.*
> *The 60s were*
>> *a lot of unnecessary war and*
>> *a lot of necessary peacefulness and*
>> *a lot of very necessary copulation.*
> *The 60s were*
>> *spiritual liberation,*
>> *liberation with word,*
>> *black liberation,*
>> *liberation of women,*
>> *liberation of men,*
>> *gay liberation.*
> *The 60s were*
>> *flower power symbolizing strength*
>> *of earth, ecology, wisdom of earthly*

relations,
interknit minds and mouths over centuries.
The 60s were
psychedelics, ending the Vietnam War
and landing on the moon.
The 60s were
a youth nation and an old age nation getting
together
in a marriage in the 70s
and then a divorce in the 80s
and then a remarriage in the 90s
with the birds and the bees.
The 60s were
fried shoes, demonic industries, satanic
Ayatollahs
coming up from the rear
and a lot of great poetry.
The 60s were
actually San Francisco Renaissance and
ripening a Beat generation into public
consciousness
and turning into political hippies.
The 60s were
the death of Neal Cassady
and Kerouac drinking himself to death
having left behind an angelic scroll.

ALLEN GINSBERG

*Allen invited us to his house in New York in 1989, at the time
of the SEVA Foundation's benefit concert ("seva" is Sanskrit
for service) for the homeless at the Cathedral of St. John the
Divine. He was working with his assistant, Robert, in his small
office off the kitchen, then announced that he had to go to
Brooklyn College, where he was teaching, and we could do the
interview on the way. We piled into a cab, cameraman in the
front seat, me holding the light in the back seat and asking
questions. Allen was so amused, he took out his camera and
shot us shooting him.*

Lisa: Can you tell me about the evolution of your work? And
are the 60s worth the nostalgia?

Allen: First of all, you are preoccupied with the 60s, but I am
not. My first book and best known poem was written in the
50s about the 40s. I'm more of a curve beginning with the 50s
and rooted in my experience as a kid in the 40s.

"Howl," which is the best-known poem I've written,
was written in 1955 and published in 57. "Kaddish," which
was a more ripe and a larger poem, and maybe a better one,

was written in the early 60s and the later 60s. I had a lot of antiwar poems, and a well-known book called *The Fall of America* about the decline of the American empire, the moral decline as well as the physical defeat.

In the 70s I was very much involved with Buddhist meditation and was working at Naropa Institute in Boulder, Colorado with a Tibetan Lama, the Venerable Chogyam Trungpa Rinpoche, who was my teacher for meditation. We founded the first Buddhist college accredited in the Western World, and that took up most of my energy. I have worked there from 74 to the present, and I lived there from 78 to 84. Then I came back to New York. At the moment I'm involved with photography, putting on photography shows—forty years of snapshots, amateur snapshots. I'm also teaching at Brooklyn College, teaching at Naropa Institute, writing poetry, and putting out big books with Harper & Row: *Collected Poems*, 1947-1980, *Deliberate Prose*, which came out in 84, *White Trout*, poems from 80 to 85, and then an anniversary edition of "Howl."

I've been traveling a lot to Russia and China, Eastern and Central Europe, Nicaragua, working occasionally with Ernesto Cardenal, the poet minister of culture, sort of trying to encourage America to lay hands off the Nicaraguan situation, and I've been making music with various musicians: Don Cherry, Bob Dylan occasionally did back-up guitar, Elvin Jones on drums, and Old John Hammond, who produced a record for me in 82. And now I'm working with a group of very intelligent rock musicians for a continuation of the old poetry-jazz: spoken poetry with jazz music. So the main activities are music, poetry, photography, teaching, and, primarily, writing.

What was interesting in the 60s was that the private insights of older people in their forties and fifties came to the surface. The poetry in the 50s reached general consciousness in the 60s, so that the realization of the possible death of the planet, the ecological fix, the greenhouse effect, the depletion of the ozone layer—all were understood by the avant garde, both in poetry and the sciences, back in the 60s. It had an effect on politics and on public thinking, so that the realization of this as a fresh planet that was in danger was an insight of the 60s which was worldwide but which then was ignored or denied, sort of like an alcoholic denies his habit. There was a sense of denial on the part of the political world and maybe the middle class. They didn't want to face the facts.

By the 80s, the ecological threat had become media property and had become disseminated sufficiently so that everybody got hip to some extent whether or not they wanted to act on it. But the main insight, which is that we were sentient beings on a living planet and that we were destroying our planet, was the breakthrough of the 60s, and an understanding that came through in the later 80s more consciously.

Lisa: Do you think that people are nostalgic about the 60s?

Allen: I don't think it's so much a nostalgia for the 60s that everybody's after. What it is is an attempt to recover the insight of the 60s, which is a realistic insight that has been denied by the war party all along—the people who see the national security threat as Russia. Now that that's dissolved, that veil of delusion is more or less dispersed. The more horrific international security threat of earth, air, fire, and water being tainted is understood. Earth—desertification, the cutting of the forests, the poisoning of the ground with nuclear and petrochemical wastes. Air—the ozone depletion and the acid rain and the greenhouse effect. Water—the death of the North Sea and many oceans. Fire—the tainting of our energy sources through petrochemicals, which cause the greenhouse effect, and nuclear, which causes universal radioactivity. So everybody finally has the alchemical elements and the practical elements, the human elements understood as being threatened.

[*Looking out car window*] This is Ocean Parkway on the way to Brooklyn College from Manhattan. Not much traffic. This used to be a very nice residential neighborhood. It still is, actually, because as Manhattan gets fuller and more crowded, the rents go up. [*Talks to driver*: Do you know where Foster Avenue is? OK, take a left on Foster and go up to 18th, and then we take a right for one block and then a left on 27th, but I'll keep you informed.]

I think what happened was that the 60s were the breakthrough, in public, of the essential insights relating to saving the planet from both nuclear and other manmade holocausts and genocides and species chauvinisms, destroying the substrate that we live off—the human substrate as well as the natural, ecological one—and that's taken plenty of time to ripen. Whereas Kerouac said in 1960, when Timothy Leary first gave him some psilocybin, "Walking on water wasn't built in a day," so it's taken all this time for the awareness to go around the world and come back and ripen. There's a tremendous denial in the 80s, so I don't know. Maybe it will take to the 90s for people to begin acting on the insights that they've got already. Otherwise, I guess the game is up for humanity. But it does seem to be like shit-or-get-off-the-pot in terms of conservation, awareness, and curbing population growth, and just the development of some kind of basic gentility toward each other and toward nature. I guess gentility is the key, and that was one of the problems of the 60s: the gentility of the Beat Generation was overwhelmed by the rancor and animosity of left-wing, Marxist-oriented politics at a time when Communism had bankrupted itself with both Stalin and Mao, so that a sort of bureaucratic political solution was looked for instead of a personal solution. But the universe is personal, and that was probably the insight of the 60s—or the 40s for that matter, or maybe the 20s with Einstein—that the universe is personal. It isn't a machine, and to try to treat it like a machine, like the capitalists and Communists have tried to do, has only made the situation worse. [*To driver*: Take a left here and go up to 28th and Glenwood.]

Lisa: You have been doing a lot of photography during all these years.

Allen: Well, you know, I've got a camera, and I've been taking little snapshots for the last 30 years or so, well since 1945-46-47, so I have photographs of Burroughs and Kerouac and all the company of Beat poets from the 50s. Burroughs and Kerouac from the 40s and early 50s and Snyder, Whalen, and many other friends who were involved in the literary world to the present. And I'm working with Robert Frank. Around 1984, I suddenly became a shutterbug and got ambitious and began having good prints made by a guy named Brian Graham, who Robert Frank had worked with in printmaking. So I've had shows with the photographs.

There's now something like 35,000 images, and they're all on the computer, or numbered at any rate. And there are probably about a thousand or fifteen hundred of them that

I've made—11 x 14 or 8 x 10 or 16 x 20 prints. So I've had various shows over the last couple of years—at the Fogg in Cambridge and the Dallas Museum of Art, the Holly Solliman Gallery in New York, and sort of an elite gallery in Washington—Middendorf—and a traveling show that went from Arfus, Denmark through Krakow and Warsaw in Poland. I'm now preparing for a show in Hanover with a big catalogue put out in Berlin, and that will circulate around the next couple of years, toward the beginning of the 90s, in middle-Europa. And a large book put out by Twelve Trees Press is about finished, except for some literary material to add to the back of the book. So that's sort of become an expensive hobby in my sixties.

Lisa: How old are you?

Allen: Sixty-two now, sixty-three in a half year.

Lisa: One more thing: The 60s were . . . You can do it five times: the 60s were this, the 60s were that—whatever you think.

Allen: The 60s is somebody else's poem. Sometimes a corny one and sometimes a rancorous one. The 60s is a nostalgic trap. Although it had some virtuous moments of awareness, [*To driver*: Take a sharp right here.] The 60s took a sharp right after in the 70s and went into the Nixon/Reagan/Bush era because the American public didn't want to swallow the 60s. The 60s were a time of a planetary vibe. [*To driver*: We'll get out here.] The 60s were where everybody said, "We'll get out here and cure the planet." The 60s were the beginning of dharma, sitting on your behind in America. The 60s were the beginning of Buddha dharma growth. The 60s were an octopus on the moon squid's head with Einstein having a bad dream. [*To driver*: How much do I owe you?]

RON THELIN

Ron and his brother, Jay, started The Psychedelic Shop in the Haight-Ashbury in 1966, and Ron and his wife, Marsha, and their kids lived down the hill from Tom and me in Forest Knolls in Marin County, California. The Thelin brothers helped initiate us into the Haight when we first arrived, and we became very good friends. We interviewed Ron, with Marsha at his side, in 1987, at their house in Forest Knolls.

Lisa: Tell me about yourself.

Ron: My brother and I were, oh! turned on by LSD—that was a real rug-pulling experience. The Chalice, I think, is the best description of what LSD was. It made one see, hear, taste, touch, smell in a highly sensitive and sort of breathtaking new way. If people were locked into a job identity or some kind of pattern of identity and couldn't free their time to surrender to the experience, then it could become a freak-out, because your normal mode of thought—how you handle form in daily routine—could be stopped by the catalyst of LSD, could be suspended. You were still you, but then you started sensing another self, one that was in touch with the senses. So I think that LSD was a profound chemical that came along, and there were other chemicals also, and we explored them. There wasn't a fear in the 60s of exploring—there was adventure and an experimental frame of mind, and people wanted to be their own laboratories, to know their own experience, based on their own experience, I think. That was one of the effects on me. So it was a real self-revelation, a real turn-on, something like a true self. It was such a profound experience, and it seemed it was happening with many other people as well. A sense was looming of some larger community that had its eye towards sort of a vision, and a whole different picture of how life on earth could be.

It was not an uneducated group of people that were involved in that awakening or coming-out party of knowledge and consciousness. A strikingly different social movement occurred. It wasn't just a trend or a fad or a change of style. It was something much deeper than that. I feel people were entertaining and acting upon, and part of that had to do with recognition of our place on earth—that we are a part of earth. We're all interrelated. "Interdependence" became a word we began to understand in a new way, and the realization that national boundaries are a figment of our imagination was more evident. These were things we needed to transcend. But I think that, first, we needed to redeem ourselves; first, we had to be a good nation. We would be good and responsible if we would extend the hand of friendship to the Russians—at least. I think freedom is stronger. We don't have to be afraid of the Russians; they have legitimate concerns. What is striking about Reykjavik is that Reagan was caught off guard—it was a telling incident. He went to Iceland not really prepared to negotiate a reduction of arms. Had he imagined! If he was serious about negotiating a reduction of arms, why wouldn't he have gone there with the imagination that in ten years we could do this? That's obvious. If you were going to negotiate with Russia, you would have considered every possibility.

That picture of the earth from the moon was living proof that we are one—we are all one. If we destroy the Brazilian rain forest, which acts sort of like a lung for the planet, we are destroying not just the forest but the biosphere we live in. That's serious business, but I think these things in the 60s have become important in politics today. There was an awakening in the 60s to our garden. Our garden—and our responsibility is stewardship of this earth, so that we just are in harmony with the natural flow that's already there. Our activities, our human activities, should be in harmony with the natural scale of things around us, the watersheds that we live in. We shouldn't have polluted creeks. That's scandalous, to have a polluted creek running right through your back yard. That's your water. People cannot live without water. Water is serious business. It is not a place where you should throw bottles or Coke cans or beer bottles. That's water, that's something we cannot live without. There's lots we can live without. And yet, right here in our valley where I live, we treat water so poorly. There are tires in there, yet there's a lot of awareness here. It happens that we have a little hatchery here, and we return salmon to the river, so there's an awareness, so it's not totally bad, but even that could be improved. These kinds of things were realized in the 60s. We started to see things in a different way. See our relationship to earth in a different way, and then the responsibility to it goes beyond just an allegiance to a country. There was the recognition of our place on the planet and there is allegiance to the oneness of the earth. Because that's reality. That biosphere is happening to all of us. All over the planet, acid rain now. Naturally, it goes all over. We make it here, and it blows over and gets somebody else.

So a lot of people were around the Haight-Ashbury at the time when my brother and I both had profound experiences with LSD. Other people had similar experiences too. The Human Be-In just happened. Nobody manipulated that. It was just this call and this feeling that something different was happening. There were a lot of people who were feeling something different happening, and who turned up? Ten thousand people turned up. It was out of sight, out of this world, that that many people were starting to feel different about their place on earth and their responsibility to the earth and what the meaning of life was. Those questions were serious to a lot of people. There was a real journey that was set out upon. People left San Francisco and went all over the world. A friend of mine was in the Peace Corps in India, and he read in a newspaper about the Death of the Hippie ceremony in the Haight. He saw something saying, "Today we're declaring the Death of a Hippie, in India!"

Michael Bowen, Allen Ginsberg, Allen Cohen, Jay, and I did our part to put on the Be-In. Jay got the permit from Parks and Recreation. We paid for a couple of posters to be made. Stanley Mouse and Michael Bowen collaborated on one, and Rick Griffin did the other. There were people that I didn't know who were spreading the word and talking to people. I just know what I did. Over ten thousand people. Obviously, other people did what they did on their own in relationship to it. That was one of the surprises about it. We were of like mind. Some people came from the south and the north of San Francisco and just kind of converged there on January 14th, 1967. It was sunny all day. I loved Ginsberg at the end chanting something about kitchen clean-up and leaving the place the way we found it. That was really good, and that act stuck from then on. Wavy Gravy used to do it. At the first Haight Ashbury street fair, when it came to the end of the day, there's Wavy Gravy handing out garbage bags, getting everyone to pick up the garbage. It was completely clean.

We were from a merchant background. My father was manager of a Woolworth's. So when we were growing up, sometimes I'd spend the evening at the store doing inventory or something. We'd be running up and down the aisles. We worked as stock boys sometimes in the summer for him. We grew up in a merchant's family, so it was a natural way for us to express ourselves: to open up this psychedelic shop, which featured books related to this new way of consciousness that people were talking about. We sold music. Indian music started to be popular, folk music too. It was all new and different. The ear was hearing in a different way than it previously had.

Our store was right across the street from Woolworth's, the first one my father ever managed. It wasn't a conscious choice, it just happened that way. We sold records, music, books, and then we started to have art shows: the Jook Savage Art Show was there, and we had a poster-coloring contest, and Steve Samuels did that wonderful mandala that we adopted as the logo for the Psychedelic Shop. That big round one, a black and fine-lined mandala that he did, sort of an American original, so that was on our letterhead for our stationery. We took a lot of things on consignment, you know, like the beginning of the cottage industry. A lot of people were

getting into making their own things at home. They didn't
want to be working at a nine-to-five job at something that
didn't become them particularly. A lot of that creative energy
was released at that time. People began finding out who they
were and what served their nature, nourished their nature so
that they could become fulfilled.

Someone converted a theater in the Haight and got
rid of a lot of seats. We put three of them in the window of our
store facing out, and when people walked by and looked in the
window, there were people sitting there looking at them. We
tried a lot of different things there: put in the meditation room.
I was hitchhiking once, and I got a ride with someone who had
conceived a baby in the meditation room. We had a lot of
paraphernalia too, and we gave away a whole bunch of papers
that showed how to make LSD—at the time, it was legal.
There was nothing "they" could do about it, but a chemist had
tied up the whole formula for how to make LSD and how to
cook it and what to do. We gave away lots of sets of those
papers.

A message board went up— another person who
lived in the Haight thought of it. A lot of people who were
private would come down there to socialize, meet fellow
seekers, start to relate on a social level. Seemed like archetypal forms of people were free—free to do or become, that's
why you all saw all these guys with tall silk stove-pipe hats
on, people in Indian shirts, acting out whatever trip they felt
they were on in discovering themselves: they would dress like
it; act like it. You could see Renaissance, ancient Indian robes,
Rome—it was all there, a living theater of people acting out
archetypal characters. They were really into "Who am I
really?" Or "What do I have to do to make money?" There
was a grace period there—when welfare was generous—and
people weren't out for a whole bunch of bucks anyway. They
just wanted to get by, and back to the land kind of stuff.

January 1st, 1966, I started the Psychedelic Shop, and
we closed it October 6th, 1967—that was the Death of Hippie
Day. We gave everything away. It seemed like people were
sort of just adopting a style of dress and habit without any
thought going into it or experience going into why they were
doing that. It became a media hype, and people started
growing their hair long without any kind of purpose in life or
statement or ability to express a purpose in life. There was a

fire, and people threw in beads, flowers, and artifacts of being a hippie. A hippie—everything then was a hippie. "Hey, I think I'm a hippie!" The coffin was marched down Haight Street. It was taken down to the Panhandle and burned, and there was food there, and I think a band played. The next day or two after that, Arthur Lisch and I bought a white panel truck, and we went off to Washington, D.C. for the exorcism of the Pentagon. What a mad trip that was! We stopped at schools and churches. We were just so jacked up. We walked all around the Pentagon, which is no small task, because those grounds go under and over. The idea was to circle the Pentagon holding hands, which would have been a monumental task, but we didn't have to, because the Pentagon put soldiers in a circle around the Pentagon. So we walked all the way around talking to the soldiers. I was there when they stormed the wooden gates. There are a number of big entrances. Huge wooden gates would open—as big as the whole wall there— and at one point, somehow or other, the gate got opened. Picture all these people pushing in and screaming and the soldiers coming out, and we all got pushed back. Some soldiers burst into tears and came over to our side. Then they kept pushing us back. At one point they made about a five-foot push. I had a Japanese flute, and I was pretty good at playing it, and I was pushed back so hard that I dropped it. I asked a soldier if he could grab my *shakuhachi*: "Could you please lean back there and hand me that *shakuhachi*, please, it's a nice instrument, I really like it a lot." They would not budge. They had to play their soldier part; it was really hard not to. We were lovable people. It was not a nasty crowd. It was flowers in their rifle barrels and stuff like that. My flute is now somewhere in the Pentagon. Maybe one of the soldiers learned how to play it.

Lisa: What else of great importance happened during that time?

Ron: Eating health food really took off in the 60s; home birthing, natural foods, gardening.

Lisa: The bomb was a big problem during those times too, wouldn't you say?

Ron: Nuclear fission has to be stopped—both in the arms race and the nuclear plants. It will come to be understood as a crime, fissioning will. Fusion is also something they're working on that is totally unnecessary—a huge monstrosity of hardware. What you have with fissioning is huge amounts of heat that are out of this world, that can destroy us. Radiation that comes out of the process can damage the finer tissues of the brain, and the waste and ash become lethal to biological life for a quarter of a million years. We have the evidences of that. That's the facts. That's what comes of fissioning. How can a people who have a written history that dates back five to six thousand years, or let's say ten thousand years, put something in the ground down in New Mexico, in Carlsbad, under twenty five hundred feet in some salt chambers? Just bury that waste for two hundred and fifty thousand years. What is that all about?

Lisa: What turned you on?

Ron: There were a lot of yogas around in the 60s, diets, meditation techniques, chanting, secret mantras, religious texts about the Bhagavad Gita, the Bible, the Koran, the Kabbala, the Old Testament, but the scripture that impressed me the most was the Shiva, a one-page sheet that takes a few minutes to read. One of the lines in there is that self-respect is the way to the life of truth, power, knowledge, and love. And that, to me, is the underlying principle for every human creature today.

WAVY GRAVY

Wavy Gravy is the founder of the original Hog Farm Com-
mune in Tujunga, California. He still lives communally with
the Hog Farm today. They have two homes now, a rambling,
two-story Victorian house in Berkeley, where we did our
interview in 1989, and a five-hundred-acre ranch in
Laytonville, California, where they teach each summer at their
performing arts camp, Camp Winnarainbow. Wavy has a very
small room in Berkeley overlooking Henry Street. It is filled
with hats, beanies, dolls, posters, framed photos, pins,
instruments, a collection of over two hundred T-shirts, colorful
jump suits (all handmade for him), collages of blues artists
that he creates in his spare time, and statues of Jerry Garcia
and Buddha, as well as an eight-armed Donald Duck. Wavy
was dressed in a SEVA sweatshirt, his golden curls cascading
down his head—a natural-born clown and Saint Misbehavin'.
He is also the only person I know who hears no ego, speaks no
ego, and sees no ego.

Lisa: Tell me about the croquet game that day at the Hog Farm
in Tujunga.

Wavy: On Saturdays we'd go to the Shrine Auditorium, and we'd do the big light show with the single-wing turquoise bird, and I'd do the big gong-bongs and stuff like that, and Sunday was kind of like Hog Sunday. Everybody would call from all over Southern California and say, "What's the theme?" And it would be Dress Like Kids, or Roll in The Mud, or once we built a theater for Tiny Tim, and once it was a croquet party. We played croquet in the hog pen, and everybody designed their own croquet mallets with sights and fur and feathers, and some were attached to coats. There was certainly a lot of creativity there. Whatever the theme was, we'd try and put ultimate creativity on it, and as the show began to move around the country, I remember pulling in with the buses to Cambridge, and we're saying, "Boston, what can we do here?"And we ended up doing a giant farting contest with about eight rock and roll bands in the huge cage where they would have athletic events, track meets, stuff like that. We had eight rock and roll bands and two huge galvanized garbage cans full of baked beans. People would eat baked beans and boogie and then, when they felt one coming on, they'd run over to the microphone and we'd tape it. And the winner would go together with us to the Winter's End Rock Festival in Palm Beach.

Lisa: What about when you painted the hogs at the Hog Farm and you rode them?

Wavy: Oh yeah, that was the Hog Rodeo. We figured we don't have beans, but we've got a lot of pigs, so the concept was just paint those suckers up and ride them and see who'd get the longest ride. It was quite gorgeous. We showed that in Paris to Salvador Dalí, and he fell in love with the Hog Farm Rodeo— he wished he was there. You had to be there.

Lisa: How did you happen to be living at the Hog Farm?

Wavy: What it was is Kesey was on the lam in Mexico, and we were doing a traveling road show, *Can You Pass the Acid Test?*, with a band called The Grateful Dead. And *Life* magazine was shooting us all for their cover, and people were posing away, and Ken Babbs stole the bus and took off to join Kesey in Mexico. So my wife then, Bonnie Jean, and I were living in a two-room cabin in Sunland, California, and suddenly we had thirty or forty houseguests. And the landlord came by and said forty-two people is too many people for a two-room cabin. And we sort of concurred from there out. We were being evicted, but in the life-in-the-bizarre-lane of kitchen synchronicity, along came Bud Pelsue and said, "Old Saul up on that mountain, he's had a stroke, and they need somebody to slop them hogs." I remember driving up in the dead of night to check out the venue, and there was Burbank laid at our feet like luminous jewels on a field of black velvet. And I stood on this knoll to get a better look, and the knoll stood up and starting walking with me on its back. It was this big old black sow. Forty-eight hog farmers a year are devoured by their livestock, so I remember feeding them in groups of two.

Lisa: And then one of those little babies became Pigasus.

Wavy: We ran a pig for President, it's true, in 1968. We had no idea when we went on the road, with one pig to remember our humble beginnings, that she would be the first female black-and-white candidate for the presidency and would require her own truck and several body servants.

Lisa: And how many votes did she get?

Wavy: We never counted. Pigasus actually informed us to vote for ourself.

Lisa: Who were the Merry Pranksters, and where did you meet Kesey?

Wavy: The Merry Pranksters were an appendage of the *Acid Test*. The Acid Testers, as it were, were a group of various Oregonian/Californian sentient critters heaven-bent on initiating the planet to its potential under the dreaded mind-warp substance, LSD. I don't even remember when I first met Kesey. He used to come over a lot when I was living with Tim Hardin in L.A. I remember that. Did I meet him before that? Maybe, but that was my first initiation, kind of. They dragged me off to Capistrano or somewhere where Babbs was living, and I was forced to watch three days of movies of a bunch of lunatics driving across the free world in a painted bus to New York City. Lots of miles of images of Mike Hagan's shoes. Mike was their cameraman and he would ingest these substances and shoot his shoes. Still today, filmmakers from all over the world occasionally journey to Oregon and try and edit Mike Hagan's shoes into some kind of cohesive, universe-solving visual substance. And they usually end up in deep therapy.

Lisa: Why did you go on the road with the Hog Farm in the buses, and what did you do?

Wavy: We're talking about a mobile hallucination-expanded family here. Every Sunday we had been doing this free celebration. And we thought, "Well, it'd be interesting to take this free celebration on the road." And then folks did a film for Otto Preminger called *Skidoo*, and mechanics had already saved up and bought one bus, and we turned it into a bunch of buses, and we painted them up and filled them with rice, beans, and our various lives and hit the road, first for New Mexico for our trial run, which was at the Los Alamos proving grounds. Then, driving around the country, we'd go to colleges and get sponsored by the inter-fraternity council and the SDS. The only thing that they would agree on all year was the Day of Lunacy with us. And then we'd fill in the middle. We'd empty out the art department, the music department, all the various departments, and pile it all up in the middle of the football field, and fall asleep. And then the next day, students would start beating on the windows of the bus saying, "When's it going to happen?" We'd say, "Oh grab a wrench or something, we're a little wasted." And the next thing you know, they're putting together this thirty-foot dome and sixty-foot dome, and we're all in cahoots doing it until, finally, it would get set up, and then the night would fall and the light shows would flash on the screen attached to the domes, and everybody was the star. That was the game we were playing: to show everybody they could be the star of this movie, which was our lives.

Lisa: What was the Great Bus Race? What instigated it? And what was the prize?

Wavy: The Great Bus Race was actually the Summer Solstice in Aspen Meadow up above Santa Fe, where we all gathered, not having any idea that we were going to have a great bus race, but just hanging out with the cosmic vibes in the high altitude, and along comes Kesey with all these cases of beer, and they had just invented screw-on tops, and we didn't know that. So we were all glugging it down and the next thing you know we are electrified, and there were the buses, and it seemed to just naturally fall into the flow of stuff that we would have a bus race. Or perhaps it wasn't that way at all. It was partly that way. God, I remember sitting on the top of the bus with a microphone and the sheriff coming over and handing me this announcement to make that John and Mary had bubonic plague and they wanted to shoot them up with some antidote of some kind. I remember looking at those two words, "bubonic plague," and Kesey leaning over and saying, "Sock it to 'em." I said, "Well, it's the Black Death." We decided all the buses would try to find John and Mary, and whoever shot them up first would win all these prizes, like the bell from *Furthur*, the chromium Donald Duck from the *Road Hog* bus—there were all these various bus mojos—and then the police come running up. "Well, we found them." But the buses were all revved up, so we decided to go once around the meadow with gusto, and I remember them all starting up like—we were going to do it in heats—but no, they just all started rolling at once! I remember almost sawing in half the Yogi Bhajan and his breathing class. There was a tent full of hippies that got—well, good thing they weren't in their tent, that's all I can say. But the scariest part was when they were all lumbering to the finish, and there was the little kid who was frozen right on the finish line, and somebody—Jerry Lamb—leaped out of the crowd and grabbed the kid and rolled with the kid, and all these buses rolled over the finish line. I remember Kesey screaming, "Press on, press on!" and I'm screaming, "Be careful!" And that's pretty much our lifestyle.

Lisa: Who won?

Wavy: The racing was the fun, it didn't matter who won actually. The Great Bus *Furthur* had to relinquish her silver bell to the bus *Road Hog*, who wore it proudly on to

Woodstock.

Lisa: What did Stan Goldstein have to do with inviting you to Woodstock?

Wavy: We first saw Stan Goldstein in New York. We were in this loft trying to evacuate New York City. Bob Kaufman, the poet, said the city should be built on one side of the street, so we were trying to evacuate to New Mexico, and this guy shows up looking like Allen Ginsberg on a Dick Gregory diet, and starts hooting at us how we should do this music festival in New York state. And we said, "We'll be in New Mexico." And he said, "That's all right, we'll fly you in on an astrojet." We thought, you know, he's just tripping. The next thing you know, he was tripping indeed—into New Mexico. There he was at the electric bus race with a valise and a whole lot of linear overlay that seemed to confirm the fact that, next thing you know, there's eighty-five of us and fifteen Indians at the Albuquerque airport, getting ready to jump on an astrojet for Nuvo Yorko, the Cement Apple.

    Well, we got off the airplane and here were all these world press people saying, "Oh, here they come. They're doing the security." I said, "My God, they've made us the cops!" I asked, "Well, do you feel secure?" The guy says, "Well, yeah." And I said, "Well, see? It's working!" He asks, "What are you using for riot control?" And I said, "Cream pies and seltzer bottles." And they all wrote it down, and I felt the power of manipulating the media—ha-ha. And we jumped on the buses, not even ours, and drove out to nowhere near Woodstock, but White Lake and Bethel, New York, where we reunited with the *Furthur* bus from the Pranksters and the *Road Hog* of the Hog Farm, who had gone ahead to clear trails and do that kind of stuff. It had been moved from venue to venue as injunctions forced us to Bethel, where we had built the kitchen dome. I remember there was a winged pig hanging in the kitchen with a big sign that said: "Fried Lice." That was where the Hog Farm free kitchen was operating out of, with Jahanara. Peter White Rabbit and Lisa Law went into New York and brought back multi-sacks of bulgar wheat and vegetables and other healthy stuff, despite our yearning for burgers.

    The farmers were sweeping people out of the fields,

and we would incorporate them into our work crew. I remember the promoters asking us how many security armbands we needed. I remember saying, "Well, what do you think Babbs?" And Babbs said, "How many people are you expecting?" They said, "Well, a couple hundred thousand." And Ken said, "Well that'd be sufficient." And their eyes just rolled, you know. We got maybe a hundred armbands, and then we started printing them up with a potato. And we'd always go out into the crowd with at least ten of them in our pocket, and if we saw people who were acting responsible, we'd give them three or four, and tell them to pass them out until, by the end of the festival, a lot of people were wearing those winged-pig armbands. That's Pigasus.

Lisa: How did you feel about the festival as an event in your life?

Wavy: I think that what was really interesting was when we were called by the promoters. Mel Lawrence, in particular, called me and Tom Law, who was the co-Please Chief and yoga teacher, and Mel says, "We're just about ready to start taking tickets now," and I looked out at the infield and there was fifty thousand people and he says to me and Tom, "Well, you wanna clear the infield so we can start to collect tickets?" And we looked at each other, and we said, "Do you want a good movie or a bad movie?" And I remember Mel and him getting on the walkie talkie to, I guess, Michael, and they had this palaver that lasted about ten or fifteen minutes and came back to us and said, "We want to make the festival free." Which I think was, to them, a very wise choice with a lot of consciousness, and to their credit they did that. That's when the great amalgam of the warm bodies began to descend on it all. If it hadn't already, that was the kicker. That's what closed the New York State Thruway.

Lisa: So how did you feel emotionally about that as an event in your life?

Wavy: I think I have a line in the Woodstock movie, "There's a little bit of heaven in every disaster area." People tend to go beyond themself, to go the extra nine yards to help their fellow sentient critters. And I began to be moved by a certain energy that was more than me. I began to feel that, obviously, and to surrender to that and be moved from working with the drug freak-outs up that long ramp onto the big stage to talk to the lots of people. It was like I felt Howdy Doody had more free will than I did. There were these invisible threads that were kind of moving me as I surrendered to that energy. Throughout the rest of my life, I'll feel that particular buzz, and I yearn for it, and it's what I exist for, I guess. I guess it's not adrenaline. It's some kind of spiritual wooga-wooga that I'm entitled to spend my days in quest of, yeah? It's all about selfishness and greed. This is a buzz that you do not find in the pharmaceutical cabinet, but if you spend a little time in the front lines, helping people out and helping people help themself, you start to get a buzz. In fact, they have determined that scientifically it's good for your health to help each other out.

Lisa: What did you say to all the people?

Wavy: I said, "Good morning. What we have in mind is breakfast in bed for 400,000," which was when we introduced hippies to granola. I don't think they had ever seen it before, and we passed it out in Dixie cups all over the festival, and people were laying in their sleeping bags, and somebody would run up and hand them a Dixie cup full of granola. "What is this, gravel?" And they were not far from wrong, but it was nourishing gravel and could get them down the road to the peace that passeth understanding.

For those who wanted to go beyond granola, they could make it back to the Hog Farm, which was kind of a sanctuary of people who had figured out their survival movie a bit, and they could get something to eat if you didn't want to pay the vendors. Or you could chip in and get something to eat. We were feeding about ten thousand people a meal. I remember when *Life* magazine took the photograph of the Hog Farm kitchen, it was all volunteers. We had all passed out in the bushes. Working day after day after day, eventually you pass out, and then you get up and do it some more, just like always. Chop water, carry wood.

Lisa: What is the Divine Dodo of the First Church of Fun?

Wavy: Oh Lisa, now you're really prying into the inner, inner sanctums of the Hog. The First Church of Fun is a new world religion I helped to found over a decade ago, installing myself as the Divine Dodo. If I was the Divine Dodo, there would be no pictures. But I'm just Wavy Gravy, sitting here talking to you all. Every April Fools' Day we'd have sacred rights and inner teachings, where you line up, take off your right shoe and sock, and get a string tied around your toe by the altered boy, and then go in the back room to meet the Dope, Peter, the 6 and 7/8ths, which was his hat size, or the Green Goddess, or whatever deity happened to be holding forth with sacrament in the first half of the riddle. After the ingestion of the sacrament, a vapor as it were, you would go out and meet the Fallen Archbishop or Cardinal Sin, who would teach the funny handshake and give you the second half of the joke, and you would be funny for that year. But you have to find where we are on April Fools' Day. That's the quest.

Also, an inner teaching of the First Church of Fun is, if you're on a bummer, you take a paper bag that just fits over your head, and do the funny mantra—brrbh—you will turn into a living kazoo, and it's hard to stay on a bummer when you're a living kazoo. This is scientifically tested. Harpo Marx says, "If all else fails, stand on your head." Wavy Gravy says, "Take a paper bag and put it over your head and go brrbh."

Lisa: Tell me how you first met Bob Dylan.

Wavy: I remember when Dylan wandered into the Gaslight in New York. He was wearing Woody Guthrie's underwear—I'm not making this up. He had a sign on his guitar that said, "This machine kills fascists," and he said, "Hey! Hey! Can I go on?" I said, "What's your name, kid?" And he said, "Bob Dylan." I said—I don't know what impelled me—I just grabbed the mike, and I said, "Well, uh, here he is, ladies and gentlemen, a legend in his own lifetime—what's your name again?"

We shared a room up over the Gaslight. In fact, "A Hard Rain's A-Gonna Fall" was written on my typewriter. It has since been eaten by a Bekins [storage] along with Lenny Bruce's couch.

Lisa: How do you feel about Dylan's contribution to the 60s?

Wavy: Well, sixties, schmixties. I'm not a decadist at all, but as far as, you know, the body of songwriting—he changed it from moon-in-June-spoon to significant kind of stuff that had to do with the people and their struggles for freedom and for something intelligent to happen in music. I think he was the springboard for all of that, and I think that his songs for a great period of that time were that incredible energy of the wind blowing the answer, blowing through his heart and coming out on the paper. I think he had very little control over it, but he had the sense to surrender to the energy and scribble it down. And the incredible legacy came out of that. I don't think he's finished at all. I think in some ways he's got his best work in front of him.

Lisa: Do you remember the Castle?

Wavy: The Castle? Do I remember the Castle? The Douglas Fairbanks hallucination? Yes, indeed, I remember it a bit. You know, all that stone and you expect to see manacles being attached to the wall, and where's the rack and the iron maiden? And I remember the opium den that Severn Darden lived in in the basement rather vividly, and the big rake that they used to stir the fire with—that fireplace you could put a horse inside and cook it.

Lisa: Tell me about Nobody for President.

Wavy: Well, we were not going to run Nobody for President again. We started out, we ran a pig for president, then we ran a rock for president. We came back from Asia to discover the Zippies were running a rock, and we called them up and said, "Well, if you liked our pig, you're going to love our rock." And so we had this rock from Mt. Ararat that had *om mani padme uummmmm*, and we had a roll for vice-president, and at the different rallies we'd have jelly rolls and bagels, and you could always eat the vice-president, and then I spaced the rock out in a taxi cab, and the idea of Nobody bubbled up the spinal telegraph there. Nobody is perfect. Nobody keeps all campaign promises, Nobody should have that much power—all that kind of stuff.

   We ran Nobody for President for three elections. And then well, Wavy says, "It takes two to tango and three to tell the truth." And Gurdjieff says, "A prayer must be uttered three times," etc., etc. So I was thinking of running a piano in 88, and the next thing you know, there's Jesse Jackson on the TV throwing in the towel and giving up, and the plastic chatter teeth that I used to represent Nobody started clicking of their own volition on top of the TV. And it just spooked me, it was like Nobody giving me the nudge to get out there one more time in our bus, which we called the *Nobody One*, because Bush was flying around in the Air Force One. And I firmly believe still that Nobody should have that much power, and at least None of the Above should be on the ballot. My God, in Chile they can say no to Pinochet, but we couldn't say no to Bush and Dukakis, even though they both put us to sleep. Once again we're into the dilemma of the lesser of two evils. Well, once again, we stuck it out there for Nobody, because Nobody was in Washington working for me, and Nobody was lowering my taxes, and all the usual reasons, and of course, if Nobody wins, Nobody loses. It's a pair of ducks.

Lisa: Why did the Hog Farm commune survive and why did other communes fail?

Wavy: A lot of communes that started in the 60s didn't make it. We made it because we were an expanded family. We weren't as "The Commune," "The Collective." It wasn't like that. We were a pile of folks knowing that we're a bunch of fuck-ups trying to do our best to make an amalgam, a group brain. We had the buses and the caravan to start with, and the shows to do, so we had that incredible focus that led us through the 60s and the middle of the 70s. Let's face it, the 60s weren't over. When your nose goes on strike, pick it. We had that incredible impetus of the shows and the celebrations, so we didn't get caught in a lot of the yammering that began to occur. After we finished the bus ride from London to the Himalayas, and the Vietnam shutdown, etc., we settled in Berkeley. The third word out of everybody's mouth was "house," because the kids were plugging up the aisles, you understand, and then we started the Telephone Answering Service, Babylon.

Lisa: What was the role of drugs in the 60s and now?

Wavy: Well, that was the jelly roll. You have to say which

drugs. Like Nancy said, "Just say no." No to what? I think
there's a vast difference between smack, crack, and smoking
flowers. So I spend a lot of time flying around the country
promoting the smoking of flowers that you can grow in your
yard. I think that's realistic. It would take a lot of the crime out
of drugs, and it would certainly be a lot better for you than
alcohol. I think in the 60s it was also the same kind of things.
We were into the soft drugs, if you will—psychedelics, acid,
mushrooms, and cannabis. I think that there was always a
stigma against speed. I remember the speed pills, "Speed
Kills," the Zippie poster, the Freak Brothers—all the various
icons of the 60s came down on smack and speed. There wasn't
too much coke around then, but I liked the saying, "Cocaine is
nature's way of telling people to spend money and be mean to
their friends." I think it sucks.

Lisa: Who is Hugh Romney?

Wavy: Oh yeah. Hugh Romney is some guy I used to know
from when I tumbled out of my mother's womb till the Texas
Pop Festival when I got the affirmation from B.B. King that I
could be Wavy Gravy. I remember getting back to Cal State,
where I had a grant working with neurologically handicapped
kids, and I told them my name was Wavy Gravy, and the
classes were filmed through one-way glass, and the professors
came running into the class after it was over saying, "Keep
that name, you saved a week's orientation." And it seems to
work that way, except with telephone operators. I can never
give them the whole name. It shorts them out. I say, "Gravy,
first initial W." They can cope with that. But Wavy Gravy
together is too much for them. They think I'm a ruse.

Lisa: Hugh Romney first came to L.A. and did the Phantom
Cabaret with Tiny Tim. Was that before the Committee, or did
you study at Second City, or . . . ?

Wavy: No, no, no, I just picked it up along the way. Hard
Knocks U. It was after the Committee. I had defected from the
Committee because California was going to fall in the ocean. I
was a tongue dancer then. I did an album on World Pacific.
And prior to that I was an intense Beat poet. So who knows
what I'm going to turn into next? Maybe wonderful garbage.

I've been that before.

Lisa: What about Viola Spolin? Did she have any influence on you?

Wavy: Well, you know, I think the profound influence of Viola was when she came up on the mountaintop where all the pigs were. We were having a celebration where we were edifying a friend of ours from Second City named Severn Darden as he leaped out of the car knowing nothing. We put him on a burro and threw palm fronds in front of him and worshipped him and idolized him and blew his mind. Viola was there, and somebody walked up to her with a turkey leg, telling her she had a long-distance phone call, and she grabbed that turkey and started talking into it, and I appreciated Viola ever since, and use her books a lot when I work with kids. I do a course called Space Eat, which is a variation of Viola's theater games that I've taken through my own life channels and Gravy'd it a bit. What it mostly does is turn people on to their first instinct and their creative imagination, which is just, once again, the wind blowing through their heart, which is just spirit taking a dance with them. Something to aspire toward.

Lisa: What is the philosophy of Wavy Gravy and the Hog Farm, that wonderful philosophy that made Woodstock as calm as it was, that makes Camp Winnarainbow so wonderful?

Wavy: Phil Osophy. I remember him. Ha! Uh, that you can do anything that you want as long as nobody gets hurt. Our leader can take it. That we're all the same person trying to shake hands with our self. That you try to put your good where it will do the most. Feel where it's flowing and flow with it and give it a push—the Keseyisms, the Gravyisms, whatever we picked up from Hard Knocks U. Basically sharing and caring. The Love Sisters sharing and caring. That's it.

Woodstock was created for wallets and looking to generate photos of dead presidents for promoters, and somehow or other those turnstiles didn't get up in time, and the next thing you know the universe took over and did a little dance, and we were archetypes of that dance. Nowadays we've had, starting with Band-Aid, Farm-Aid, Live-Aid, the Amnesty Shows, Home-Aid, my Cowboys for Indians, and Third

Eyeball—people are doing it for the right reasons.

Lisa: What were the 60s to you?.

Wavy: Well, after 1959 came 1960, followed by 1961, 1962, 1963, 1964, 1965, 1966, 1967, 1968, 1969. That was the 60s. Then it really started to get interesting in 69 into the 70s. The 70s were part of the 60s, 71 was part of the 60s, 72 was part of the 60s—I mean, if we're talking about that whole upheaval where people were trying to really believe that they could in a short time make the planet a better place. What we did start to realize is that we're in it for the long haul, and what we learned in the 60s is to do it with a sense of humor, because it's joy that helps us turn the wheel of our ideal, or, as my friend Abbie Hoffman used to say, "Dare to struggle, dare to grin."

Lisa: What's in the future for you?

Wavy: One breath at a time. The sand goes through the hourglass one grain at a time. Or, as my friend Steven Ben Israel once said, "I have nostalgia for the future."

JAHANARA ROMNEY

*Jahanara is the main foundation of the Hog Farm commune
and Wavy Gravy's anchorwoman. She runs Camp
Winnarainbow and is on the board of directors of the SEVA
Foundation. She occupies a small room in the back of the
camp's office, on the same property as the main Hog Farm
house. Her room, where we interviewed her in 1989, was filled
with fabrics from Guatemala and Mexico, rugs from Tibet, and
photos of herself and Wavy throughout the years as well as of
the Guatemalan friends she has made.*

Lisa: What were the 60s like to you?

Jahanara: Most of the 60s in my memory is like one long blur
of trying to cook dinner from the inside aisle of a moving bus
with pots and pans tied onto it. The Hog Farm started off with
a lot of men and me, and then one fine day, Dorgie and Helena
came up the hill and I was so thrilled, because then I wouldn't
be the only one cooking anymore. They would help me 'cause
they were women and, of course, that's what women did—
sorry, folks, but it's true. And we did that for a long time

without questioning it. We used to have this wheel called the Dance Master Chart, 'cause we started having a lot of people come up and look at us and see what we were doing and interview us and stuff, 'cause we were unusual. We were a commune, and there weren't many. And we needed to know who was in charge in case anything happened. So we had this Dance Master Chart that would go around with the names of all the men, and we'd turn it one notch every day, and whoever the arrow was on, that was the person who was the boss that day. But it just went around the men. And then we decided that, because there were three women now, we should have a Dance Mistress Chart. So we made a Dance Mistress Chart, and she would be the one who would cook. It never occurred to me that there was something inappropriate about this until a couple of guys showed up in the Hog Farm who just started cooking, and it blew my mind. And they were good at it. So after that, no one thinks twice about anyone who lives here taking their turn cooking. So I guess that's one of the main differences. Certainly the role of women is much more expanded—everywhere, not just in our family.

Lisa: What was the Hog Farm's role at Woodstock?

Jahanara: We went to Woodstock to do life support. They had called us up and said that they wanted us to prepare campgrounds that were going to be for probably several thousand people—maybe as much as ten or fifteen thousand people coming to camp—and they needed to have fire trails and a free kitchen set up, and would we please come and do that. And we said that we would. We were living in New Mexico on a fifteen-acre farm with no running water or electricity, and I used to go down in a pickup truck every day and stand at the one pay phone in Peñasco and talk to Stan Goldstein on the phone, and we set this whole thing up.

We went in with a hundred people in an airplane—the Jook Savages and the Hog Farm—and our role was to do life support. What we actually ended up doing was setting up the life support systems. We set up the free kitchen, we set up the fire trails, and we set up the various systems. But then, once Woodstock happened, the event took over. I remember working very hard along with a lot of other people to set up the free kitchen, and then once the music started, I never went in there again. The people just came in and did it. I spent all of Woodstock in the medical tents, working with people who had taken too much psychedelic of one sort or another.

Lisa: Did the Festival Committee elect the Hog Farm to take care of that?

Jahanara: Well, Woodstock kind of got out of hand. All of the things that were planned to go down in a certain very prepared, careful way, like you did at a rock concert, just went all to hell. So they didn't have any choice, really, whether they were going to let us or not let us do anything. Things were out of control, and people who would go in who were capable of organizing things and making things better—everybody just did that. No one was into stopping it, because there wasn't anything to replace it with. We very quickly got a mutually respectful relationship going with the doctors and medical personnel, for instance, who got flown in by helicopter 'cause they got set down in the middle of this sea of breathing people in every possible condition of mind, and they didn't know how to deal with it. So they used us for state-of-mind consultants, and we used them for medical consultants, and we all worked together. It was actually very heaven-like. All the barriers broke down.

Lisa: What part do you think Woodstock played in the 60s? Some people say it was the end, some people say the 60s were the Woodstock Generation. What do you think?

Jahanara: Well, the further we get away from Woodstock, the more people forget what it really was, you know? But to me, what I think about when I think about Woodstock and its role in whatever generation, it was a time when a lot of us were together where we actually got to live our dream. The outside was cut off. There was a lot of gorgeous, wonderful music and wonderful people. And we were able, for a few days, to develop all our own systems in communications. I mean, when you have a major-sized city where Abbie Hoffman is organizing the medical tent and running the newspaper, and the likes of me and Lisa Law running and organizing the free kitchen, I mean, that was amazing. It's a time when we got to live our dream for a minute and see how it would be if we were running the show. It was pretty nice at Woodstock. That's what I think.

Actually, I think the 60s happened because the 50s happened. I was a teenager in the 50s, and it was an extremely repressed, untruthful kind of way to be raised. Society was repressed beyond belief. I mean, the clothes, the morals, what we were told about sex, what we were told about life—it was just so full of crap. And so I think we all sort of grew up in our little nuclear families, where our parents were doing their best to raise us well and essentially just lying to us about what was important in life. And we all just burst free. So there was a decade of us all trying to be more truthful with each other and what was important about living. And I think it's left its mark on today. After we unzipped the tight suit of the 50s and stepped out and danced around a while, we didn't need to do that anymore. It's like we were already out, we didn't have more suits and more suits to keep unzipping, and so then people thought, "Oh well, that was that."

But the truth is that the things that we changed in the 60s are changed forever. I mean, it's not going to be like it was before. People can live with someone they love without marriage. People can love and have friendships with people of color. People of different races and religions are tolerated. The toleration of other religions is the norm, not being tolerant of other religions is the aberration. It wasn't like that in the 50s. So, in a way I feel like the work we did together was successful, and things are better, and our kids now are better off because of what we did in the 60s. I'm proud of it.

Lisa: How do you think they're carrying on the work that we did?

Jahanara: Well, I still live in the Hog Farm, and we have a bunch of kids here that are teenagers now. And those are the kids that I know best. So they are children who were raised in this sort of unique family and communal lifestyle. But I find that they are so much more aware of issues of justice, for instance, than I was. My son is beginning to discover issues and truths about the rain forests. He did a demonstration a couple of weeks ago where he sat down, and the police came and hauled him and about fifteen others away, for making a statement about the rain forests in front of the Japanese

Embassy—the Japanese cut down the rain forest and haul it away to build their houses. He was very well-informed about this issue. It's very exciting for me to see the kids informing themself, taking stands, having the ability. This is kind of subtle. But something I really notice in our kids is that they have the ability to see things from another person's point of view, to look at it when they're arguing with somebody: "Well, this is how I feel," and "It must look like this through her eyes." I could never do that when I was seventeen. I learned that at about thirty. Our kids seem so much more awake than we were, and it's thrilling to me. It makes me feel OK about getting older. We've raised these splendid, splendid young people, and they really care. They're informing themselves, and they're going to take care of it, and it makes me feel right about the planet.

Lisa: Can you give me a little background on the Hog Farm?

Jahanara: Well, the Hog Farm is the name of a group of people who live together, and we started living together on a hog farm in 1965. A surprising amount of us still live together here and at our place up in Northern California. And we still have a farm in New Mexico. What we are is just a group of people who live together in sort of the way that an extended family would live together. Rather than being a kind of commune where you all get together based on philosophy—like, we're all vegetarians, or we're all Buddhists, or something like that—we tend to attract members based on who falls in love with whom, you know, or somebody's friend comes to town, and they end up moving in. And so it becomes like an ex-tended family where there are different kinds of people, and we don't all do the same thing, and we're not all alike. If somebody grows up and becomes different in their 40s than they were in their 20s, they don't automatically get . . . like, I have a credit card now, and I didn't get thrown out of the family! Although none of us had credit cards in the 60s, it's OK to stay who we are and stick around. And the thing about the Hog Farm that is the most special to me, I think, is that, like a marriage, if you try to hold together for twenty years, it's very hard to do. I don't know many people who've managed to live through twenty years of being married to the same person. There are a lot of struggles, and it's like being in a marriage where you have to do all that with twenty-five or thirty different people—all the while you're raising your kids—with different philosophies and going through all the stuff that people go through as they pass through twenty years of their life. I'm not the same person I used to be. The same things aren't important to me.

So we have struggled to not get divorced essentially over the years. And now we're getting to the point where it's paying off. Because now we live with all these people that we know so well, and when we go through times like when Cedar's mother died, and it was such a horribly difficult situation, and she was just exhausted, and she had three kids to take care of—she could just go and do that and leave the kids here, and we all know them, and it wasn't like they had to move to a stranger's house. There is a kind of a support in the family, a kind of depth of knowing and loving each other, that you just don't get even in people you've known ten years! It's just so deep and natural that it's a real reward for sticking with it. But I tell you, we went through some very hellish times. Just like in my marriage. I went through some really hard times. For some reason, Wavy and I decided not to get divorced. And so we stuck it out, and now it's very sweet. That's how it is in the Hog Farm.

Lisa: Is there a common ground in the Hog Farm as well?

Jahanara: We love and support each other. That's really the common ground. There's nobody that's really Republican— there may be, they could if they wanted to. So I suppose we're rather liberal politically, but some of us are very spiritually oriented. And some of us aren't at all and don't want to hear about that. Some of us go out in the world and have businesses—run offices and go to work in the morning. And some of us sit around and draw and play guitar.

We don't all do the same thing. We try to get everybody to put in an equal amount of money—enough to cover our basic needs. That's an agreement we've made: that everybody will put an equal amount into, say, the food fund or the rent fund. But other than that, we're very free to become who it is that we are.

Lisa: Remember Steve Gaskin's group?

Jahanara: Another wonderful group that stayed together for a very long time. I always felt that the difference between us and Gaskin's group—who I respect and admire tremendously—was that the people who were part of that group were part of it because they would adhere to a certain philosophy. In order to go live at Gaskin's farm, you had to put all your money in a pot, you had to live in a certain way, and you had to be a vegetarian, and it's not that way here. We live and change and grow and, as a result, when we become different, like you do in your 40s and 50s, we don't have to leave.

Lisa: How many Hog Farmers are there who live at the house?

Jahanara: If you were going to say how many are there, we had a family reunion—we put out a call—and two or three hundred people showed up. Who knows? But who lives at the house—we have this house here, and we have a farm up in Laytonville, and people go back and forth between the two—there's probably about fifty people, and maybe a third of them, maybe almost half of them, are kids now. Between the two places. In the summer we're almost all up there. And in the winter, more of us are down here.

Lisa: Tell me about your pet—Camp Winnarainbow.

Jahanara: Camp Winnarainbow is a circus-arts camp, and Wavy started it with a friend. I got involved in it about six years ago. It's a place where kids come to unleash their creativity and learn to live in the country and walk around on stilts and learn to juggle and stuff like that. It's a performing arts camp. But it carries with it sort of a spirit of the 60s. For instance, you have to have rules in a children's camp, you have to have rules to keep people safe and nurtured and fed and their teeth brushed and their hair combed. But we try to put a lid on rules and, as Wavy says, "Let the wind blow through the spirit" at camp.

It's a very wonderful and exciting place. I've been working on the scholarship program, because my fantasy dream for Camp Winnarainbow is that we try to make it like a small world. We have lots of people of color and people who come from Europe and people from Indian reservations in South Dakota. We truck them out so we can all live together

with all of the races and all of the cultures and have an
agreement from the get-go that we all respect each other's
basic cultures, and then see if we can create peace on earth—
and have fun doing it. That's a very important part of it.

Lisa: It seems that the Hog Farm, in the 60s and now, bases a
lot of what they do on having fun and, to me, it's a very
serious world right now. That you can still take care of those
issues and have fun at the same time is very healing.

Jahanara: You have to keep paying attention to keeping your
heart light. I mean, the situation in the world, if you start to
think about it, is so grim, you can just totally drown in
suffering. And I find that if I am drowning in suffering, then I
don't have the kind of zip that it takes to get up and try to fix
it. So, keeping a light heart is part of the medicine for what's
wrong with the world.

Lisa: You said that you were constantly creating what you had
in the 60s, and you mentioned magic.

Jahanara: For a long time in the 60s—for ten years—I lived on
a bus. I lived on a painted bus with a lot of other people. We
used to say that eleven people on the bus was just right,
fourteen was a little crowded, and seven was lonely. So that
was the kind of range of crowdedness that we would have on
the buses. And I lived that way for ten years.
        Sometimes we had as much as six buses traveling
around in the Hog Farm, and the Jook Savages and all of us
living sort of from minute to minute. And I wonder how we
did it. People would get ten bucks for their birthday—their
mother would find out where they were, and they'd send it on
to Denver. I did some television shows back in my early 20s,
and sometimes they'd show a *Peyton Place* in England, and
they'd send me forty bucks, you know. And it just happened
by magic. When we'd get totally flat broke, we'd make paper
flowers and hustle them on the street, or we'd go pick apples
somewhere. God knows how we managed to get ourselves
around. I remember a time, no kidding, when we drove into
Boulder, Colorado, and there was nothing to eat, and we
pulled up behind a shopping center where they had a Safeway
and a Kentucky Chicken kind of thing, and we started looking

in the garbage cans. There were twenty-two hot chicken dinners with gravy and corn and mashed potatoes, all in plastic covers, just like you'd take it out, sitting in the garbage can. It's like someone called up and said, "The Hog Farm's going to be coming here." I mean, someone must have literally called up and ordered them and then not shown up, and they threw them away. And we served ourselves dinner.

But it went on like that. It's as though, as long as we were traveling around, trying to bring a certain spirit to the country, we'd be all right, and I think this is what we imagined we were doing—and maybe we were. We were trying to make it better going, and we were doing free shows around, and as long as we were doing that without any look to where we could get our food—it's like the hand of the management reached down and fed us every day. I don't know how we survived.

After a while it was time for that to stop. We started having kids, we needed a house. And now it's like the hand of the management that carried the magic said, "OK, you guys are on your own now. We'll go and take care of someone else." And that's OK. Now I pay my rent, and we have a PG&E bill, and we go shopping, and all that stuff. And we don't go in the back of the Safeways anymore. We go in the front door. And I like to think that somebody else, somewhere else is getting that, now that we're not using it anymore, you know? Like we had our turn.

Lisa: What did you do on the road with the Hog Farm?

Jahanara: Transforming the world. To make it loving and creative and wonderful and fun. We were young, so of course we were quite certain that we could do this single-handedly, no problem. And we started out by getting a bus, and we had some friends—the Merry Pranksters—who had a bus, and we thought that was a good idea.

Wavy and I lived on that bus for a while, and so we got a bus, and we fixed it up so we could all live in it. And we built bunks and storage spaces. The space we had the bunks in was three feet across and two people would sleep in that amount of space. And I image Wavy and I now, in a space three feet across—forget it! Then, underneath the bunks, there were footlockers. So we could lift them up, and we stashed all our gear under there. And then we went off: "The United States of America, driver, and step on it!"

We would go into a community, and we would try to find sponsors to do a show. A lot of times we would have it on campuses, and we would try to find sponsors from different ends of the political spectrum. Like, if we could get a Unitarian minister and the Students for a Democratic Society or a fraternity and a women's rights group to sponsor us, we used to like that, and we would say that we were going to do a big show, and the star would be YOU! Please come and star in our show. And then we would just set up toys. We would set up a pallet—we used to travel around with a big dome, two big domes, actually: one that we would stick white plastic sheets half way around so it would be a screen for a light show, and the rest would be open; and one that we could cover up with a yellow tarp made in the form of a dome house in case it rained. And we would set that up. We would get great big Tinker Toys and sheets of paper and paint and color crayons so people could create large murals together. And we'd find a band, and we'd find out whatever they did locally. If we had the champion birdwhistle guy living in the town, we'd say come on up, and we'd give him a mike. And we would do these shows. And people would get into it.

Lisa: The media keep wanting to make like the 60s didn't exist, and it's now more obvious than ever that those things are really important. Especially now, since we have ozone depletion and nuclear waste and all that. And now is the time to say, "Hey, it still lives today."

Jahanara: Yeah, I get upset when I hear, particularly news people, constantly say, "Well, now that the 60s are dead, and no one's doing anything like that anymore, how do you feel? Do you feel like an anachronism?" And I feel like, "God, look around. It's totally transformed. It's nothing like it was before that decade happened." The reason that we're not doing it or it's not being done to the same extent is because so much has been transformed. As far as the life of the people that I'm close to, like Wavy's life and my life, we're still doing the same thing from the same place that we did in the 60s. I dress differently when I walk out the door sometimes, and sometimes I don't. Sometimes I dress just the same. But the 60s weren't about love beads, you know. They weren't about wearing a peace symbol on your forehead. They were about sort of an inner transformation and a spirit of joy and freedom and a spirit of trying to create a system of justice, right here, right around us, not out there somewhere, but between two human beings. And that's very much alive. It's very much alive in our children, I hope in children everywhere. It's still the same thing that motivates me when I go out to work on the stuff that I care about. You know, when I go out to work on SEVA Foundation, which is something I do—working on projects in Central America that mean something to me—I do it from the same place that we did free shows when I was twenty-two.

Lisa: Tell me more about women's lib and the Hog Farm.

Jahanara: When the Hog Farm first began, I think women did all of the things that we used to call "women's work." Remember, back in the old days, when there was such a thing as women's work? Mostly, it was anything to do with kids or cooking or arranging things for something important that was about to happen, which was always done by men. And I have to say that I was part and parcel of all of this, and it didn't occur to me that anything was wrong with it. It carried on like that when we got on the buses and when we would start to travel. The women would do all the preparatory work, the men would drive the bus. And there was a big deal about who would drive the bus. We always had to give him the nicest cigarettes and the nicest meal, and he would get his choice of what he got to eat. All of the honors went to the person who drove the bus. And women were never, never allowed to drive the bus.

And I remember after a while that began to irritate me. Why couldn't I drive the bus? I could drive a car—you know what I mean?—I could learn to drive the bus. Well, if you can't fix it, you can't drive it. So I could learn to fix it— you learned somehow! And it started to really bother me. Then I got into a situation one time that was really scary, where I couldn't drive the bus, and I needed to be able to, very much. The American Indian Movement had taken over the Bureau of Indian Affairs. They had stormed the building and were holding it—we were in Washington, D.C. There were police everywhere, and the men were all standing out in front of the Bureau of Indian Affairs building with guns and war paint on. We had pulled our bus up there, and some of us had gone inside to film. Our bus was parked right in front of the BIA building. Wavy was in the back with a body cast on and he couldn't walk—he had had some surgery. And I had a little baby in the bus. Lo and behold, the police came and said, "You better move this bus, or we're going to tear gas it." And I have a husband in a body cast and a little six-month-old baby, and I couldn't move the damn bus.

So I had to go through the enemy lines. I had to get permission to get through the armed line. It took me about a half an hour to get inside the BIA building. This was an armed encampment. I get in, find Red Dog in there somewhere, and I get him to come out. It took us another half hour to get out. Thank God they didn't throw the tear gas. He came out and moved the bus, and I remember: I just put my foot down. I said, "I've had enough of this shit. I can move this bus. Somebody teach me. Is there a key, is there a button you push?" And I remember the furor that went up about this. "Bonnie Jean wants to drive the bus. Well, it's not right. Who do you think you are?" And it was a big scene. But I was just adamant. That is my first memory of any stirrings of some sort of women's-rights feeling within myself. I was so outraged that my husband and my child should be endangered because women weren't allowed to drive the bus. After that, things began to open up. And a couple of men came and joined the family who came from some other planet. God knows where they came from. But they walked into the Hog Farm and started cooking food.

I remember very well. We were camped in a meadow in New Mexico, El Valle Grande, and Ken Babbs takes this wind-up sewing machine off the bus, and he sits down there and he starts making himself a pair of pants. Unbelievable! A man sewing! This couldn't happen! And he cooked too, and so did Peter White Rabbit. He came along and cooked, and then Rick Sullivan said, "Well, jeez, I can cook rice and vegetables, maybe I'll do it once in a while." And then little by little, it all just sort of changed over. I think the women did some pushing. I think we said, "Enough of this, you can't just assume that we'll cook." I remember saying to a couple of the male persuasion, a couple of times, "You eat, you cook. That's how it is in this family if you want to live here." But I have to say, for the most part, I think it dawned on the men the same time it dawned on the women that this isn't right, you know. And so they started making changes at the same time we did. It seems the role of the women in the 60s was to create, was to do all the logistics that allowed the men to be wonderful. The role of the women in the 70s was transition, and the role of the women in the 80s was co-creating with the men as equals—absolutely. And the men know that, and the women know it. It's something we all support together.

Lisa: What role did Bob Dylan play in the 60s?

Jahanara: I really thought that Bob Dylan was a spokesman for the generation in the 60s. I felt like the Hog Farm and our buses and stuff were on the forefront of what was going on in the 60s, and his music was always going right along with us. Other people who were still living in houses and were maybe a little bit behind us in the revolution would find that he always surprised them. He would come in with some whole new sound or some whole new philosophy, and pretty soon they would be following that way. So I think he was like the lightning rod. Very exciting musician and poet, and a real, genuine spokesperson for the generation. Now I think of Dylan as a consummate musician, you know. He's really slick, he's really professional, and I have a lot of respect for him as a musician, and I enjoy listening to his records, but it doesn't stir my soul the way it did twenty years ago. Maybe that's because my soul is twenty years older, and music doesn't make me shiver to the same extent it used to. But his music meant a lot to me, and I think to almost everybody during that time. He spoke our hearts, and he was the first one.

Lisa: Describe a day in the life of the Hog Farm in the 60s.

Jahanara: Wavy and I had a bunk on the bus, and we slept under a patchwork sleeping bag that we called Homeplate, and so I would wake up on the bus, maybe the bus was moving or maybe it was parked somewhere, and I would look out the window, which was exactly level with my eyes. I'd just open my eye, and there would be what was right outside. One day I remember waking up, and there was the Gem Spa on 42nd

Street in New York. More often we'd be rolling down some highway and there'd be street lights going past me, and so we would wake up on the bus, and then we would pack all our stuff and our blankets. We'd put the blankets in the overheads and pack all our gear underneath the bunks and then fold the bunks down, so there'd be an aisle going down the bus.

And then we'd start to work. Mostly, the women would start to work on figuring out what we were going to have to eat that day. And the way we ate was, we would buy hundred-pound sacks of powdered milk, rice, flour, and then big containers of oil, and we would try to make something that was based on whatever staples we had with us. Our food fund was most often $2 a day or less, and with that $2, first we would go see what was available behind Safeway. What had they thrown away? Could we make a salad? Could we make a tomato sauce? And then, after we saw what was thrown away from Safeway, we would then see what was missing. Maybe we'd take the two bucks and buy cheese and make a cheese sauce for the rice to put over the broccoli that we found in the garbage and that would be dinner.

Breakfast was usually cereal—oats or something else that we had in a big sack—and powdered milk. So the food would be the first thing of the day and then whatever our mission was: if we were on our way somewhere and we weren't setting up a show and figuring our logistics of who was going to bring the Tinker Toys and stuff, then there would be a lot of riding on the bus. And I spent a lot of my time trying to do beadwork on a moving bus without very good light. That was my thing. Nowadays I get up for work. I see if my son's awake and make sure he's not going to sleep through his first class at high school. I dress in something that looks respectable enough to go to an office in, often with some sort of high heels with it, which are shoes that I would never wear unless I was forced to. And I go to an office and spend at least half my day in an office at a telephone answering service to earn a wage, and then I come back here and work in my office in the house, being the administrator of Camp Winnarainbow. Or else I go to the SEVA Foundation office and work on a project that I do in Central America.

Lisa: Tell me about SEVA.

Jahanara: The SEVA Foundation is a charity of which I am a member. I'm one of the board members, as is Wavy, and we do two things. We do projects in the world that try to alleviate suffering wherever we find it—a large blindness project in Nepal, and smaller projects that I partially run with Native American people and in Guatemala and with Guatemalan refuges in Mexico. We try to do it with as much love and clarity and integrity as we can possibly infuse into doing that kind of work in the world. We feel that just things like keeping personal relationships clear between the people involved have as much to do with how a project turns out as making a good business plan or making a clear budget. So SEVA's something that means a lot to me, and I've been able to bring to the SEVA Foundation kinds of projects which I personally care very much about.

Lisa: The 60s were . . .

Jahanara:
> *The 60s were a burst of freedom and joy.*
> *The 60s were about living your dream.*
> *The 60s were doing what you believed in.*
> *The 60s were about unzipping from the suit of the*
> *50s.*

The 60s allowed us to escape from the repression of the 50s and really be ourselves. It was a wonderful time. And the 60s were when I was in my twenties and that has something to do with it too. You know? If the 60s happened now it wouldn't be quite the same for me as it was being lucky enough to be in my 20s in the 60s. That was great.

PETER COYOTE

*Peter Coyote is a passionate master of words, an actor, author,
singer and historian. His insight into the soul of the 60s
became the hub of my interviews. He felt he could do his best
if we went right to the heart of the Haight-Ashbury, where he
took us on a little tour in 1989, stopping at places of historic
interest and significance.*

Lisa: I remember a lot of theater going on in the Haight.

Peter: About all you really need for theater is public space and
actors. The first theater I was involved with here was the San
Francisco Mime Troupe. They used to come into the Panhandle and set up a stage, bunch of platforms, a backdrop.
While the actors were changing, a band would play drums,
bugles, and recorders to call up a crowd, and we'd put on
plays—topical stuff about issues of the day, and always
comedies.

   Most of the Diggers came out of that band of people.
We shared the thought that theater as it was constituted was
not a vehicle for change because it was too like a business.
When you paid money at the door, you knew that it was a

business. And if you didn't like the content of the play, you just ignored it. It was like going into a shop and not liking the merchandise. So we used these areas here and didn't charge money in advance. The Diggers took it a step further. About here [*pointing*] we set up free kitchens and free food and a big yellow rectangle, about 6 feet by 6 feet, called the Free Frame of Reference. In order to get a meal, people stepped through this Free Frame of Reference and were given a miniature frame on a cord to wear around their neck and "regard'" the world through. They were invited to look at the world from a free frame of reference—to revise their cultural premises. And although many people came for the hot food and to eat, they also came for the act of theater—to get food that they didn't pay for in a different way and to engage with their brothers and sisters in this piece of theater which was "Food."

I'd say that if the Diggers had a genius, it was, to use Peter Berg's phrase, "To create the condition they described." To create events which had their meaning implicit in them and which, by performing them, created the culture that you'd rather live in. You didn't have to propagandize, you just performed the acts, and they invoked the change itself. The free food wasn't exactly my thing, but a lot of people in the Digger family took responsibility to do that. And I would participate somewhat.

Lisa: I remember there was a Digger Free Store.

Peter: The Digger Free Store was a perfect piece of Digger theater. Everything in the room was free. There were counters, there were racks full of clothes, goods, television sets, chairs. Everything was free. And even the roles were free. Meaning not only the food, but the roles of manager, superintendent, what have you, and people would come here thinking it was a store, and we would play with their expectations.

One morning I remember seeing a very, very large black woman who was obviously stealing from the free store. She was looking around and shoving stuff in paper bags. So I went over—I was the manager that day—and I began helping her. And I was keeping an eye out and shoving stuff in bags, and she checked me out as an ally and really dug it and said, "Where's the boss?" And I said, "I'm the boss." And we just kept shoving the stuff in, and she just stopped, and I said,

"What else do you want? What else? Come on, quick!" And her mind—you could just see it turn over. The ball bearings froze. And she just got up and took it all and straightened it and left. The next day she came back with a flat of day-old donuts and left them on the counter. This woman got it.

A lot of soldiers came to the free store. They'd come on liberty, maybe coming back from Nam or on the way out, and they would go through the racks of free clothes and take their uniforms off and hang them neatly on the rack and put on a watch cap and some blue jeans and a denim jacket and disappear right into the streets. And if they knew how to ask, there were people around who could get you perfect draft cards—all the codes intact—everything just right. This was a stopping-off point. It was a conduit. And it's now a very good restaurant. I've eaten there. Organic food, really nice. But it was the ideal Digger theater. Nothing announced it as a play. You were in it whether you liked it or not.

People figured out how to play this particular act very quickly. And the Free Store was a place I liked to hang out. It was one of those set pieces that changed people by their not knowing it was theater. It changed their relationship to goods. If there was machinery that could make a television set for every man, woman, and child on the planet, and you didn't have a television because you didn't have the money, the money was scarce, not the television. Money was a way of creating scarcity artificially. So we created a free store to show that the stuff wasn't scarce. People were throwing away the stuff. You want the stuff? Come take it. Now, what are you going to do with it?

In this spot, right here [*pointing to a grassy lawn in the panhandle of Golden Gate park*], was where all the vernal equinox celebrations and summer solstices were held. One of the tricks of the Diggers was to have planetary events as the occasions for these parties—not to have them honor a person, because we always operated anonymously. "Free" meant not only without money, but it also meant without telling who you were, without doing it for credit or fame. So every vernal equinox and autumnal equinox and summer and winter solstice, we would have some kind of celebration. And this is where the Grateful Dead would play and Janis and Quicksilver Messenger Service, and you'd see Tonto walking with a Shiva princess, and the Lone Ranger might be running around with

Annie Oakley or Dick Tracy, and people came together to act out their fantasies and create acts of public theater. To create the culture that they wanted to live in. And they did it by assuming the authority to do it. That's what made it happen, and that assumption of authority is what made the Diggers so different from traditional Leftist groups.

[*Walking down Haight Street*] When I came here in 64, the street was undeveloped, kind of a hodgepodge, but the Thelin brothers had opened up The Psychedelic Shop, which was an information center about psychedelics, and then two years later, Haight Street was the center of the national theater of redefining who you were and what it was. And the street was jammed with multitudinous ideas of human identity. You might see anyone, anyone who had ever wanted to act out publicly come walking down Haight Street. One night Willie B. Hart and Jason Mark Alexander [two of the black actors from the San Francisco Mime Troupe's Minstrel Show] and I started singing in the street right here. And before long, enough people had joined us that the police barricaded Ashbury Street and Stanyon Street [blockading Haight Street], and the street was filled with people dancing and playing volleyball over the street-car wires, and every doorway was full of doo-wop groups, singing rock and roll. A whole bunch of black guys came up from the Fillmore to check the climate and see if they were welcome, and they were, and they stayed and sang and partied, and it was a very idyllic and high night. Absolutely devoid of racial tension. People were getting high and singing and making music, and having doo-wop competitions between doorways where they congregated. And salt-and-pepper integrated groups would get the best voices and move down the street. And that was the way things could take off—spontaneously. People were up for theater, and what theater meant was a new way of acting. It felt more human and more spontaneous and more authentic than what the 50s—the Eisenhower years—had offered them. And the stage for that was the Haight-Ashbury.

Musician [*passing on the street*]: Well, anytime you can get some good publicity for this neighborhood, I mean, this neighborhood has had so much bad publicity, you know.

Peter: Well, yes and no. I mean, yes, there has been bad

publicity. I think a lot of the publicity emanates from people who want to move capital into the neighborhood and move the street people out. And it was that way in the 60s as well. After the Haight-Ashbury, tour buses started to come, then all the dentists from Far Rockaway, who had bought into these stores, wanted to get the street people who made the scene off the streets. The street people said, "Well, fuck that," and that's why there were riots.

Lisa: Why did the Haight become the counter-cultural center?

Peter: I think the Haight became a counter-cultural center because it was basically free turf. University of California Medical Center is up the hill. It's kind of an anonymous, quiet, lower-middle-class neighborhood with cheap rents, and when people came to this neighborhood they weren't displacing an urban poor or dispossessed population like they did, let's say, on New York's Lower East Side. You know the coast of California, the west coast of the United States, is plunging into the sea, smashing into the Pacific plate. Geologically it's the most active place on this continent. It's the newest ground that's being churned up, and something about the energy of this place attracted all kinds of people. They were just here at the right time. It's like the film business in Hollywood in the early 20s, when the Laemmles and the Warners and the Zuckers and all those people happened to be at the right place at the right time. It was a social epiphany. That's what the Haight was like. And the media disseminated it and made it an event, and it became one of the first public theaters of that time.

Lisa: What was happening socially?

Peter: At that time we were coming out of the Eisenhower years, and I think of golf and Republicans. I think of Perry Como, and guys in limegreen pants and girls in pale pink sweaters. People had built a permissive loony bin in the suburbs for their kids. They'd come out of World War II and the Depression and decided that their children would never go through anything like they'd been through: experiences, by the way, that made them, the parents, cunning and resourceful and smart and crafty. And so they built these loony bins called the suburbs. which deprived their kids of adequate tests of their own worth. And the kids intuited it and understood they were growing up somehow inauthentically and without the opportunity to test themselves. And they took off in search of it. And when there's something that people really, desperately need for their health and well-being, they're going to get it. And they came here. They created a turf here where you were invisible, "With no direction home, like a complete unknown." [Bob Dylan] You were who you presented yourself as, and how you acted and whether you stood or fell was really up to you. And how seriously you played the game and committed to it was up to you.

Lisa: What was the purpose of the communes? A lot of people left the Haight-Ashbury in 67 and went out and started to live in communes.

Peter: Well, communes are just a natural response to lack of resources. This is a pretty indulgent society, made indulgent by wealth. If you had a big house like this [*pointing to the house he once lived in in the Haight*] it could hold perhaps thirty people, and it might have taken part of thirty people's incomes in those days to pay that rent. Communes were both a social experiment in living with less, using less, and an economic reality. No one had any money, so people had to split rent. It was also a richer and fuller way to live than the nuclear families. It was wonderful to sit down with thirty people at a dinner table and to play music with twenty of them after dinner, to split chores and duties. And in a lot of cases, people were self-consciously hunting for alternatives, for an America that they knew could not sustain this level of indulgence and wealth forever. So there was a spectrum of reasons that accounted for communes.

Lisa: Where did the 60s come from?

Peter: It's probably because I'm an actor that I regard things in terms of theater, but the seed of the 60s was the moral awakening of the Civil Rights movement and the folkmusic movement of the 50s. Black people fired the consciences of the nation, and the music that was associated with them was folk music—earthy, authentic, and compelling. People began rejecting canned music in favor of creating their own, and once they did that, they began considering what kind of life produced those sounds that were so compelling and true, and that led to a search for new experiences. The first events that I remember were people coming together in Washington Square Park in Greenwich Village to play music. People would dig up old 78 records, and they'd share knowledge of obscure musicians and they'd trade folk music and new songs they were creating. The music was an occasion for a kind of theater, or the central event for a kind of theater, which was concerned with proclaiming new values and new groups and new identities.

Communes were theater. Haight Street was theater. The events that the Diggers threw where the Dead and Janis and everybody played were not created by the music. The music was the expression of people who were formulating a new culture, self-consciously trying to empower themselves and act out an alternative. Because remember, the world that each generation receives is just a theater of past generations. It's the generation before you that determines whether or not you're being social or anti-social. Taking drugs or psychedelics is not inherently anti-social. An Amazonian kid taking *yage* in the middle of a jungle clearing surrounded by the village elders is participating in a profoundly social act. And one of the insights that was missing in American culture was lack of transcendental vision. There was no room for the transcendental. People were locked into a purely materialistic, kind of Protestant, mechanistic worldview, with no real opportunity to express worship, devotion, awe. This created a hunger, especially in young people who were anxious to get off the hook of their quotidian reality. I'm not apologizing for the excesses of drugs. There were a lot. People damaged themselves. People died. But the impulse behind it was profoundly moral. It was an opportunity to try to contact something that was bigger and more human and more vital than what they were being offered. And it was the older generation that defined it as anti-social. Because their world could only be held together by excluding the transcendental and the sacred.

Lisa: What did Dylan do to express the times in his songs?

Peter: I only met him very briefly, but, from my point of view, Dylan was the voice of the 60s. No one else came close. Not only his lyrics, but the attitude that he embodied. The contradictory ironies, sarcasms, and cutting insights and honesty, and particularly the detachment. He scooped it, and he scooped it for twenty years, as far as I'm concerned. I mean the Beatles are nice musicians, the Grateful Dead are nice musicians, but Dylan was like Mozart. Or like in the 40s, when white people were listening to Glenn Miller, and dancing, the musicians knew that it was Count Basie and Duke Ellington that were really happening. And the musicians everywhere know that it was Dylan that broke the really new ground in popular music. The guy may never have sold a gold record, but he brought poetry into music, he brought insight, he brought truth. He brought a lot of imitators, but that's not his fault. He expressed what was inexpressible. He gave it voice. "Like a Rolling Stone"[Bob Dylan] became an anthem. How many times I witnessed people being initiated by hooks and crooks, it had happened to me, and Dylan says, "You used to ride on a chrome horse with your diplomat / Who carried on his shoulders a Siamese cat / Ain't it hard when you discover that / He really wasn't where it's at / After he took from you everything he could steal." Well, everybody who made a transition from middle-class homes to the streets had that experience. I mean, he copped it perfectly. "Well, six white horses that you did promise / Were fin'lly delivered down to the penitentiary / But to live outside the law, you must be honest / I know you always say that you agree / But where are you tonight, sweet Marie?" It was his spin on the word "say" that made it so hip: the offhand, slicing judgment, the calling-it-as-it-is accuracy of it. Everybody who was on the street had been there. So to me, he was the guy. He was Mozart.

Lisa: You said that once you've done something with 100% of your being, you can never go back to being a lunchbox Johnny.

Peter: Yeah, people ask me what the 60s were about, and are they over, and I don't think so. I think what the 60s did was liberate people from the expectations that were laid down for them by their parents. People learned that they were completely free to commit themselves to what they chose to do.

And once you've committed yourself 100% to something, you can't settle anymore. It's very difficult to go out and be a lunchbox Johnny and to take a job that you're alienated from. Your body just won't let you condemn it to alienation and boredom.

Whether you wear long hair or short hair or punk or even wear a business suit, if you got turned on to full potential and hitting on all twelve cylinders, and you carry that commitment into your life today, you've got it. If you look at that period of time, and you look at the women's movement, the peace movement, the environmental movement, the holistic-medicine movement, the natural-food movement—all of those things came out of a fundamental re-evaluation of America, a dissatisfaction with what was being offered, and were the direct fruits of people who wanted to be completely committed to their life.

You can see what happens to people when they're not committed. Because if you look at crack cocaine today, the one thing people are not talking about is how come so many Americans want to be stoned. They're talking about every kind of sociological bullshit, but they're not talking about the coke high and why people seek it. The coke high is an omnipotent high. It makes you feel committed, powerful, and engaged. And people who want to be stoned all the time are people who are disengaged. People who need to feel omnipotent are people who feel powerless.

The reality of America today is that almost everybody has minimal power to make decisions over their lives, and that's something that young people seized in the 60s and have not given up. And now that a lot of young people today have bought their BMWs and yuppified their house and got the kids in private school, they look around and find they're being sold, or are selling, Tampax and toilet paper every day, and that does not reflect their reality or their perception of the universe. Those people are hungry for something, and I think that's why you're seeing the nostalgia for the 60s today.

I'm not nostalgic for it myself, because I'm still living it, and the people I know have still kept their principles and kept their intentions even though they may look different, even though their lives may be more complex and more mature. For instance, once upon a time, I wouldn't have felt that a businessman could be worth anything. Today I know that if a businessman is serving his customers and really helping and giving quality goods and not making stuff that's going to break down and waste, if he's applying intelligence and skill to what he's doing, he's doing the work. He's doing the right thing.

Lisa: Is this an addictive society?

Peter: The word that comes to me is "indulgent." We're so rich that we've been allowed to get lazy and soft. We've become indulgent. We have a world in which everybody can have a car, whether or not it's good for the planet. Anyone can take anything on the earth and turn it into anything they want— plastic hair dryers, dildos, electric light machines—and it's all the skeleton and the meat and the flesh and bones of the planet. Primitive people don't have that fat and don't have that edge. They do what they have to do and they don't waste, because they can't. I think that the great wealth of America has in some way ruined us. We could go back to the 30s and have radio and labor-saving devices and be a lot simpler and a lot quieter and a lot more in charge of our existence. I think we'd be a lot healthier. I can't wait until the oil runs out.

One of the things that is useful to remember is that no social movement or philosophy comes out of thin air. We came out of the Beatniks. The Beatniks probably came out of the Dadaists and out of the Whitman-American transcendental-ists—Thoreau, Whitman, and Emerson. Gary Snyder calls this lineage "The Great Underground." It probably began with Paleolithic shamans and priests forty thousand years ago doing interspecies worship and rituals to talk to the animals. And it's been a kind of underground lineage of poets and shamans and yogans and seers and musicians and singers and healers and witches for forty thousand years.

So whether it's punks or whether it's poets or whether it's political resistance, all those people have been fathered by people and backed by a movement that goes back into antiquity. And so talking to a woman here on the street who's kind of replicating the reality of me and my friends twenty years ago, it's not that she's copying, it's not that we were copying, but you come out of a tradition and somehow the knowledge of that tradition is reassuring, because it's genera-tional, and it's the real tie to values that are essential to be

fully human. Without them you're just a citizen of a nation
state, and that's a thin soup.

You walk down Haight Street today and you see a lot
of punks in the street, and I have a lot of affinity for those kids
because the Diggers were a lot closer to punks than we were to
Flower Children. Flower Children was a kind of ram-a-lama
mythology that the media used to spread as a way of creating a
philosophy for people. This movement was essentially
anarchic and revolutionary and re-constructivist. You know,
we wanted to change the country. The Diggers were quite
angry and quite like the punks and much more kind of ready-
to-go.

The strength of this culture is that it absorbs everything and sells it back to you. The Haight-Ashbury in a way
was ruined when outside investors bought the local shops and
wanted to kick the street people off because they got in the
way of the customers coming in to buy. The only guys you see
with really long hair today are rock'n'roll musicians. They're
the only ones that can afford it. Everybody else has to work.

So the culture has this elastic ability to incorporate
something and then sell it back to you as a style. The punks
were ahead for a little while. Now you just turn on MTV, and
there they are—motorcycle jackets and leather whips and what
have you and the next cut of kids will be a step ahead of them
and the cutting edge is always pushing far enough out so that
it can't be co-opted. But I think what you learn as you get
older is that any style can be co-opted. You have to get below
style.

So the punks are trying to stay out ahead of the edge,
and maybe the skinheads are trying to stay ahead of the edge.
But when you get a little older, you learn that any style can be
co-opted, and you begin to opt for a more secret practice. You
begin to operate on the level of intention and just doing what it
is you want to do. It doesn't matter what you look like.

In the 60s, long hair and beads and all that was a
tribal identification system. It was a way of letting other
people know what your values were. But today, you can tell by
looking in somebody's eyes if they've been stoned or not. You
can tell if they're alive inside, just by looking at their eyes. It's
kind of like the way gay people survived in the 40s and 50s.
Just by looking at each other you pick up a scent of real life.
And that can't be co-opted. I think that that's probably what a

lot of the refugees and the survivors of the 60s are now doing. Their style is seamless. They can't be identified by style. But if you look at the way they're living their life and what it's dedicated to, it's dedicated to the values that they expressed in the 60s and felt were important then. I certainly haven't changed. Even though I have a lot more money and a lot nicer place to live, my intention is still the same, and so it is with all my friends.

Lisa: So how do you think the values of the 60s are now, in the 90s?

Peter: Well, I think one thing is you have to say that we frightened a lot of people in the 60s. We moved so fast and so hard on so many fronts, and we also asked so many questions that couldn't be answered, that the country got frightened. I think that they threw the country to Reagan as a housekeeping gesture. I don't think that the whole country really embraced his conservatism, but I think people kind of intuitively felt there were all these problems and all these questions, and we didn't know what to do: let's just throw it to the conservatives, and they'll just take care of it until we work out the answers. Little did they know.

I think what's happened now is the kids have come up through the Reagan/Bush corporate American playpen. They've had all the goodies. They've had the brand names. They've had the BMWs. They've had the status competitions, and it just wears thin. And it's just like all the workers that are basically alienated from their work. They're not empowered to make decisions about what they do. They're not given the authority to solve problems, so it means that their life on the job is a waste. I think kids are growing up with this feeling of emptiness and abandonment. They look around, and they can see that the generation older than them—the people in charge—are just selling the country off as fast as they can sell it. They're shipping out the topsoil, they're poisoning the water, they're selling the timber off to the Japanese, they're selling the assets off. And the kids are realizing that they're not even going to get a bowl of porridge. They're going to be working on a Japanese assembly line. They're going to be working on a Saudi Arabian assembly line. And I think those kids are angry. And I think they should be. Because they've been betrayed by the generation that's supposed to look after them and deliver them a world that's at least been as cared for as the one they received. So once those kids start to get angry, they plug into something very authentic and very real, which is what we plugged into, and those are the values of the 60s. They have different codes and different meanings, but that's what it is.

Lisa: What about the other kids, the children of the hippies?

Peter: There are kids who've been there all along. There were a lot of kids who were raised in the 60s and they just basically sidestepped a whole neurotic loop. Not all of those kids came out great. But I'm amazed by the proportion, the number of kids that *Good Housekeeping* might have predicted would be juvenile delinquents and drug fiends that in fact are resourceful, wonderful, committed, dedicated kids. Cleaning creeks and taking care of the salmon and helping the old people in the hospitals and playing music and having a great life. They learned early that life is supposed to be joyous. We're not all supposed to be Swiss watchmakers. We're supposed to love our lives, and love the time, and watch the oak leaves blossom, you know. We're supposed to have a good time in this life.

Lisa: Kids today?

Peter: I think that the real reason that the older generation is so critical of the younger generation is because on some level they know they're right, and the young people are forcing their elders to ask questions and justify choices that they've taken. And to the extent that you can't justify the choices that you've taken, you have to shut your kids up. Well, there are some people that just missed that whole loop. The kids just grew up actively sharing their parents' values, just like a lot of rich middle-class white kids, who just grew up actively sharing their parents values. They're not in any conflict about having a Mercedes at sixteen. I think that's a healthy thing. If you pull back and say, "Which set of values is going to be most conducive to the long-term health of the planet?" I think you have to opt with the 60s.

Lisa: What role did drugs play in the 60s and what is the role of drugs today?

Peter: Well, drugs are a complicated issue. All people all over the planet in all space and time have needed to get off the hook. The hook is kind of the small-mind, everyday reality— all the rules. And whether you meditate or whether you're a Bushman smoking weed or whether you're a be-bopper smoking hashish or whether you're taking *ayahuasca* or *yage* or a martini or coffee or tobacco, everybody is getting off the hook.

I think that one of the problems of the 60s was that people were so lied to by the Harry Anslingers and the narcotics squads and the police about marijuana and about it leading to heroin, that when they got turned on to marijuana and hashish and found out it didn't lead to heroin, they thought maybe they'd been lied to about everything, and they tried everything. I think another element that admitted drugs into the culture was the fact that people felt that they had to overcome cultural training and cultural habits, and they thought that by deranging the mind, much like Valéry and Rimbaud and Baudelaire, that they could free themselves from their kind of middle-class roots. And the training—you know, you've been in school from the time you're six to eighteen or twenty-one—that's a lot of brainwashing. People wanted to look at the world with fresh-washed eyes. They felt that drugs would do that. And in some degree they do. But the problem is that there were no teachers and no elders, and people were prey to indulgence and they were prey to mistakes.

It's hard to say what the role of drugs is today. It's not popular to say they have any role, except that nobody's trying to stop alcohol, and nobody's trying to stop nicotine and caffeine, particularly. I would say that anything that hurts the body, that violates the limits of the body, doesn't really have a place. But I would say that human beings need the transcendental. It's a vital nourishment, and if Catholicism and Judaism and Protestantism don't do it, you've got to find your own sacraments and your own practices that do. I've been a student of Zen Buddhism the last fifteen years, so I get high by meditating, and I get my transcendental insights by meditating, because I find it doesn't hurt the body. I found that a lot of drugs hurt the body. I certainly think that anything that's done as a sacrament is probably OK 'cause it's not going to be abused—whether it's mushrooms or LSD or hashish or marijuana or one of those non-chemicalized ingredients. I wouldn't urge it on anyone. I wouldn't suggest that this is something everybody ought to do, but I have to say that people need sacraments, and they need transcendental visions.

Lisa: Tell me about Emmett Grogan.

Peter: This guy shows up at the Mime Troupe—real street-wise, street-tough, Irishman—and he does an audition, gets in the Mime Troupe, and he and I are taking a walk, and we get so engrossed in conversation, we walk from 5th and Howard back to Fell and Stanyan—it's maybe three miles. Just talking and talking, and he winds up in our house, and of course it's Emmett Grogan.

   If Dylan was the voice of the 60s, Emmett was the archetypal Digger. He was a life-actor, a handsome and very charismatic guy. Nobody seemed to know exactly what he did. But he did it with such style and such panache, and what he really seemed to do was work a city. He and I went to New York once for about three and a half months, and we must have spent three hours a day on the telephone, calling up people, newspaper columnists, arranging meetings between the Puerto Rican gangs and the police, and he would just go through the newspapers every morning and he would create a role for himself, and a role for us as the Diggers as unaffiliated free agents. We would just invent something to do. He was extraordinary at it. Very inspiring. Fearless. He was a consum-mate life-actor who invented the most heroic, glamorous role for himself on the everyday streets of America that he could, and he lived it all the way out. He was the archetypal Digger.

Lisa: Have your values changed, evolved?

Peter: Well, it feels to me like there's not so much of a difference between the work that I do today and the work that I did in the 60s. I make more money, but I'm still dealing in cultural images. I'm still trying to inspire people so that they'll govern their own aspirations. I make money in film and television, and I use that money to support my writing. Hopefully those films that I write will do the same thing my work in the Diggers did. It's like holding something bright and shiny up in front of people and saying, "Don't you think this is a little better?"

When you work for other people, you don't have quite the autonomy that you do when you own the means of production, but I'd say unless I'm desperately hungry or my family's going to get thrown out on the street, I haven't yet had to do anything which violated my political beliefs. And only occasionally had to step all over my artistic standards. I feel pretty lucky to make my living as an artist. It's kind of what I held out for in the 60s—to do what I wanted to do with my life and not waste it and not feel out of control any more than the universe is out of control.

Lisa: If you were to say one line about the 60s, what would you say?

Peter: Well, I'd say that the 60s were about permission, and the 70s were about the cost of the permission. The 80s were about synthesizing what you learned from the freedom of the 60s with what you have to know to stay alive and be an adult. And the 90s are about revisiting the 60s as a competent, disciplined adult and getting it right this time.

Lisa: The 60s were . . .

Peter: *The 60s were absolute freedom.* Absence of limits. In the 80s, I learned the utility of limits. And if you're an artist, you know that you need limits. That a piano is a very rigid instrument and has to be in perfect tune, and the struggle against those limits is where the art comes. If you play it with a chain saw, it's just kind of a one-shot number. It's funny, because the 60s were really the 70s. The 60s didn't get in gear until 67, and that momentum carried on until maybe 75 or 76. And then there was a period of maybe ten years of recovering from the absolute freedom, some of the excess and some of the mistakes, and, in my case, getting my health back. And from then on we have been trying to synthesize what we learned from that absolute freedom.

Lisa: What was a typical day in the 60s?

Peter: A day in the 60s? Wake up, have a little sex, build a fire, have some coffee, smoke a cigarette, scrounge some money for gasoline, fix my truck, play music, get high, eat some food, maybe have some more sex, go to bed. That was a good day. The trick was to get into whatever you were into and stay into it until you felt it beautiful to stop.

Lisa: Any final thoughts?

Peter: Each and every one of us has absolutely everything we need to be perfect in this very moment. Realizing that and expressing it: absolutely understanding that there is nothing to gain, nothing to perfect, nothing to alter will probably take me the rest of several lifetimes.

RAM DASS

Ram Dass is not a guru, he has told me, but a mouthpiece. His books, lectures, tapes, and videos have helped millions find inner peace and acceptance of themselves. He and Timothy Leary were two of the first to introduce us to psychedelics and mind-expansion. Ram Dass is one of the founders of the Nim Karoli Ashram in Taos, New Mexico. In the ashram, a statue of Hanuman lies on its side, his head resting in the palm of his right hand. Twice a year people come from all over the United States to pray and chant to Hanuman, and Ram Dass visits and moves among the devotees, telling stories and greeting the crowds. Early one morning in 1989 we met with him behind the temple on a great field of dark green grass, with the Taos mountains looming in the distance and the clear blue skies of New Mexico overhead.

Lisa: What were the 60s about?

It's probably too soon to understand what the 60s were all about, but it was a mushroom explosion of consciousness that has left in its wake a transformed culture. It was as if we regained our faith in the possibilities of the universe, as if we broke out of a strangling mind-hold that was a combination of Puritanism and the Protestant work ethic and a whole lot of values we carried with us. We had so much worship of the intellect, and suddenly at that moment, as Tim [Leary] said, you turn on, tune in and drop out. But at any rate, you turn on and tune in. And you go to see that there are many planes of reality, and that the planes that we were stuck on, that we thought were really real, turned out to be only relatively real.

First mushrooms, then acid, did to our perceptions of reality what Einstein did in physics to Newtonian physics, which took it from treating a certain plane as real to Einstein's saying, "It depends on where you're standing." That's what we understood, and the minute we understood that there was relative reality, we were empowered to change things. It was as if the childhood nursery stories we had read were suddenly possible—they were real. People lived with love and joy. There's not much joy in culture, it's all such serious business. And there was dancing and playing. We played with time and space. We started to go behind time and space and see the relative nature of those things, and the nature of social relationships changed.

That was the major input of what went from vertical power structures to this whole networking, horizontal thing, where there were suddenly many voices speaking. People had an intuitive validity, so they weren't just trying to impress someone else, they were trusting their own inner voice.

For me, in 1963, as a Jewish, middle-class boy from Boston, to take on Harvard and get thrown out for something that was so intuitively valid that I had experienced through LSD—to deny that experience in order to stay at Harvard would have been a quality of hypocrisy that I couldn't live with.

I'm living so much in the moment, and that was part of what happened to us then. Instead of being so future-oriented and past-oriented and carrying our baggage and our personality with us, we started to experience the fullness of being here now, the fullness of this moment, and realizing that process and product were the same thing. You couldn't keep justifying cruelty and viciousness and a lot of stuff because of some ultimate good. It wasn't good enough. And it scared the culture a great deal, what happened in that time. It scared the culture because it felt chaotic, and it felt like the institutions were in jeopardy. And indeed they were, because we saw those institutions, those monolithic structures like the Pentagon and the White House, as just these papier-mâché things created by the human mind that were extremely vulnerable because they were rooted in fear, not in love. And we began to sense the possibility that love was a stronger power than fear.

What happened later on was that we flexed our muscles to take on the social institutions and the anti-Vietnam movement, and once we got into the marketplace of social action, a lot of our old habits started to re-assert themselves. While we had tasted all of this, we weren't yet rooted in it. And we could go up and down. We'd get high, and we'd come down. We'd get high, and we'd come down. And then we started to take on the world. The evolutionary and revolutionary forces were coming together. They were complementing each other at that point, and so the anti-Vietnam movement was both revolutionary, which had in it the anger and the violence and the polarization of the culture, and it was also part of an evolutionary process in which we were just coming to appreciate who we really were or weren't. We weren't who we thought we were. At that time we thought we would create new economic and social structures—alternative cultures, the communes, bartering instead of money. We had all sorts of ideas about how we would do it, and a lot of us went off and tried it, and we learned a lot that has been useful since then. But we were also very naïve. Our innocence was colored by our naïveté. There is a certain kind of innocence that is rooted in wisdom, and there is an innocence that is naïve, and we thought we could translate that vision directly into action and, indeed, it's taken us twenty years now—through the 70s and the 80s—to come to appreciate just how to do that. And we're learning that the work inward and the work outward have to go apace. You can't get ahead of your wagon train, in a way.

Sometimes I think that what happened to me in my first psychedelic sessions, I'm still, twenty-five years later, growing into. It was that profound. I'm still learning how to manifest that vision in daily life, because I came in contact with a part of my being that had nothing to do with my social roles, my psychological identity, my body. It had nothing to do with time or space, nothing to do with being born and dying. And over the years, when I've studied maps that have become available to me, I found in Hinduism and Buddhism and the

Tao, and in agnostic Christianity and Kabbala, a cartography
for my own mind's transformation. I'm beginning to understand how you live with equanimity in the presence of
suffering and be joyful. And that's a big one. It's taken me
many years to do that, because, when we would have trips,
some of them would be good trips and everything would look
precious and beautiful; and sometimes we would have bad
trips, and it would all look horrible. Well, that's all true. What
we always want to do is avert our eyes from what's horrible
and look at what's beautiful. But if you're really going to be a
mensch, if you're going to be a really conscious being in the
universe, you've got to be able to keep your eyes open and
keep your heart open in hell. Just be fully present.

That's part of what the 60s started me on a journey
for. And it's interesting because a lot of the memories of those
very profound psychedelic experiences could have been
interpreted as, "Well, life isn't like it was then. Wow, weren't
the 60s great!" But what I see now is that the 60s were like
baby steps: they gave me the faith to go ahead, and they gave
me a template against which to see where I was as time went
on. What I've done over the past twenty years is to check back
every year or two with an acid trip, just to see what I was
forgetting and how it was integrating, and it's extraordinary to
feel it integrate, to feel that I can look at other people with this
much love and this much compassion and this much spaciousness, and meet them in the place behind the drama that we're
involved in all the time, and feel this equanimity—that's all
the product of the 60s.

When I look at the culture now, and when I look at
my audiences who come to my lectures now—twenty years
ago they were between fifteen and twenty-five years old. Now
they're between fifteen and seventy-five years old. It's not just
the audiences growing old with me; it's a much broader range,
a much more heterogeneous range, too, culturally, and still
under-represented in the minority groups, because they have
another agenda. And in Des Moines, Iowa, or Kansas or the
states in the Midwest, there are 500, 1000, 2000 people each
time, and I'm saying the same stuff that I was saying twenty
years ago when only a few people could hear it. And I look at
them now and 70% of them have never smoked a joint,
they've never taken drugs, they've never read Eastern philosophy. How in the hell do they know all that stuff? Because

when they nod, they must know that they know it. And what I realized then is that it's permeated the culture. These values, these perceptions, these shifts, that started with psychedelia in the 60s and went through the rock lyrics and the whole ambiance of that culture, are not just a generation growing old, they are feeding into the culture. What's interesting is that there was, because of the revolutionary component of what we did in the 60s, a pendulum swing. Evolution is always generational. So the next generation was very conservative. They just wanted to go into engineering and law and make money and be yuppies, and that was a part of the reaction to the impurities of the 60s. But the deeper parts of the 60s that were true are in there, and slowly they come out. The truer parts of the 60s are starting to be honored rather than just unconsciously adopted. They're starting to be consciously adopted, and that, to me, is a very exciting process. I think that history will remember the 60s as a critical turning point in this culture.

Lisa: What do you feel was the main impetus?

Ram Dass: A key impetus for what happened in the 60s was psychedelics or mind-manifesting chemicals. They played a very powerful catalytic role in the whole process of transformation. And when people ask me, "Would it have happened without it?" . . . Conceivably. How could you know? What happened, it seems, is that the psychedelics frightened the culture, and the use of drugs fit in with an addictive personality that we have in our culture. When I look at them now, I see that the addictions to drugs like crack and cocaine represent to the middle class the failure of the American dream to fulfill the way it promised. And when they don't feel fulfilled, when they did the whole yuppie number and got all the stuff, then they say, "If the American dream doesn't work, it'll work with more. More is better." It's also a sign in the inner city that we are not attending to our people, that we are leaving a lot of people disenfranchised in our culture. They're screaming, and that's part of the screaming. They're dropping out with drugs, and I'll tell you, I don't much blame them, for what their alternatives are. I think we have to turn around our thinking about what is a healthy culture in terms of much more inclusiveness rather than exclusiveness. I think that the

present-day drug problem that Nancy Reagan was so concerned with, as she held up her martini, was really just a sign
of a shifting culture, a sign of the culture screaming that the
way we've designed it is not good enough, not humanely
compassionate enough.

I live so much in airports and motels and stages and
meeting halls that sometimes I lose my connection to the
earth, to nature, to cycles, to the heavens, Then I come back
here to New Mexico, and I just sit down and feel the presence
of the Spirit, the way it manifests in all these forms. There's a
very special light here in New Mexico, and just the quality of
the earth-connectedness, of the adobe structures, and the way
people live close to the elements is very elemental. I think I
need that to understand the present moment.

And here, for me, in New Mexico is the Hanuman
Temple which, in Hindu culture, is the representation of the
way of coming to spirit through service. My name is Ram
Dass, which means Servant of God, and I'm named after
Hanuman, actually. What I'm learning how to do is called
karmic yoga, which is to awaken into the spirit of this moment
through the way in which I relate to the suffering of the
universe around me.

I've got to learn how not to burn out, how to stay
equanimous and get my hands dirty and get into it and stay
open. So Hanuman helps me do this. I just came down from
Lama, which is a commune that we started in 1966 or 67, and
it's a continuing community that is strong and clear and light
and growing, and it's really like a mastery school.

It is a transformative space in which people live very
close to the earth with their firewood runs and outhouses and
very simple vegetarian food, and the kids are there and the
gardens, and as I walk in the woods and sit by the fire in the
circles as we chant together, I feel like I'm reconnecting to the
roots of my being, and that's part of being in the present
moment for me.

I'm not terribly familiar with the communes here. I'm
aware that the experiments we started in the 60s have gone in
a lot of directions. Some of the people have preserved the
original social structures that were there. Some have become
very ecologically oriented. Some have become very socially,
politically oriented. I teach up in Brighton Bush in Oregon,
and that's an old commune community that is basically

ecological in its orientation—holding on to the old trees. And then there are others that have kept the anarchy: it's mellowed into a kind of gentle anarchy and use of dope and a life that is very slow and immediate. We are a complex organism, and I think we're all part of an organism. We need each other, and we need to play all these different parts. I don't see that it's better or worse.

There are a lot of us who are on a journey together, and what we do is get together now and then to compare notes—describing the path we're on and what we're hearing—and, over the years, what I've become is a mouthpiece for a process that a lot of us are going through.

It's not that I'm going through it first or I know the answers, it's merely that I am a mouth for that process. And so I will be mouthing it again, and we do it through a thing called Darshan, where people come and they ask questions and I play with them, and we sort of reflect together to hear where we are and what we're learning and how we're integrating the spirit and life and where we're getting hung up in relationships and sexuality or drugs or whatever—the stuff we have to keep thinking about.

Lisa: You work with SEVA.

Ram Dass: SEVA is another thing that really comes out of the 60s and 70s in an interesting way. It's an organization, a group of people who include people like Wavy Gravy and Jahanara Romney and Mike Jeffrey, who is now a judge in Alaska but who used to wash dishes in the temple in India when I was there, and Mirabi, and there's so many of us from so many different walks of life who have come together with the multiple objective of collaborating and relieving suffering in the world, growing spiritually in the process of doing that, and having fun doing it. We are ten years old now, and it is such a rich experience that none of us would miss a single board meeting for anything.

And what projects we've taken on! We work with the blind in Nepal. We do cataract surgery in Nepal and work with children who have various blindness and life-threatening illnesses. We work in India with blindness. We work in Guatemala, in the villages that have been decimated by economic and political suppression of these incredibly beautiful Mayan Indians. We are helping them redevelop their villages. Being down in Guatemala has affected me tremendously. It's politicized me, because I feel very much that our government is culpable for what the conditions are in Guatemala. I feel very called into political action to try to change that situation. All SEVA does is provide seeds and help them with their weaving crafts, and their wells, and help them get their lives together. SEVA has no political part in it, but I personally feel the pull to be political. We also work with Women of All Red Nations, the American Indians in the Dakotas with a lot of health problems, and the Porcupine Clinic, which is just opening next fall, which is part of the dance that SEVA has played a part in helping. It got going through Jahanara's efforts. It's just a joy. We have on the Puja table at the middle of our board meeting a pair of clown glasses—they're usually called the serious glasses—and if anybody uses the word "serious," you have to put them on and continue with what you're saying, so that we won't take ourselves too seriously.

Lisa: Tell me about your relationship with Timothy Leary.

Ram Dass: Tim was my psychedelic guru. He introduced me to psilocybin mushrooms in 1961, and he was one helluva good guide. He was so much looser. I was such an uptight, middle-class, neurotic person, I'm amazed that he had the patience to hang in with me. He loosened me up an awful lot over the years and taught me how to live with chaos. He certainly did that. And then we came to a parting of the ways in the middle 60s, when our work was completed. It was difficult, because I felt that he was busy in a way fighting the Establishment more than I felt was necessary, and I didn't really want to play that. He was the Irish taking on the English. So I split and went off to India, and that was a big part of my life. What happened to me in India gave me a whole other reference for what had happened to my consciousness and gave me a bearing and a direction to it, which a lot of the people who just took drugs in the 60s didn't have. They didn't have a process for integrating what had happened to them into their daily lives. I had a whole set of cultural traditions in Buddhism and Hinduism, and I really treasure that a lot.

I think that Timothy and Aldous Huxley and Ralph Metzner and Alan Watts all guided me in that direction at one point. The interesting thing is that Timothy then went in a very different direction. I don't mean his political stuff with prisons and all that, I mean the way in which he became enamored of the games of the mind, if you will. And I became much more enamored of the awareness that exists behind the mind, so that he went into computer software and playing with his mind a great deal.

Recently, he and I spent an evening together in Hollywood at Spago's and Helena's, and we had an absolute ball together. At one point I turned to Timothy, "You know, Timothy, when I look back at the 60s, I think we won. I really think we won." And he said, "You know, I think we did too."

I feel this incredible love for Timothy even though we really can't dance together. We have different values, we've gone in different directions, but I think we really appreciate and honor each other a lot. I think the kind of connection that happens when you've taken as many acid trips as Tim and I have together—even though the going gets hard between us at times on social and political levels, and I don't think that he is very much honoring of my spiritual work particularly—I still think that the love is really strong and clear.

I am on the Board of the Albert Hoffman Foundation, which is a foundation formed to create a psychedelic library and to preserve the dignity and the potential opportunity of psychedelics in a culture that is hysterical about drugs. This culture has very naïvely massed together all the opiates—all the psychotropics, psychedelic agents, and the triptomines, and the opiates—and they're entirely different. You use them for different reasons, and it's very naïve to group these things together this way. Before the crackdown on psychedelics and the stopping of a lot of the research, the potential for psychedelics in terms of dealing with people dying, for example—like a nurse who's dying of cancer: she takes LSD and says, "Yes, I know I'm dying of a deadly disease, but look at the beauty of the universe." It's important that the culture not lose that preciousness of a shift in perception.

Lisa: Who is Ram Dass?

Ram Dass: I have no idea who Ram Dass is. I'm not even interested, to tell you the truth. I think that I've been in Nobody Special training for so long now that I've sort of stopped. It's just a form that I play in, and people project onto it this or that. It has very little meaning to me at all. I just am. I'm right here. I have no idea who I am, and I keep figuring I can costume up anyway I want to. I think that even "Who will I be when I grow up?" is kind of irrelevant, because I decided I'd never grow up anyway. It's just not a relevant question. I like the "I don't know," the openness, because every time I get a model of who I am, it's like a prison to me. It's much more fun to keep that spaciousness. I can give you all sorts of astral story lines—I'm just the messiah that's just arrived, or something like that—but it's just a bunch of crap. I don't believe any of it.

But it's interesting, because you keep meeting people, and they project onto you, and the game is how you don't buy their projections, how you make yourself like a sieve, so they go through you. People say, "Oh Ram Dass, thank you for what you've done for me." Somebody else says, "Hi Dick, how are you doing?" And it's all the same blah-blah. It just runs through you. Instead of "Oh thank you, would you like to kiss my ring?"

TIMOTHY LEARY

Timothy was invited to give a speech at the 1989 Whole Earth
Festival at the University of California, where he spoke to a
young crowd on the quad. Wavy Gravy was the MC.

Timothy: Thank you, Wavy. Well, we must have done something right to end up here, at UC Davis. In the middle of the
Reagan/Bush/Quayle/Ollie North decade, we come together to
start something new.

     Before getting down to business here, I'd like to take
a couple of minutes to pay tribute to a great American—a
friend of Wavy Gravy's and mine and most of you—a man
who was a legend in his time. I'm talking, of course, about
Abbie Hoffman.

     Abbie was a man of many, many lives and many
roads and many incarnations. He lived life in overdrive and
laid down an incredible track record. Many of you in this
meadow probably never had the fortune to see Abbie Hoffman
in action, but Abbie invented rap: if he was given a microphone, he would take off like a rocket.

     There are many misconceptions about Abbie and
about that period—the 60s and 70s—because what Abbie was

doing, and what many of us were trying to help him do, was something totally new—certainly in American politics and Western culture. We were trying to perform a cultural revolution without price and politics, or without guns, or without any of the trappings of power. It was being done with intelligence and heightened consciousness.

Now, most people don't know that Abbie Hoffman was a graduate student at Berkeley in psychology. Maybe many of you don't know, while we're on the subject, I got my Ph.D. from Berkeley in psychology and believe many of the spokespeople and the cheerleaders of the 60s and 70s came from the traditions and practices of thinking deeply and sharply about issues. And that's what the 60s is all about: attempting to raise consciousness and encourage and empower people, particularly young people, to think for yourselves and question authority.

Let me tell you a little of that. I was honored to be with Abbie on the occasion of his last public appearance. And I'm going to share with you the last public words uttered by Abbie Hoffman in a minute. But before I do that, I think it's important that we understand a little bit more about Abbie. Abbie was not a traditional politician. He wrote a book once called, *Revolution*—not for Marx or for Lenin or for Mao—*Revolution for the Hell of It.* Many, many righteous, right-wing conservative Americans think that Abbie Hoffman was not only the devil, but a Communist. Well, Abbie was not a Communist. As a matter of fact, all of us who were involved in the 60s understood that we wouldn't last for five minutes in a Communist state. We were bitterly opposed to Communism. Abbie used to say that he was a Marxist—a Groucho Marxist! Well, there's one thing we all agreed on, and that was that we hated Communism, because Communism represents a political power. The Communist Party is in cahoots with the military and in cahoots with the police, which controls the press and which controls industry, and there's a little elite of commissars who run the whole thing, and they specialize in imperialism and nationalism. So we hated the Communist Party.

We also hated the equivalent of the Communist Party in the United States, because when you think about it, there's one party in this country that is in cahoots with the military. Like, how many of the generals and military do you think voted for Jesse Jackson? There's one party in this country that is always in cahoots with the police and the CIA. There's one party in this country that certainly controls the press and controls the money and controls the industry and which has a little elite that attend private schools and go to Yale University and end up running Texas oil wells. And, of course, I'm talking about the Republican Party.

This does not mean to say that Abbie or any of us who were involved in this cultural revolution were Democrats. The whole point was, we're not going to vote out the scoundrels and vote the rascals in. The idea was politics of consciousness, a politics of intelligence. If you could get people thinking clearly, they'd obviously act with more common sense, and they'd free themselves. The key is freedom. So everything that Abbie would do was to get you to dissolve, or to undermine or to undercut or to loosen up the shackles that keep all of our minds from being free, the shackles that are laid upon us by our parents, however well-intentioned they are, by the schools, by society, by organized religions, and of course by most politicians.

I can't think of anything better to do than to have a little five-minute celebratory wake in honor of Abbie Hoffman. He would love this. He would love to be here. There was one time when Abbie wanted to demonstrate the greed of Wall Street. Good God! You know, under the Reagan administration, Wall Street and savings-and-loan people have stolen one trillion dollars! Well, Abbie was trying to make this point back in the 60s. He got one hundred dollar bills, and with a friend of his, they went to Wall Street, and they wanted to get into the visitors/spectators balcony above the stock market—that pit of greed. So Abbie and his friend, of course they were dressed with wild hair and dirty blue jeans and scruffy T-shirts with some obscene things probably written on them, and the guard looked at them and said, "You can't come in the Wall Street spectators balcony." And Abbie, in a loud voice, said "You're not letting us in the Wall Street Stock Market because we're Jewish! Is this the policy of the Wall Street Stock Market, to keep Jews from coming into the spectator section?" And the cop said, "Get in, boy, get in, boy." So then Abbie and his friend leaned over the balcony and started throwing handfuls of dollar bills. Well, the trading stopped immediately, and the brokers were running around, jumping and fighting and knocking each other over on all fours, picking up the dollar bills. And after he ran out of dollar bills, Abbie threw pennies, and they booed him. Now all that was well reported in the press, to give you an example of how you can make a point without violence or bombing or even bad vibrations. Abbie used to say all the time, "You can't do good unless you feel good." Which is a formula for intelligent politics.

I'm sure you've heard of the occasion when we tried to stop the horrible war in Vietnam. Abbie organized these fifty thousand young Americans to come to the Pentagon, surround the Pentagon, and try to levitate it. Abbie had people all over the country getting corn and maize from the Indians, and incense, and everybody was armed with some sort of a magical technique to levitate the Pentagon. And some say they did, some say they didn't—who knows?

On the occasion of Abbie Hoffman's last public appearance—his last words—I had met him about an hour before, at a restaurant, and I was shocked at the way Abbie looked. He had had an auto accident. He was walking with difficulty, and that incredible enthusiasm and almost megalo-maniac joy and garrulousness were gone. He was very quiet. When Abbie was introduced—oh, by the way, it was at Vanderbilt University—when Abbie walked on stage, he walked like this [*walks slowly, with head down*], which was really shocking, because Abbie never moved under less than 55 miles an hour. Whatever the speed limit was, Abbie used to always violate it. But it was shocking to see Abbie this way. And I was a little concerned, but I need not have been con-cerned about Abbie, because the lucid intelligence and that powerful mind—he just laid down a talk that fortunately is taped and you'll get to see it someday.

At the end of his speech—his last public appear-ance—Abbie was summarizing the effects of the cultural revolution of the 60s and 70s. And of course everyone is trying to prove that nothing happened, or that America has gone back to apple pie and mother and right-wing militarism and so forth. And Abbie was demonstrating that the victories that were won in the 60s can never be undermined, because they're victories in people's minds. And once you free people's minds, it's very hard to turn them off again. So Abbie said, "When we came to the 60s, America had a state of legalized apartheid. Black people could not ride in the buses. Black people could not go in certain theaters." He said, "We did not end racism, but we ended legalized apartheid in this country. And they will never go back on that."

Before the 60s, everyone knew that women were there to help men—Mamie Eisenhower and that crew. Abbie said, "We did not end sexism, but consciousness is raised, so that everyone now is aware of this issue and has to deal with it on an individual basis." He said, "We did not end militarism in this country, in the world, but never again will the American people allow a military clique in the Pentagon to send a million American young people nine thousand miles across the globe to fight a war that the people do not want." His final words: he said, "Yes, we were young, we were silly, we made mistakes, we were obstinate, we were naïve, but we were right. I regret nothing!"

I still get a chill in my spine every time I think of those words. Now somewhere, right this very minute, Abbie Hoffman is taking the rainbow bus up to cloud nine in the sky, and right now I know Abbie is having a little reunion with Jimi Hendrix and Jim Morrison, yeah, John Lennon, and I know that Abbie is very happy in the last two weeks, because something has happened. Television is everything, you know that. Who controls television controls the minds of the people. And to my amazement—and I'm sure to your pleasure— we've seen things on television that are as good as I've ever seen on television. In China—*China!*—one hundred and fifty thousand young people openly defying one of the toughest dictatorships in the world. China! I'm sure if you looked at those films, it was heartpounding to see those young Chinese with the same innocent, naïve faces that the American young people had in the 60s. In front of cameras, because they understood the lesson of Abbie Hoffman: "Get yourself in front of a TV camera, and you're going to change things." Where did they learn this? They learned it from watching Abbie Hoffman and the hippies in the 60s. Young Chinese started talking in English: "We want freedom. We want democracy. We want an end to corruption. We are patriotic Chinese. We want China to be free."

Now you see, that's a new kind of revolution. It's not Marxism overthrowing Capitalism. It's not royalists fighting with socialists. It's basically issue-orientated. Abbie was very active politically, but he never ran for office. He was not running around trying to get you to vote for one crook or another. He was fighting the politics of the environment and stopping pollution. Now Abbie was very happy in his last days. And other things were going on in television.

Believe it or not, the most totalitarian dictatorship in the world—the Soviet Union—is suddenly having their Summer of Love, and young Russians are going around growing their hair long and listening to punk rock, and there was a little hashish situation from Afghanistan. And the English translation of "glasnost" is, you know, Summer of Love. South Korea, the South Korean dictatorship is a real gangster. They think nothing of killing each other with machine guns. Young people in Korea standing up throwing stones at tanks. Where'd they learn that? Well, in South Korea they learned that from the Yippies and from theatrical politics. No guns. What Abbie used to do at Berkeley and other campuses when the National Guard would come out to threaten the students—they would put flowers in the gun barrels.

You notice the Chinese students—I was delighted—suddenly there were explosions, the explosions around the Chinese students were not bombs—they were celebratory firecrackers, like the Chinese New Year's. Because it was a new year—they can never go back, because in every Communist country, in every fascist country, where they showed the news, people went, "No shit, if the Chinese can do it, certainly we Japanese can do it, right?" If the Japanese can do it, certainly the Koreans can do it. I mean, just think. But see, this is invisible politics. You never hear about it in the news columns, and the political scientists will write about it in twenty years, when it doesn't do any good. The Ayatollah Khomeini, you know—he's got a billion people of Islamic descent who, five times a day, get on their knees and hit their heads on the ground. The word "Islam" means submission. Now, I'm not making fun of all Islamic people. The Islamic religion probably has as many intelligent people who think for themselves as the Christian religion—maybe five percent. I'm going to make fun of everyone. I'm very nondenominational. I'm going to make fun of every organized religion.

Now, brothers and sisters, I'm now going to quote you the word of God, the Christian/Jewish Bible, where God has told us what's what. Here is the theory of human intelligence that comes from Genesis, Chapter 3, boys and girls, look it up in your Bible. God said, "Adam, Adam you're my boy here. This is what I've done, Adam. Me, I did it all. On the first day I made the heavens and the stars. On the second day I made the planets. On the third day I made the oceans. On the fourth day I made the land, the creepy-crawly things. On the fifth day I made the whales. On the sixth day I made the ultimate Club Mediterranean destination resort—it's called the Garden of Eden! And I put you in it, Adam. You can do whatever you want. And because you're all alone, I'm going to give you a servant, OK?" God says to Adam, "I'm going to take one of your ribs and give you a servant that will work for you, call her woman, but no guts, no." The Bible is not a women's liberation tract, as you've gathered. Then God said to Adam and Eve, "Listen, in this garden you can do whatever you want, just live it up. But there are two food-and-drug regulations. You see that tree over there? That's the Tree of Eternal Life, and the fruit of that is a controlled substance. Just say no! Just say no to immortality. It ain't good for you. 'Cause, if you have immortality and live forever, you'd be a god like me, and I can't allow that." He said, "Now, you see that tree over there? That is the Tree of Knowledge, and if you eat of that, the blinds will fall from your eyes, and you will become as wise as I am and a god, and I can't allow that to happen."

Now, that's pretty cold-blooded, don't you think? Well, we're now in a period where it's possible, with the communication devices we have for individual humans, to learn how to think for ourselves and question authority. I have been unhappy and discouraged, as perhaps many of you have been in the last ten years, to see how conservative college students have become under the Reagan administration. I've talked to many professors, and you know, the professors are pissed off, because most of your professors went through the 60s and the 70s, and they brought about great changes, and they thought the next generation was really going to kick ass. But instead, many—not all, but most—of the general tendencies of college students during the 80s was, "Build this administration, career." Even racism is coming back on campus. The ROTC, which was a laugh—grown men dressing up like boy scouts, like Ollie North, trying to march around the campus. The ROTC got back in fashion! Can you believe that?

Well, the reason for that, as explained to me by some professors, was this: the college students during the late 70s and 80s, their fathers and mothers became teenagers and college students during the 50s, when the same thing was happening: you had an old senile general for President, who was Cold War, and we had Joe McCarthy, like Ollie North, running around scaring people, and there was careerism, and no one in the 50s had much concern for social issues.

But that is all changing. It is changing so visibly, and I think you will be amazed in the next few years to watch this change. In the steroid-cocaine-Reagan era, steroids, booze, and cocaine were the drugs of choice, and they're not friendly drugs. Twenty years ago, four hundred thousand kids—young adults—were at Woodstock. There were probably ten thousand young people—babies—conceived during that weekend. How old are those kids now? They're in their twenties! The first wave of college students who are the children of the 60s children who are the grandchildren of Dr. Spock, now they're in college. Suppose you're eighteen, seventeen, fifteen years old now, and you say, "Hey Mom, hey Dad, were you there in the 60s?" "Well, yeah, mom and dad were." "Were you all at Woodstock?" "Well, sure." "You mean you ran around bare-assed, smoking marijuana at Woodstock?" "Well, we were younger then, but we did." "And you levitated the Pentagon with Abbie Hoffman?" "Well, yeah, we did, matter of fact." "And you stopped the war in Vietnam? If it weren't for you, we'd still be killing American and Vietnamese over there?" "Well, yeah, your mom and I did that, yeah, OK." Do you think kids like that are going to become business administration majors? [*Audience laughs*]

This may be wishful thinking, but I want to share something with you. Tuesday night I lectured at a very large California campus, and I went out to dinner with the head of the lecture committee afterwards, and I said to him, "What are you majoring in?" Typically, they say marketing or business administration. And he says, "Well, I was in marketing and business administration, but I changed my major." I said, "What do you study?" And he said, "Environmental protection." And he's a campus leader. I said, "Why'd you change?" And he said, "Well, I thought about it—working in a bank and making a lot of money—and it didn't seem to be doing any good. I believe that the planet is in bad shape, and I can work and try to help the ozone layer or stop the rape of the Amazon rain forest, and I can always go back and make a million dollars, but I may not have a chance to save the planet."

Last night I lectured at, of all places, Stanford. Stanford! Mr. Republican Stanford. And afterwards, I went out to dinner with one of the guys that might be the next student-body president, and I said, "What are you majoring in?" He said, "Ecology." He had read the books of John Muir and he said, "I want to really find out what's going on with the forests and natural resources. I've got to help save the planet, or what good is it to make a lot of money?"

These young kids are coming along. They saw their parents being a little too materialistic, so many of them are more realistic and more practical, and not as young and naïve as they were in the 60s. The new generation of young actors and actresses coming up will reflect the new attitude. Winona Ryder, for one—you listen to her in interviews, and she's the daughter of political activists and psychedelic leaders of the 60s, so she's sophisticated, and she's realistic and deep. So I'm going to leave you with this notion: you're going to see in the 90s—the 80s were the 50s, and the 90s are going to be the best of the 60s, with an enormous amount of realistic intelligence thrown in. We can only hope.

After Timothy gave his speech at the 1989 Whole Earth Festival, we sat under some trees off to the side of the stage and did this interview.

Lisa: In 1967 you were at the Human Be-In. Could you tell us how you feel about that—that day, that special day in your life?

Timothy: Oh, Lisa, I can hardly remember. There are three dangerous side effects of psychedelic drugs, as you know. The first is long-term memory gain, and the second is short-term memory loss, and the third I forget. But we had so many wonderful Be-Ins. The great thing about the San Francisco Be-In in 67 is that it was the first. And it will always go down as that.

Lisa: How do you feel about what you said that day?

Timothy: I deny everything. Who knows what anyone said that day? As Robin Williams says, "Anyone who remembers the 60s wasn't there."

Lisa: You were the man who popularized LSD. How do you feel about that?

Timothy: I think Cary Grant popularized LSD, and certainly John Lennon, the Beatles, with "Lucy in the Sky with Diamonds." I was a humble Harvard professor. I certainly did my share, but I certainly give most of the credit to more eloquent and popular spokespeople.

Lisa: So you feel that that day when you said, "Turn on, tune in, and drop out," that you weren't . . .

Timothy: Actually it was Marshall McLuhan who taught me that. He said, "That's a good motto," and what Marshall McLuhan meant by that, and what I meant by that, was this: "Turn on" means activate the divinity or the great spirit inside you. That's been said for thousands of years by every great philosophic person. Activate what's inside you: turn it on. And "Tune in" means: once you've done that, to go back to the society and to tell everybody else about it—paint pictures, do computer programs, write rock'n'roll to express it. And "Drop out" doesn't mean drop out and spend the rest of the your life smoking marijuana and listening to Beatles records. "Drop out" means change. "Drop out" means drop in and drop out. You have to do everything the same every week. Drop in and drop out. That was a bumper sticker, and it was a pretty good one, and now we've got new ones that say: "Hang in, hang out, hang on, turn around, tune in, tuned out, fine tune."

Lisa: What were you doing before you took LSD?

Timothy: I was a Harvard professor.

Lisa: What happened to you after you took it?

Timothy: Like millions of people who have made this voyage, I discovered that there were enormous universes inside my brain which can be reached if you have the vehicle or the rocket fuel to get you there. This has been known for thousands of years. The wisest philosophers—men and women—have known that we have all these universes within. Most people when they experience them can only say "Wow," but sometimes great painters like Hieronymous Bosch would come back and give us paintings and illustrations of what you can find in your brain. So I made that discovery, which has been made by millions of mystics and visionaries throughout history. And it's there, inside your brain, if you know how to get it going.

Lisa: So now today what's happening is that whole mystical thing about LSD. . . . People are becoming more aware of it, like with the Albert Hoffman Archives. Oscar Janiger is getting information together, Ginsberg, and you, are helping . . . can you tell a little bit about the Albert Hoffman archives?

Timothy: Albert Hoffman was a Swiss chemist who discovered LSD and synthesized psilocybin—a great organic chemist and a great scholar and a gentleman. He's 80 years old and he's still as lively and as sharp and as energetic as he ever was, which is saying a lot for a Swiss. A group of people in Los Angeles—Oscar Janiger among them—are going to get an Albert Hoffman Archives together in which the writings and the movies and the films and the music and the memorabilia about this psychedelic experience will be kept in one place. When they first announced this last year, Albert Hoffman came over here and announced that LSD has been made legal in Switzerland. Isn't that amazing? Conservative, uptight Switzerland has made LSD legal. Doctors and psychiatrists and ministers and respectable people can be licensed to prescribe LSD. So the spirit goes on.

Lisa: Can you give us some quotes about what the 60s were to you?

Timothy:
>Well, the 60s are the 90s.
>The 60s are and will be the twenty-first century.
>The 60s appeared in Spain after Franco died.
>The 60s appeared in all places. (In the Soviet Union "Glasnost" and "Perestroika" mean turn on, tune in, drop out.

Didn't you know that?)

The 60s are now appearing in China (where one hundred fifty thousand students in May 1989 are revolting peacefully and happily against that terrible Chinese dictatorship.)

So the 60s are and will be happening wherever young people begin thinking for themselves and do something to make it a better world.

The 60s, I guess, are beginning all over again with the new college students in the 90s. Now what could be more inspirational? What could be better than that?

PAUL KRASSNER

Paul Krassner lives a few blocks from the beach in Venice, California. He is continuously working on writing projects—either his magazine, The Realist, *or a new book. He works from the second story of his home in a room filled with filing cabinets and a computer, and there are stacks of newspapers lining the hallways and the walls of his room. He's a serious bookworm as well as a satirist, stand-up comedian, and historian. He never fails to make me laugh. I did this interview at his home in 1989.*

Lisa: What were the 60s all about?

Paul: First, you know, I've copyrighted the 60s, so that any time anybody mentions that decade, including me, I automatically get royalties. The 60s lasted from 1958 to 1974. During that time, there was a mass awakening.Those of us who had felt like the only Martians on our block found a sense of community. Sex, drugs, and rock'n'roll were only the visible signs of what was basically a spiritual revolution. Religions of repression were replaced by religions of liberation. As Lenny

Bruce said, "People are leaving the church and going back to God."

Lisa: What role did psychedelics play?

Paul: Psychedelics was one vehicle among others—zen, yoga, aikido, meditation, fasting, chanting, advanced breathing—that served to put folks in contact with their consciousness, to understand their motivation and behavior and to change them. The CIA originally planned to use LSD as a control mechanism, but young people used it as a sacrament to de-program themselves from an inhumane society and to re-program themselves into a value system more in harmony with nature. The CIA's scenario backfired. Not to mention that a massage on acid was a truly colorful trip. We took our credo—"Make love, not war"—literally. Sensuality became a way of life. Sexual exploration replaced "Wham, bam, thank you, ma'am."

Lisa: What about free love?

Paul: Discovering the beauties and pitfalls of free love didn't fail, in the sense that an experiment never fails. The process is a success simply because you try it. From marijuana to mushrooms, music has been enhanced—in the performing and in the listening. And the dancing—"Dancing in the Streets" was our soundtrack.

Lisa: Looking back, can we blame those people who burned their draft cards, escaped to Canada, and avoided the draft in other ways?

Paul: The underground press flourished as young people saw the difference between what they experienced on the streets and how it was reported in the mainstream press. They could see the connection between busting a kid here for smoking pot, and dropping napalm on kids on the other side of the globe. It was the logical extension of dehumanization. Dodging the draft was an honorable occupation.

Lisa: Do you think it was a good move for our lawmakers to make marijuana and LSD illegal?

Paul: As long as a government can arbitrarily decide which drugs are legal and which are illegal, then those who are behind bars for drugs are political prisoners.

Lisa: How did Native Americans influence the youth?

Paul: Countercultural youth realized that from the very beginning, even before slavery, this country was the scene of violent intrusion, starting with the European invasion of Native American Indians. It had been their land, and it was their sense of intimacy with the land that hippies tried to recapture.

Lisa: What were the good values that came from the 60s, and do those values still work today?

Paul: Every individual that I know from the 60s (*ka-ching!*— that's the sound of a cash register) has tried to remain true to the values that they learned in the 60s (*ka-ching!*). There's an old saying that a liberal is a radical with a family. And some are now conservatives. But compassion can be nonpartisan.

Lisa: What did Woodstock represent to the world, and why are so many people trying to recapture that feeling?

Paul: Woodstock was the second Martian convention, with music. It was a follow-up to the Human Be-In, which was known as "a gathering of the tribes." The government tried to understand this. The Criminal Intelligence Division of the Army was at Woodstock, realizing that these kids in the mud were not willing to kill or die in Vietnam. The Hudson Institute, a conservative think tank, concluded that hippies were delaying the guaranteed annual wage. Everybody saw us through their own subjective filters. We were a threat to the establishment, because they perceived us—correctly—as an alternative to their own, embedded insanity.

Lisa: Did communes work?

Paul: Some communes worked and some didn't. The Hog Farm, the Merry Pranksters, the Farm in Tennessee—these have evolved along with their participants. Even many of those that didn't work out still remain in force as extended families.

Lisa: What was so special about the Grateful Dead, and why did they have such a following?

Paul: Like the Pranksters, the Grateful Dead were a traveling commune. A Dead concert was really an extended family reunion. A healing ceremony. A pilgrimage. A renewal. A rebirth. And a fucking good time. I will never forget Jerry Garcia's final instruction to the band in Egypt: "Remember, play in tune."

Lisa: What are your thoughts on marijuana?

Paul: Medical marijuana is now a crux issue, since 97% of the American public seeks medical help for pain, and marijuana has been proven to relieve pain. Everyone knows that tobacco is legal, and it kills 1200 people a day in this country alone, but pot is illegal, and the worst that can happen is maybe you'll raid your neighbor's refrigerator. I was in Amsterdam for the 10th annual Cannabis Cup. Pot is legal there, and civilization thrives. The drug war has transformed the military-industrial complex into the prison-industrial complex. The bottom line is, it provides jobs in an insecure world. Fascism is already here, it's just friendly fascism, with spin doctors galore to explain how it protects you.

Lisa: What kind of legacy are we leaving for our children?

Paul: Perhaps the main legacy of the 60s (*ka-ching!*) is the children of the counterculture. They were treated with respect as individuals, and now the ones I meet are intelligent, funny, hip, and proactive. They needed less deconditioning than their parents. They balance nicely between technology and humanity. They see through bullshit. They buckle seat belts automatically and take recycling for granted. They realize that responsibility can be fun. Harry Chapin said, "If you don't act like there's hope, there is no hope." So even if it's a placebo, I feel optimistic. It's probably due to chromosome damage.

Lisa: There were a lot of movements that really took on

momentum in the 60s: civil rights, women's rights, gay rights. What do you think allowed these issues to gain such momentum?

Paul: Out of the Eisenhower-Nixon years, exploding from the repression (McCarthyism), the piety (Norman Vincent Peale's *The Power of Positive Thinking*) and blandness (Snooky Lanson singing "It's a Marshmallow World" on "The Lucky Strike Hit Parade"), the progressive movements of the 60s (*ka-ching!*)—from civil rights to women's liberation—all stemmed from that desire to break out of the chains of racism and sexism, and those battles continue to accelerate today and tomorrow.

Lisa: Are the 60s dead?

Paul: The values of the 60s are not dead. They've changed, you know. Condoms used to be party decorations. Now they're responsibility. Sex, drugs, and rock'n'roll were our credo, and now they're all being attacked again. I think that maybe the principal value of the 60s was to live in the present moment. And so what's going on now is not so much nostalgia as people finding their own countercultural roots. And that's important in any society—to know your roots.

Lisa: What are your feelings about Wavy Gravy?

Paul: If he were dead, he would be a folk myth already. But I'd rather have him alive and wait for the folk myth. He's like that missing link between responsibility and fun. I mean, he has made being a fool a spiritual path. And I have too, but not as visibly as he has. I mean, Wavy is so into not making a separation between his work and his play that, more than anybody I can think of, when he takes off his clown makeup, he looks *more* like a clown.

Lisa: How about Abbie Hoffman?

Paul: Well, you know, on different levels, I miss a friend that I loved, and I also regret that he cut short all the additional stuff that he had to contribute to the culture. But he once said that he felt that Che Guevara was more effective in his death than in his life, and, in a certain way, it's true of Abbie, because his death has served as a catalyst for reuniting people in a spirit of community, which is what he did during his lifetime. So that's his legacy, that it's possible to fight city hall in creative ways and to use wit and imagination as your weapons. He was a very unique individual.

I remember once I told him that my brother, who had worked in a corporation told me that his job was to make himself replaceable. And Abbie said, "Wow, my job is to make myself irreplaceable." And he is indeed irreplaceable.

Lisa: Can you give us a quick day in your life in the 60s?

Paul: There was no typical day. That was the thing. You made the day up as you went along. You made up your timetable as you went along, and sometimes something else would come along, and, if you trusted yourself, then the priorities that you would choose would be done in an organic way. And so the priorities would shift throughout the day. That's what my typical day was. I would just juggle priorities. But I try to make no separation between my work and my play, so there was no typical day. It's the same thing now, you know. Partly because I've never had, or hardly have ever had, a regular job. So, therefore, I haven't had to structure my day according to a time clock or to a boss. I'm fortunate in living that way. I think my typical day was spent trying not to find a job, and to not keep it if I found one.

Lisa: What do you think religion will become?

Paul: Every institution is evolving, and that includes religion too. In the 60s, there was an influx of eastern religion, so that people could compare religions of control (western religions) with religions of liberation. The message of these alternative religions was compassion, nonviolence, and the notion that the spirit and the flesh are not mutually exclusive and, in fact, they enhance each other. I've always been an atheist, but I've also been an absurdist, so I've always thought the most absurd thing would be for me to develop a relationship with a deity that I don't believe in.

Lisa: Can you tell me what you feel about Dennis Hopper as

an artist?

Paul: The word "fuck" is written forty-seven times all around the paintings in different subtle ways. It's very impressive.

Lisa: Where's that?

Paul: Any of his paintings—every single painting has "fuck" forty-seven times. It's his personal trademark. It's like Leo Herschfield always has his daughter Nina's name in his caricatures. Same principle. It's just his private joke, but now we've revealed it to the world. Actually the art work of Dennis's that remains in my mind is a scene from *The American Friend*, the movie where he's lying on a pool table with a Polaroid camera above him and taking pictures of himself, and the pictures fall to the billiards table. When I think of Dennis Hopper, I think of a billiard table. I guess I mean art should be for itself, you know. I mean, if you're going to show his art, the audience can decide for itself what it is. Right? Don't you agree?

Lisa: You should see his new art, now. His new art is painting over imaginary graffiti.

Paul: Over imaginary graffiti? Well, I think he's not only pushed the envelope, he's sealed it.

Lisa: What do you think of Ken Kesey?

Paul: Kesey is a dear friend, and I don't see him as often as I would like to. I do know that he recently taught at the University of Oregon and collaborated on a novel with his students, which was kind of symbolic, I think, of what's happening in the 90s, which is again a community effort. Very collaborative—people realizing their interdependency and acting accordingly.

Lisa: Lenny Bruce?

Paul: Lenny Bruce used to say that you could judge a society by the mere fact that they were sending kids to prison for smoking flowers, and I think his gentleness comes through in that remark.

Lisa: If you were President . . .

Paul: If I were President, I would appoint a cabinet that would serve the needs of humans, not corporations. To ensure that, I would require all campaign donations be anonymous. And if I weren't such a First Amendment nut, I would outlaw bullshit.

Lisa: The 60s were . . .

Paul:

> *The 60s (ka-ching!) were a mass awakening, an*
> *evolutionary jump in consciousness.*
> *The 70s were anticlimactic—a mass retreat.*
> *The 80s were festering with greed and acquisition.*
> *The 90s are reeking of spin doctors with everything*
> *coming to a head,* so that the people can

celebrate the year 2000 as if their religion and their corporation were the only things that mattered. And so it's going to be very interesting. More interesting than this answer, certainly. The millennium will be a battle between individual freedom and friendly fascism.

MOUNTAIN GIRL (Caroline Garcia)

I found Caroline in her home atop a hill in San Rafael, California in 1989. She was busy being mama to her girls. Her husband, legendary Grateful Dead guitarist Jerry Garcia, was in another room and stuck his head in to say hello. I taped Caroline in her room, which had a loom in it and a colorful piece of her weaving hanging on the wall. Weaving is her special talent, one of many she has, including juggling the daily life of a family and being wife to a musician in one of the few bands to make it from the 60s right into the 90s—still truckin' until Jerry passed away in 1995.

Lisa: I interviewed a Vietnam vet in the Haight, and, by the end of the interview, we were all in tears. What a great loss that war was.

Mountain Girl: Women my age can't get a date, because all the eligible men went to Vietnam and got all screwed up, shot up, killed, wasted, lost. There's nobody to go out with. We miss them. It's like the males of our generation sort of got truncated right there—chopped off. I know so many people who talk about the friends they used to have. It's really sad.

There was the whole high school class that signed up en masse out of Roseberg, Oregon in, I think, 1966 or 1965, and only three or four guys came back. They all signed up to be in the same unit, and they were all killed on Hamburger Hill or one of those awful places. I happened to meet the guy who ran away, and the FBI chased him all over Europe because he went to sign up with the rest of the guys and then got cold feet and split. He's the only guy left from his high school class.

Lisa: Where did you get your name?

Mountain Girl: One of the Pranksters, Michael Hagan, gave it to me. At the time, I was living in a little rustic cabin on the side of the mountain in Skylander, which was right above La Honda. He asked me where I lived, and I said, "Oh, I live in a cabin up on the mountain." And he said, "Oh, you must be Mountain Girl then." And it stuck. I've had to deal with it ever since.

Lisa: Well, a lot of the people have their names changed.

Mountain Girl: Yeah, but nobody else got stuck with theirs like I did.

Lisa: The Prankster called "Hassler"?

Mountain Girl: Hassler got stuck with his, that's true. No, Babbs, Gretchen got stuck with theirs. Gretchen Fetchen is still Gretchen Fetchen to this very day. And as a matter of fact, I think it's on one of her kids' birth certificates, so it's causing her a lot of trouble. But that was a fun thing to do—to change names and become somebody else, and it was all involved with this concept that we were kicking around, which was to make life more like a movie. And this making your lives over as a movie gave you a certain amount of freedom of action that you don't get in normal life. You're able to become more. You take on what seems like a larger role. It's like an expansion on life. And it's really a lot of fun to do that. And the excuse of making a movie—you could use that excuse for doing all sorts of crazy stuff: "Oh, it's part of the movie."

Lisa: To me, the Pranksters were this group of people who had nothing but fun and theater. Tell me what a Prankster was.

Mountain Girl: The Pranksters were a clever invention by deranged people. The derangement was deliberate, and the concept of Pranksterism was an attempt to keep it kind of light, and I would say mischievous rather than hooliganism. The idea was to startle and to shock and to bring about a change in the perceptions of the people who were watching the Pranksters. A lot of them wore red-and-white-striped shirts, but that was part of the movie—they photograph marvelously. Even in really bad light, you could see the motion of a red-and-white-striped shirt a mile away. And there was a lot of fluorescent paint and fluorescent rubber balls and color moving.

Lisa: *Furthur* was actually the first bus of all the buses, right?

Mountain Girl: I believe it was the first bus. I don't know of any other buses that were previous to that. It was a yellow school bus that had been converted to a camper by a guy with a big family—a 1939 International, with funny headlights that set up on top of the fenders with a big sort of silly-smile bumper kind of thing. It was a sweet bus. It was just a darling bus, but it had an extremely low ceiling that everybody had to get used to. It was three inches lower than my head, which meant that everybody that ran around in there was ducking. All the time, you were running around all hunched over.

The conversion of *Furthur* from a school bus into the Prankster mobile was pretty spectacular. They welded a big rack on top, and then they took a beautiful curved windshield out of a Corvette, I believe it was, and stuck that up on the front, so you could ride on the top without getting your hair blown off. Then they cut a porthole in the back with a ladder that you climb up to a turret. The turret itself was a recycled dryer drum, and that was all painted and added onto. And then there was the ladder, so it was a lot like a Mexican bus. When we got to Mexico, we said, "Wow, these people have buses like this all the time, with ladders and racks and platforms on the back." They knew how to make buses more friendly. So *Furthur* got a big coat of paint too, and everybody worked for a long time on it, getting it painted and colorized and named.

Lisa: How'd you meet the Pranksters?

Mountain Girl: How I got involved with the Pranksters is a
short, sweet story. I was sitting in St. Michael's Alley on
University Avenue in Palo Alto. I had lost my job, and I had
lost my erstwhile boyfriend just moments previously 'cause he
was called back to Kansas (by his mother). And I was sitting
there, feeling sorry for myself and having the St. Michael's
Alley Special, which was a huge cup of coffee with a big
scoop of mocha ice cream in it and then whipped cream on top
of that. I think I was eighteen years old and I had a motorcycle. I had gone all over California on my motorcycle, so I
was feeling very independent, like I could handle anything.
And these two weird guys came up to me and asked me if I
wanted to go out and smoke a joint and I had nothing to lose at
that point and one of them was really cute, so I said, "Sure."
        We went out and got in this old white station wagon,
and this older guy just flings it into reverse and backs screech-
ing up the street to the railroad tracks, and backs onto the
railroad tracks and drives down the railroad tracks to a little
park—Menlo Park. And I'm going, "God, this guy is driving
down the railroad tracks. I've never done this before. This is
really wild . . . *berump, berump, berump*, down the tracks."
These guys are giggling and laughing and they were really
neat. He whips off the tracks just as a train goes by, and it
turns out that that was Neal Cassady who picked me up, and
his sidekick Bradley, who was a tennis star for a very short
period at Stanford. They took me up the hill and introduced
me to Ken Kesey. We got up to La Honda about 4 o'clock in
the morning, and there was the bus under the redwood trees in
the dawn light. It was an incredible-looking bus, all painted up
garish and wild. I cracked up. I couldn't believe it. It was the
wildest thing I had ever seen. I was so pleased to meet people
that had another vision, you know.

Lisa: How do you compare the 60s to now?

Mountain Girl: Well, the thing about the 60s was it was all
new. It was an explosion of new ideas. Now, all those ideas
have been out there for thirty years and a lot of them have
gotten to be old hat. A lot of people scoff at that stuff that was
so new and bright and fresh at the time. You have to remember

that the 60s all happened right after Kennedy got shot, which was such a huge disappointment for people. When that happened, there was so much sorrow in the country, especially in the young people, because Kennedy was a real shot in the arm for this country, and to have him assassinated—that was a crushing blow. And when the revolution came along a couple of years later, it was a direct offshoot, I think, of the Kennedy assassination.

Lisa: Do you think that the 60s are going to be important in history books?

Mountain Girl: Well, one of the things I think that has been ignored about the 60s is art. It took a giant surge in the 60s. Suddenly art was accessible to everybody. Everybody could do art. Anybody could be an artist. You know, like Timothy Leary says, "You can be anything you want this time around." That silly thing he used to say. And it sounded really silly at the time, but actually he was right. He had boiled it down to the thing that people want to do. They want to be able to create their own lives. They don't want to be just shuttled off into a job or whatever it is—that American way. Because the American Dream just went to hell when Kennedy was shot and when the Vietnam War became such a problem.

I felt like the revolution in the 60s was the reverse of that direction—180° in the opposite direction. I think that people will be able to look back and pinpoint in art history where the 60s happened to artists, because they were a big part of it. And writing. Well, you see what happened with something as simple as "Dragnet." Suddenly on "Dragnet" they're dealing with acid-crazed hippies. You can go back and dig out "Dragnets" where they're following buses around, you know. "God, that looks like a real infraction of L.A. County law," and it seeped into everything. It was like yeast for the dough that America had become.

Think of all the writers and people that wouldn't be able to get a job today if it hadn't been for the 60s! People like Tom Wolfe, Hunter Thompson—these people would be bums, begging for a handout on the street. They wouldn't be able to get a job. Radicalism became very popular.

Lisa: Do you think that psychedelics had anything to do with the changing of art, or did it just happen at the same time?

Mountain Girl: I think that psychedelic drugs are what changed the visual perceptions of artists. Obviously, artists had been going to Mexico and getting high before LSD hit the streets in the mid-60s. But as far as the idea of a lot of people getting together and getting high and having a party atmosphere and working with colored light and film and weird sound—you can turn on the radio today and hear what 60s musicians were doing with sound. Now it's become popular.

Lisa: Well, do you think the fact that the drugs were so prevalent in the 60s has anything to do with the fact that there's so much addiction today to other drugs?

Mountain Girl: That's a tough question. I don't think so. Before I got turned on, I became aware that there were people strung out on methedrine. That was like the first drug that I noticed. In high school, kids were taking methedrine to cram for their exams, and it started out with No Doz. You could take a pill and study for your exam. I think that was going on in colleges a lot. I don't think that the drug revolution in the 60s did a damn thing for the actual attitude toward drugs in this country. Everybody already had an attitude about drugs. You took diet pills to become thin, you took Valium to calm down, you drank coffee to wake up, you took speed to study for exams. I think it was already all going on, and then the war brought hard drugs into the country. So heroin and alcoholism pretty much were emergent from the Vietnam War. But as far as psychedelics are concerned, I think you can pretty much point the finger at 1965 and a few chemists and a few very dedicated people that put it out there, because they felt it was not only saleable but also very valuable.

Lisa: How do you think it's valuable?

Mountain Girl: Well, it's valuable because it alters your perception. It gives you a much wider view. You blow off the filters that have been placed on you from early childhood by your education and by your family and by society. You're brought up to see and think and hear in certain ways, and the psychedelic experience removes those things for a few hours and gives you an opportunity to experience a whole other level. For sensitive or artistically motivated people, I think it gives them a freedom of thought that they otherwise might not get. And a lot of people who are artists and photographers and musicians will always talk about their LSD experiences as being something wonderful.

Lisa: Is it good for the kids to do LSD today?

Mountain Girl: Speaking as a parent, it's one of the things I've worried about quite a bit. My own children, I don't mind if they experiment with the stuff as long as they can talk to me about it and I know that they're going to take certain precautions to protect themselves from unnecessarily bad influences when they're in an open state. When you're high, you're just wide open to all sorts of things, so you want to set yourself in a place where you're going to be safe, and it's going to be calm and gentle, and you're going to have friends, and there's not going to be a lot of outside disturbance. I prefer a natural setting, out in nature. That gives me the most pleasure.

Lisa: You also have to be careful that the stuff you're taking is good.

Mountain Girl: Right. Actually, we had a bad experience in our family with a strychnine-laced LSD dose that was terrible. There are bad things out there, and everybody should realize that. They should be absolutely certain of their source before they risk themselves. Most important is to be in a place where you're comfortable and secure.

Lisa: How about you? Do you like to take drugs today still?

Mountain Girl: Actually, I've stopped. I felt that what I did in my earlier years wore me out, on a certain level, and I exhausted my capacity to enjoy it. I learned an awful lot and maybe sometime in the future I'd do it again, if I was in the right place. But it's very hard for me, as a parent, to find a time when I have no responsibilities. When is there time? Besides, I think I'm a little afraid of getting high now. I know what it means, and sometimes it can make you change your life in unexpected ways. Things happen. It cuts things loose, and I'm a little afraid of that right now.

Lisa: I was just going through a really hard time, and I went out and took mushrooms with my son.

Mountain Girl: How did that work out for you?

Lisa: It was great. I needed a change of direction.

Mountain Girl: I think when you come to that part of your life when you need a change of direction, when you feel yourself getting stale, and you reach down inside and you're not getting anything, well, that's a way to break it loose. I'm serious about needing that. I think people need that.

Lisa: The Native Americans knew.

Mountain Girl: When they feel the need to contact that greater thing and to give up on their humanity for a while and become another kind of spirit and make contact with the wider world of spirit, they know what to do.

Lisa: What was your role as a woman, what were you doing with the Pranksters when you were on the road?

Mountain Girl: I was a sound tech. I wired microphones and could repair projectors and fix light bulbs and all that kind of stuff—even stoned—and I was good with the soldering iron. I liked doing all that stuff. Running mikes around. Being competent.

Lisa: You weren't in charge of cooking or anything?

Mountain Girl: Not at all. I really avoided that. I swore when I left home I was never going to wash dishes, or cook, or iron, or do any of that stuff. I would never ever do any of those things that women were forced to do. And lo and behold, shortly thereafter I found myself with a baby and no washer, no drier, no car, no money, no nothing. *No* husband. I didn't have anything together. I had this darling baby. And I moved in with this rock'n'roll band and was greeted with open arms, because here was somebody to cook and wash and sew and do all that stuff. So I was cooking for nine people. And I would go around and get fifteen dollars a week from everybody to cover food, and then walk down to Haight Street and buy food at the Chinese grocery store down there, haul it back up to the house with the baby, and try to have dinner ready when they came back from rehearsal. That's the way it was for quite a while. I was the only girl living at the house for over a year. Yeah, I felt kind of strained by a lot of that, and it was very difficult, and I threw my back out about that time, hauling the groceries and the baby—all that stuff. It was a lot of work. Anyway, there was only one other person around that we knew who had a kid, and that was Jim Gurley's wife, who is now dead. She had a little boy named Ishi, who was my daughter Sunshine's contemporary. They were the same age, and they were blonde, and they were both adorable.

Lisa: Women's roles changed in the 70s with women's lib.

Mountain Girl: I remember reading somewhere—a Richard Brautigan piece or some funny thing about the 60s—saying the bohemian's ideal was a wife who worked, so he could stay home and fool around and do nothing all day. Well, that's not really fair. I feel like the role of women in the 60s was not necessarily to go out and get a job, but to keep the houses running and to keep stuff going. And it seemed like there was a lot of camaraderie and brotherhood and love and all that stuff. But not a whole lot of men really cooked or did big vegie meals or any of that kind of stuff. We were still expected to keep that together. And I expected myself to keep that stuff together. I feel like I had a personal expectation about my role that people needed to eat, and this was a good thing to do, and we'd all eat together, and it was a togetherness kind of thing. And I think, in the 70s, people kind of grew apart as they established their own homes and got their own cars. It eroded the communalism of our scene. And I know our scene is not like others. You could look at The Farm and ask them who cooked. In all of those scenes, everybody took turns. Not in our scene. *I* took turns—lots of turns.

Lisa: What about the role of the woman now?

Mountain Girl: I have a feeling that they have a better chance to be an individual, but I'm not really sure that a lot of it isn't just window dressing. I think in the 60s, women felt as good as they do today about going out and doing whatever they felt like doing. There was a great deal of free expression in the 60s. And I think that that's still going on. But I think women feel more like they have to get a job and earn money. I think they feel more responsible than they did then. I felt very irresponsible. I had no interest in getting a job or earning money in those days. Sorry. There were other ways to get along.

Lisa: Tell me about your weaving.

Mountain Girl: In the last year I've taken up weaving, and it was something that I always wanted to do. I used to fantasize about it as a child—being able to weave. I think it had to do with reading a lot of mythology as a kid. I had sort of a mythic impression of weaving: that it was this marvelous, dreamy, spacey kind of thing, but actually it's an intensely mathematical and difficult and exacting art. And what I love about it now is the mixing of color. There's something about color in fiber, and when you cross colors that are in fibers over each other, you get these gorgeous effects that you don't get with paint on the surface. The color and fiber are three-dimensional, and it's flexible, and it's really beautiful. I'm very tripped out by it.

Lisa: You're taking classes at college?

Mountain Girl: College of Marin. There's a wonderful weaving class there. Soon to be probably a thing of the past. Weaving is not considered an important art right now. And all weaving that's being done that's considered to be important art are these huge things that you see in hotels. They're just ridiculous, and they're not really good for anything except to hang there and look fabulous. Whereas weaving is really the art of dressing and wearing and comfort.

Lisa: Let's get back to the role of the woman. Do you feel happy with what you were able to accomplish personally through your life from the 60s till now?

Mountain Girl: I don't feel satisfied. No. I feel like there's a great deal more that I could have done and more that I feel I should do, but one thing that I learned from my youth is to be aware of the word "should." And you know, they have that thing about the "me generation." I always felt really bad about that. I never thought that was true for me. I always felt like I never had a chance to do the stuff that I really wanted to do. I was always caught up in a group thing. And now with my family—that's another extension of the group consciousness, which was what we were doing in the 60s—expanding on this group consciousness. And it's still expanding, and it carries with it a certain loss of ego for the individual, or a loss of personal expression. I feel like I've suffered with that.

Let me tell you, my ambition at age fourteen or fifteen was to rob a bank and get $100,000 and move to South America. That's what I wanted to do. I wanted to move to South America and get a little piece of land down in the jungle and then protect it, because I was very conscious about the rain forest and all the environmentalist issues—I was raised by environmentalist parents. And that was my ambition as a kid: to just shuck off this North American freeway bullshit and move to South America and live in a little grass hut and be a hermit—an artist and a hermit. And I got derailed, and I still haven't been to South America. I got shanghaied.

Lisa: What makes you feel proud?

Mountain Girl: Well, I'm proud of my daughters. I think children are the most creative and long-term project that I can imagine taking on. And they're three wonderful people. I'm very, very proud to have brought them up with hardly any mishaps. We've been fortunate, and it's been a lot of hard work on my part to keep the good fortune going on that level.

Lisa: How was it living with a bunch of crazies and trying to raise kids?

Mountain Girl: It was dangerous. You had to really watch everything all the time. I felt very vigilant, and it was very difficult to bring the girls up in that kind of situation. I mean, during the 70s, things got really weird there for a while. It was very hard for us to live without being hit on and impinged upon by the masses of interested—this has to do with

rock'n'roll—trying to live within a rock'n'roll scene. It's
tricky. And I'm sure that a lot of those other women who have
tried to raise kids within a rock'n'roll scene would agree with
me. It's a tricky doggone thing. Because you don't want your
children growing up seeing a lot of spoiled people, or sick
people, or crazy people, or a lot of the things that can happen.
You don't want them to see that. So I feel like I spent a lot of
time protecting our home scene from the hordes that would
have loved to get right in there and camp in our living room. I
became afraid of them. I became security-conscious and, at the
same time, I wanted to be right. I still wanted to be politically
correct. And that's a tough balance—try to protect your family
and stay politically correct. I felt like I was walking a tight-
rope for a long time with it, with the girls. We wanted to have
a good time. We wanted to have horses and cats and dogs and
birds and do everything. I wanted the children to have a good
childhood, and I think they have that.

Lisa: So what is it you feel the kids are faced with today?

Mountain Girl: Well, an overpopulated earth. They're faced
with every environmental poison and pollution and crushed-
together people and unhappy people. I know there were
unhappy people in the 50s, but I don't think there was the
percentage that there is today. I don't think there was as much
poverty. I don't think there was as much deprivation. I'm
talking about this country. Other parts of the world are way
worse off. And it's not going to get any better. It's up to the
professional people who run the world to take the time to help
people to see that there's another way to do things. There
really is enough to go around. There really is. Drinking water,
there is enough food. It's just not being distributed properly.
And I feel like one of the great things that happened in the
60s, one of the reasons Kennedy was so important, was the
Peace Corps. When you look around now, what happened to
all those people who were in the Peace Corps? Boy, they're
out there. They're still working. They're still holding and
carrying the ideals of the Peace Corps—to look after the earth.
I think they're disbanded and disbursed, but the effect is still
there—very greatly. The need for the Peace Corps-educated
mentality is very great. But we've got to get these people in
office. They've got to be running the show.

Lisa: What makes you happy?

Mountain Girl: Oh, let's see. I like getting phone calls from my kids, and comedies. I think John Cleese should be sainted. Good family events, seeing my friends, knuckling down and working on a project. Knuckling down and really getting into a project makes me happy. Putting colors on top of each other. I really like doing that. Running on the beach makes me very happy when I remember to do that. Usually I forget. I'm happy when I remember to have a good time.

Lisa: What role do you think music played in the 60s?

Mountain Girl: First of all, it was an excuse to get together, and to have a scene, an event. And during the 60s, we all became event junkies. It started out as a party ideal, and then they became events, and now, I mean, we've got a whole generation of people who love events. I love them. They're so fun. You go and everybody goes, and it's a huge scene, and it's great, and music started that, because it gave us an excuse for an event. I think that, for a while, the events took over from the music. We had the Trips Festival, and Earth Day is now an event that people come to from all over the place. The Whole Earth Expo, where they have all kinds of neat stuff. I think it was a direct offshoot of the music—creating an event. People became aware of the need for events in their lives, so they would travel great distances and go to all sorts of lengths to make an event.

Lisa: And you think that's why the Grateful Dead are so popular—because of the fact that they're an event?

Mountain Girl: Absolutely!

Lisa: And not just the music?

Mountain Girl: Well, the music is lovely too, but the event is definitely a large part of it. It's some of each in that case.

Lisa: It must be something that happens during the concert. What is it that's created that following?

Mountain Girl: I don't know. But I know that the event has a great deal to do with the fact that there's a huge following. You have the things—look at the Rainbow Gathering, or the Oregon Country Fair, or the US Festival, or Woodstock—any one of those things. They were huge events. Everybody got jammed in on top of each other and met all sorts of neat people and ran into their friends.

Lisa: Did you go to the Human Be-in?

Mountain Girl: No, I didn't. Unfortunately. We missed that because we were still in Mexico with the bus on the lam. We didn't get back until just after the Human Be-In.

Lisa: What's Ken Kesey like?

Mountain Girl: Ken? Oh, he's a crusty old fool. You know. If you put him up on stage and put a spotlight on him, he'll entertain you—he'll make you laugh till you cry. He's wonderful. He's a dear friend.

Lisa: And what's Jerry Garcia like?

Mountain Girl: Oh, he's crusty too. He can make you cry for other reasons, and he's a great musician and a good father.

Lisa: The 60s were . . . Finish the sentence five or six different ways.

Mountain Girl:
> *The 60s were post-Impressionist, gala, exuberant*
> *fluff and marshmallows, flying through the air.*

It was a charming time, when you could speak to anybody on the street and be sure of getting a smile. Where I grew up, people didn't smile at each other—upstate New York—terrible place in those days. And it was so nice to reinvent society where strangers were already friends before they'd met. Just like Will Rogers said, "A stranger is just someone you haven't met yet."

The 60s for me were a time of knowing that whatever I did was going to have an effect on the people around me and on the world at large. We *knew* we were having an effect. And it was exhilarating to know you were having an effect of that sort. For a lot of my friends, I think the 60s were an opportunity to make friends that we were going to have for life, outside of college. We were told by our parents that you went to college where you'd meet the friends you'd have for the rest of your life. Well, that didn't happen to us. We did it a little differently.

It was a chance to be freely youthful, and not live up to anybody's expectations, and to re-create the world in the way we thought was right, which really didn't happen. But we made the world a lot more colorful.

Lisa: Why didn't it happen?

Mountain Girl: Because the world's a stubborn place. And it still belongs to the power brokers.

Lisa: You think the values of the 60s are still valuable today?

Mountain Girl: Absolutely. Of course they are. And they spread throughout society on every level. Lyndon Larouche, eat your heart out. The 60s—the revolution—is over, and it was won. But people are still afraid to sign up and vote. I feel that politically the 60s have not really had the impact that they could have had, had America learned to trust its own people a little bit more. And I feel like the lack of trust is dangerous. We have to trust each other.

Lisa: Any more the 60s were . . .?

Mountain Girl:
The 60s were a big red balloon.
The 60s were Jacques Cousteau on mushrooms.
I got to see the Pyramids. That was one of my big ambitions in life, and we did it. It was wonderful. I highly recommend it. It's such a wonderful place.

Lisa: Do you think that this group of iconoclasts who came out of the 60s are capable of admiring leadership or believing that people, individuals placed in power, can be good rulers? Or is it, rather, a question of groups, community groups, grassroots organizations that can actually make these changes happen?

Mountain Girl: I think that if the professionals—a professional real estate agent, for instance—took it upon himself to do something about the homeless question two hours a week . . . I think that if all real estate agents did that, the homeless question would go away very quickly, because they would be able to put political pressure in a very focused fashion on the issue. In other words, the professionals, like lawyers, are very good at writing legislation, doctors are good at getting medical bills passed—this is the way things need to happen. People who are experts in their field need to have a conscience about society and act on it.

BEN FREIDMAN

The Posterman, Ben Freidman, had his store on Broadway and Columbus in San Francisco. He displayed posters from floor to ceiling, and also had several adjacent rooms that displayed many more posters and postcards. He even had a room of black-light posters that glow in the dark. Ben was flanked by two lovely young women who worked for him when I interviewed him in his store in 1989.

Lisa: How do you happen to possess such a collection of posters?

Ben: Bill Graham called up in a panic on a Sunday morning to tell me that his warehouse, which was next door to the old Fillmore, was being occupied by the city, and he had to get rid of the old posters that he was storing there. Chet Helms and Berkeley Bonaparte were also storing their posters there, and they wanted to unload the whole stock right away. So we asked them how much they wanted, and they each said $10,000. We got the money out of the bank—we had to help them out—and we bought them. It was $30,000 altogether, and the banker was frantic. He said, "What are you buying?" I said, "Well, posters." He couldn't believe it. He says, "You mean to say that you're spending $30,000 on pieces of paper with scribbles on them? You could have been buying property." And I said, "Well, those aren't pieces of paper with scribbles on them. They're art. And I'm buying them." It was my money. He didn't have anything to say about it. We got stuck with them for twenty years. They just lay in the warehouse. But I considered them art, and I felt that they would be worth money later on. Now they're collector's items, and people are buying them from other countries and from all over the United States.

Lisa: Who are the main artists?

Ben: Wes Wilson was the first one who worked for Bill Graham. Then there was Kelly and Mouse, who worked at the Avalon. Rick Griffin was one of the leading artists. Victor Moscoso, David Singer, and Randy Tuten were very good. Some of the artists didn't do that many posters, but they were all very good. Everybody was competing for the poster of the day, and they all created works of art.

Lisa: And the price of the posters, when you started selling them, was how much?

Ben: Those posters were given away free at the concert. Then, after the concerts, they'd put them in various stores and record shops, and our price was a dollar. The people would say, "A dollar! We get them for nothing when we go to the concert." And I'd say, "Well, you're not at the concert." So, it was a dollar. Several years later we started charging $5 for some and even $10 for some others—the rare ones. At that time, we didn't have them all. We got most of them, but not all of them. So the scarce ones became worth more. Now they're worth from $20 up. Some, $100.

Lisa: You say that you won't sell the Dead in Egypt.

Ben: I don't have any to sell. I only have the one framed.

Lisa: I understand that you sell Jerry Garcia and Pig Pen dolls?

Ben: We don't make them, but we get them from some lady in Florida who makes them. They're $30.

CAROL HINTON

Carol Hinton is very much at home in the adobe and viga *house she and her husband, Steve, built at Lama Mountain, New Mexico. Her kitchen/dining room is heated by an old wood cook stove. She fixed us some tea and sat by an old pine table, light flowing in from the small kitchen window. At various times during our interview, she would gaze lovingly out the window at Lama Mountain, covered with ponderosa pines. Jenna is one of her five children, and she reflects the sentiments of the 60s in her desire to save the environment from being trashed by short-sighted industrialists and money mongers. Our interview took place in 1989.*

Lisa: How'd you happen to come to New Buffalo?

Carol: We were in San Francisco and went to Mexico and then came up through Taos, partly because of Lao Tsu, of course, and we had a nice little adobe house at Ranchos de Taos while we were there. We were living happily ever after with our little family in the early 60s, and then, later in the 60s, this flood of people came through Taos.

Jenna: And everybody stayed at your house?

Carol: Yes, I don't know how they found us, but they would just drop in. We were like the wayside inn.

Jenna: So you had three kids by then, right? Elecko . . .

Carol: Right, Elecko, Miles, Jesse. So all these people were homing in, and then we heard about this commune that was going to start. So we thought, "Well, hey, if these people want to be together, why don't we just go out there and see if we can help them do it? We can't do it by ourselves." So we went out and gave it a try.

Jenna: Were there some good aspects about it?

Carol: Living outdoors is my favorite, but it's hard for a family. I think for single people it's easy.

Jenna: 'Cause then they sort of create their own family in the commune, right?

Carol: Right, right, and they need each other. We had our own family together already. The gals were running around with their shirts off, and the men were all looking around.

Jenna: You ran around with your shirt off?

Carol: No, I didn't. I was a married woman. But it was really interesting trying to do things together without a plan. That was the problem in this particular commune There was this idyllic idea of being able to live in peace and harmony together, right? But how to do it was the thing. I mean, if they had just simply known how to make outhouses, if they had done some research, it would have made a difference, right? And if I had just been able to stay home and make tea—I had a tipi then, a lot of people were living in tipis— if I had just been able to stay home with my family in the morning and make tea, I think I would have been all right. But you had to just give everything to the communal effort. There's nothing left. Nothing personal or individual left. All for the one. While there was a good aspect to that too, I really needed my little family situation as well.

Jenna: And that's why you came up to Lama? To get your own family scene and home?

Carol: Make our own home. I realized how much it meant to me at that point, because I had been trying to give it away. So we shared what we could of our home life, but people need to make a home for themselves, so we left them there to do it.

Lisa: What is your home like now?

Carol: It's wonderful, 'cause you can go anyplace in the world, and you still have a base, you know? A place to come home to. It means a lot. Especially when there're so many people without families, without homes, it's really amazing. Hunger—I don't even know what it is.

Jenna: So you feel that's a much stronger outlet—to have a family-based home.

Carol: For me. I think a lot of people like the nomadic life, though. Look at your sister out there, traveling around. She might not be back for years. There's a whole community of people just traveling alone in the world. It's another kind of family.

Lisa: But you've also chosen a place out here in the middle of the woods.

Carol: Yes, out of town, thank you.

Lisa: Describe that feeling of serenity that you find up here.

Carol: It's indescribable. There's nothing like it. I certainly couldn't find that in the city, but I guess if you were actually living there—if you needed to be in the city—you could find tranquillity somehow, on your roof or in your room.

Lisa: You got sick at New Buffalo?

Carol: Yeah, I got really sick. It was the flies. They brought hepatitis, and a number of people got sick. I finally got smart and got myself and my family out of there, so I could have my family together again, instead of giving it all up to this mass of humanity, who, I guess, were looking for some new kind of family. I don't know. Anyway, we went back to our home in Ranchos and reconstructed our family and finally got off the highway there and moved up here to the woods. Just brought it home, started over, started a new home. It was too public down there. So now we have what we want. We have our own home away from town, and town's out there if you need it.

Lisa: You were talking about how the young hippie girls were running around with their shirts off, and there was free love—how about the drugs?

Carol: They were prevalent. I think people brought out everything that existed—mostly acid, I think, but lots of pot and stuff. I don't know. I didn't get too involved in that aspect of it really. I didn't realize how much of a family gal I am till I was out there and losing it, you know? Families get dispersed in those places. Can't run around being everybody's momma. It can't be done. One thing that did happen from having been there was that a lot of our life following that time stemmed from that—the people. You, for instance—we met you there. And other people we've met at that commune continue to be involved in our lives. In fact, one of our sons is involved with one of the gals who was a little child at that time. Now, right now, twenty years later.

Lisa: Tell me about the role of women on the commune.

Carol: Work, lots of hard work. The role of the woman on the commune was to feed everyone, sort out the old boxes of vegetables from the supermarket, take care of all that stuff, and see if you could maintain a family or not within all that. We helped make the bricks, we helped peel the *vigas*, and do everything, 'cause there was no building there. People had tipis. We started making an adobe central building there, chopping straw. Some people came out from the pueblo and helped us understand what we were doing. And some neighbors—the neighbors were really nice out there—they were very curious and aghast at first to see this influx of people out on what had just been a piece of farmland, and then they started coming over and bringing us things and teaching us how to build.

Lisa: What was the influence of the Native Americans? How did you feel about the Indian culture around you?

Carol: Well, they're pretty far removed, being down at the pueblo, but they would come out too. They were interested in this commune as well, because they related to what we were trying to do: just start from the earth, start from scratch, having a little reverence for life and making your home and so on, instead of just moving into a Sheetrock box and calling it home. Yeah, they were good friends. And some of them were good farmers who helped start us out, because, of course, in the beginning, you have to start the garden and then, when you get a chance to grow things for everyone, you have your good fresh food, and you don't have to go downtown and get all that stuff. That was part of the plan—to be self-sufficient.

Lisa: Why did they feel a need to be self-sufficient? What was it about society that they were leaving?

Carol: I don't know. I guess each person had their own reasons, but there were certainly a lot of people with their reasons. It was incredible—this influx of people, almost all from the cities, just dropping it, just leaving it behind, and coming out to start fresh. Start life over. Start in a good way, in a way that felt right to them But it's a hard time learning it, you know? It was good to have that help.

Lisa: Were there a lot of people giving birth to babies in the tipis and trying that out and breastfeeding?

Carol: There was one child born while I was there, just one. We were there about a half a year. Yeah, that was a good birthing—happy momma. She loved it.

Lisa: We wanted to get back to the basics of everything.

Carol: Right, that's why we came to Taos in the first place. We were on our way back to the Bay Area, because I knew there was a birthing center there with natural childbirth. We'd been in Austin, Texas and the last doctor to home-deliver had just quit. He was scared, he wouldn't do it. And then later I learned that there were midwives around Taos County who had always been birthing, but we were camped up in the mountains. Here I was eight months pregnant, camped in the mountains above Santa Fe, on our way back to somewhere in the Bay Area, and thought we'd look into Taos. We found this doctor hoeing his garden. He'd delivered four thousand babies, and so we just found a way to stay here. There was no place to stay. No one rented or anything. No one new came to this town at that time. So we found a place in Talpa, and that's where Jesse was born, and we just stayed and stayed, and we're still here and it's home for sure. I can go back to San Francisco and visit. It's a nice place to visit 'cause I grew up there—that's where I was born—but I sure don't need it. I miss the ocean. I used to really miss the ocean, and then I realized the sound of the wind through the ponderosa needles is like that. The same kind of soothing sound. You can sit right here and have it all. People from all over the world come through here, if you want to be involved. There're people out here, they're here in Taos County. I think that, in a sense, we've re-created up here what we had originally in Ranchos before we went through the commune and through all those changes, and then we've come back home in a sense. Made a home for ourselves, which is what we really needed. I don't know what all those other people are doing, but I hope they're doing OK. The commune has turned into something really good. It's a seed-growing place now. They're trying to bring back the old seeds that are being forgotten about because of the hybrids. So the land is being put to good use. I don't think people need to live together like that anymore. They must have found whatever it was they were looking for, because they've gone off into all these different ways of life, and I guess they're doing OK. You don't see people coming together like that anymore, do you? Not that way.

Lisa: Well, that was new!

Carol: It was very new. But it did get old fast. What was it that changed it? What was it that dispersed the communes? Hard work! I think lack of focus, actually, because we were talking earlier about the commune up here, and the fact that their idea of expanding people's consciousness is a focus they've been working on, and it's held them together, and that place is still functioning in a good way. It just keeps expanding and growing. Lama Commune is still working, absolutely. They have this focus. They've had all sorts of different religious things going on up there, and they're very eclectic. They take the gems from each of these practices and put them together and make what works for them. I think it's been about twenty years they've been going on. They started at just about the same time as New Buffalo.

Lisa: And who started Lama commune?

Carol: Steven and Barbara Derky, and I think Ram Dass was involved, and Jonathan Altman. I think the four of them, I don't know, but we used to go up and visit them.

Lisa: Didn't they do the book *Be Here Now* up there? Printed it up there, by hand?

Carol: Oh yeah. That was their first book, wasn't it? It was our bible.

Lisa: It still applies to today, that book.

Carol: Yeah, that will never end.

Jenna: I was at New Buffalo when I was only two years old, but I feel like what they were doing there was a really good thing—just coming together and trying to accomplish something together and having that group energy. And I feel like it's really important again. Like, into the 90s, to have that, to all come together, and there're a lot of issues that we really have to face. In the 60s they were facing a lot of those issues, changing society so much from the 50s to the 60s, they were rebelling, and I feel like we really have to concentrate on a lot of issues just to be able to go on. There're major issues now, like the ozone changing, and for us to have a good life and be able to feel OK about having kids come into the world, we have to face the issues—making plastics, for instance. At the time, it seemed like a really good thing just to have a trash bag that didn't leak, and now we just have to look at those and say, "This isn't working." We need to find a different way to do it. We really need to get a handle on it, especially now since it seems to be getting so out of hand.

Lisa: So what do you see for your future?

Jenna: I just feel like we really need to get back to ourselves and have sympathy for ourselves as human beings. We just need to say, "OK, look, we created some things we thought were good, and they have been really good," but we need to look at them now and say, "They're not really working, and they're destroying things," and it's hard when there's this massive amount of blindness going on, like cutting down the rain forests. I think we just really need to be able to focus on that. Because otherwise, there's nothing. Like, they're just saying that the rain forest is a cradle of life, and if that just keeps getting destroyed, just those insects, for instance, if all these species of insects are getting destroyed daily, then it's like the balance gets really off. Would you want to get back in an airplane when they start taking little screws out? Would you be willing to do that? You think it doesn't really matter. But after a while, obviously it does. And I think that's something that we really need to face. It would be really nice if we could just find our own growth and expand our own consciousness. But I feel like we don't really have the time to play like that anymore, or to experiment like that anymore, and it would be so nice just to be able to just go to school, and learn some things that you really want to learn, and be able to go hiking and traveling and stuff. But we really have to do something about what's happening now. We can't create an alternative society. We have to face the society we have. We have to work within it. Just like you can say, "Oh well, we all suck, 'cause we're using Styrofoam." But you have to deal with it from there. It just has to involve all of society that we have now, and not be just a society on the side. Not an alternative society.

GRAHAM NASH

I call him Saint Graham. He is a one-hundred-percenter in my book, always willing to go the extra mile for a project, for a friend and for peace. I first interviewed Graham in front of St. John the Divine Cathedral in New York during a rehearsal for the SEVA benefit for the homeless in 1989. We finished the interview in the backyard of his two-story home in Encino, California in front of his studio, where he works on art, music, and photo projects a good part of every day. We also did a follow-up in 1998 with the last few questions by e-mail—one of our favorite ways to communicate in this electronic age.

Lisa: What were the 60s all about?

Graham: The 60s were mainly about finding myself. I can only speak from my own personal experiences, but that's what the 60s were about. I grew up a little. I experimented a lot with drugs and self-expression, and I found a certain kind of peace in being able to move around in my environment without looking over my shoulder. The whole nation of young people discovered that to love was better than to hate, that peace was better than war, and that helping was better than being isolated from the people around you. Not everyone felt this way, of course, but a great many of us did.

Lisa: What influenced the music so much?

Graham: The music was influenced by this apparent freedom. We were free to express ourselves in any way we thought possible, and this included trying different subject matters, different ways to record, and different ways to take care of the business end of things. The record companies were actually being run by "music people," and although the bottom line was important, it was not more important than the music itself.

Everyone was being inspired and learning from each other. It was a wonderful time to be alive and playing. Using psychedelics was a way for me to break free from bonds, bonds that kept me down and stopped me from any forward movement. I began to realize just exactly what was most important and just where I fit into the grand scheme of things.

Lisa: Did free love work?

Graham: I don't believe that free love worked for me. I was basically a shy man and still am. It was good to know, though, that should the urge arrive, that people were looser about making love and not so uptight. People were really rebelling against their parents and everything they stood for. The old times were gone, and they'd better get out of the way for the youth of the world to have their say.

Lisa: Did communes work, and what do you think they were trying to accomplish?

Graham: Communes were, I think, a way of self-preservation for people of like minds. We had all long admired the way the original peoples of this land had lived their lives, and people wanted to emulate this peaceful way of coexistence.

Lisa: Looking back, can we blame those people who burned their draft cards, escaped to Canada, and avoided the draft in other ways?

Graham: The Vietnam war was a galvanizing force in the 60s. It brought together all these kids to whom killing hundreds of thousands of people was lunacy on a grand scale. Military madness. Once they had seen, night after night, Walter Cronkite giving us daily body counts over TV at dinnertime, it didn't take long for people to get into an action mode to help bring this war to an end. People must stand up for their beliefs, and if going to Canada and burning their draft card was the way they were going to resist, then so be it.

Lisa: Have we really taken care of our veterans, who were subjected to the atrocities of a war in Vietnam that we now know should never have been? What could we do to make it better for the vets?

Graham: We have never done right by our veterans. They were never treated with the respect that veterans of past wars were. It is a demonstration that very few people ever really supported the war, and because of events like My Lai, the image of our veterans became one of murderer and not hero. I believe that things like the Vietnam War Memorial in Washington go a long way to help heal the wounds and bring us closer together, but the majority of teenagers knows very little about the war, and so it slips ever further from our collective memory. This is shameful.

Lisa: What were the good values that came from the 60s, and do those values still work today?

Graham: The values of the 60s are still alive and well today. It is the adults and the kids of the Woodstock generation who are now running the banks, the TV studios, and the businesses in today's society. These people still believe that love is better than hate, etc.

Lisa: What did Woodstock represent to the world, and why are so many people trying to recapture that feeling?

Graham: Woodstock has become, as most things do, a myth. The truth is that it was wet and miserable, and the music was mainly out of tune. The technology of sound reinforcement in those days was appalling. No one could hear each other, and yet such a great time was had by all. No violence, good cooperation between people, and everyone enjoyed the music. If every person who told me that they were at Woodstock was actually there, then the world would have tilted on its axis.

Lisa: What do you think allowed issues like civil rights, women's rights, and gay rights to gain momentum in the 60s?

Graham: The youth of America in the 60s was really trying to undo some of the bad things that were being perpetrated by the previous generation. There was a deep feeling of shame about what had already taken place, and the younger folks wanted to put things right. We wanted everybody to be able to coexist with each other and thereby make a stronger strain of humanity through the process of cross-pollination.

Lisa: Why do you think Eastern religions became so popular in the 60s?

Graham: It's quite easy, if you have any mind at all, to see behind the smoke screen of most mainstream religions. I truly believe that there is a *God*, but what it looks like and where it is, is beyond me. I have to think that some force is responsible for the creation and running of this magnificent machine, but the hellfire-and-brimstone aspects of religion, designed for keeping masses of people in line, is a ridiculous notion.

Lisa: We were both at Woodstock. I was with the Hog Farm Commune, in the fields with the masses, being the good Jewish mother and making sure everyone was fed. We would go to a neighboring farm and buy rows of food and bring the food back and all the volunteers would prepare and serve it. I think we fed over 160,000 people.
    When you got to Woodstock—and you were flown in by helicopter, right Graham?—David Crosby said he wasn't scared of the masses, he was scared of the people who were there, the big stars who were there. That's what scared him more than anything. But when you saw these masses of people brought together through music, how did you feel? What did that mean to you, to see that many people getting along and even loving the mud?

Graham: I'm amazed that Crosby remembers at all. We were all pretty high at the time, and you know what they say about the 60s—"anyone that tells you they remember the 60s wasn't there"—but, let me see. There was quite a group of people back of the stage checking us out. I mean, we'd had a record gone to number one, it was a relatively brand-new group, and no one had ever seen us, including ourselves, and they wanted to see who this Crosby, Stills, & Nash animal was. As far as the people in front—it was very obvious at the time that this was an awakening, a flowering of the power of youth, to see them come together as a group like that and still be able to enjoy themselves and not slaughter each other by the thousands, which is basically what the adults do when they get in any amount of over, you know, one hundred thousand.

But these kids were having a great time, and they did love the mud and they did love the rain and they did love the music and they did love each other. There were scenes of sharing, scenes of caring, and that Woodstock spirit still lives on today. All those people that were there at Woodstock are now the film producers and the documentary photographers and the cameramen and the sound people and the producers of movies, and they're controlling the media and controlling the press. All those people grew up and brought with them into their new life the Woodstock spirit. And it still is very prevalent today. I can feel it a lot wherever I go.

Lisa: Your concern for the world is shown by all the benefits you work on so selflessly, and it runs deep.

Graham: You must have written that, right?

Lisa: At the same time, your concern for each human is so evident as well. Who is Graham Nash, and why is he so positive, passionate, concerned and loving?

Graham: Who is Graham Nash? That's an interesting question. I think, above all, I'm a man whose father died at forty-six. And I'm now just forty-seven and I spent this entire year wondering if I was going to make it, and I made it, and I want to live life to the fullest. I want to treat everybody the way I want to be treated. I want the world to be a better place for everybody, including myself and my children. And I am positive because I am constantly faced with the beauty of life. In all its many forms.

Lisa: That's the passionate side of you, Graham?

Graham: Yeah, absolutely. My father died younger than I am, and if he felt anything like I feel, it's amazing to me because I guess with people's parents, you always figure that they're old, you know. But I'm now forty-seven years old and I don't feel forty-seven years at all. I'm still waiting to grow up, and it's kind of amazing that I feel as young as I do inside. I know the outside shell looks forty-seven, but I sure don't feel it. In fact Crosby's father, when he was eighty-two, told me the same thing: that he was waiting to grow up. I guess the insides remain young forever if you really let them, and I have every intention of remaining young inside forever.

Lisa: What hope do you have for your kids? What future do you envision for them?

Graham: I hope they make it back from school. And then I take it a minute at a time. You can't protect children, you know. No one can protect me. No one can protect my friends. We all have our own destiny, and I just hope that in bringing them up the way I am that I'm giving them the best chance to look at the world, and see the beauty in it, and take whatever slice of the world they want and just run with it and have a great time as people. I don't care what they are. I don't care what they grow up to be, I don't care what vocation they use, what sex they want to be, what religion they want to follow. I just hope that they're happy as people. If they're happy, I will have done my job. Because our job as parents, of course, is to put ourselves out of a job.

Lisa: How about your relationship with David? Has what he has been going through with drugs and spending time in jail been hard on you?

Graham: I believe in him. I believe in David. I always have. He saved my psychic life once in England when I was feeling very depressed about how I was being treated by the Hollies and how our music was being received by the Hollies. And here comes David into my life, in his cape and his walking cane, and made me feel OK about myself. Made me feel that I was worth something, that I was a decent writer, and that I should be given the chance to use my voice. And he gave me that chance, and I'll always remember him dearly for that. But that's only one of the millions of reasons I stuck by David. I see myself in him, and our partnership is very strange. It's like a mirror image of the same person: there but for the grace of God I could be when he was at his lowest point, and when he's at his highest point, there by the grace of God will I go. I just love David. I think he's worth fighting for. I've always thought he was worth fighting for. And fortunately, he thinks he's worth fighting for, which is more important.

Lisa: What makes you cry, what makes you upset, what makes you passionate?

Graham: Lots of things, you know. It's very hard to be specific about it, but I feel very passionately about waking up in the morning and looking in the mirror and realizing I'm still here. You know? It's an incredibly tough life to live, but within it there is great, tremendous beauty. This country specifically is a truly wonderful place. That's why I became an American citizen. I didn't want to comment about this place—its hatred and its beauty—if I wasn't a part of it. I would have felt a little hypocritical that way, so I became an American citizen many years ago. I don't know. The smallest thing can set me off, or I can be amazingly strong in other circumstances. I'm just like everybody else you know.

And so I try to experience as much as I can with him—my father—in mind, that's why I try so many things, that's why I explore so much, because I'm doing it for him too because he never even got a chance to do it. That's why, when we played in Wembley Stadium in 1974, the first thing I did when we got there was take a football on the grass and start kicking it around. Because my father's ambition all his life was to go to Wembley Stadium, and he never even made it, you know. And that's down to a football ground which was two hundred miles south of where we lived, and he still never made it. So it's just things like that. I just, you know—I put my mother in the royal box—silly stuff, really.

Lisa: And your mom, she wanted to be a musician and that's why she let you do whatever you wanted to do?

Graham: Yeah, and I didn't find that out until much later, of course, and she was almost dead then, but yeah, I guess she lived her life vicariously through me. I often wondered why my parents did not discourage me more from creating music when I chose that life. A lot of my friends' parents kept telling them to get a real job and be respectable and all that. My mother and father really encouraged me to be happy, which is one of the things I'm trying to do with my kids, which is one of the things that I have to teach them and that they can teach me. It's a funny life, isn't it?

Lisa: So you had very loving parents?

Graham: Well, you know, after World War II, and with rationing and housing shortages and being young and trying to live their lives, they did their best. Sure, I had a lot of love, obviously. I feel great about them. They were just trying to do their best, and in hindsight, now that I'm doing it—I have three kids of my own, as my mother and father did, cause I have two sisters—it must have been terrifying for them. They must have really subjected themselves to a great torment in that they could not be the people they wanted to be because they had to come out of World War II and try to make a living as lower-middle-class people in England. Whereas I have the opportunity to live like this only because they taught me not to fall for mediocrity, not to fall for the party line of doing what your father did and his father before him, and getting a gold watch and then going to lie down and die. I never fell for that. My parents wouldn't let me fall for that story. A lot of friends' parents, that's what they taught their kids to do: work at the mill for twelve hours, come home, drink a pint, listen to the radio or watch TV, go to bed, get up the next day and do that for the next fifty years. That wasn't for me. My parents didn't want that for me. But I didn't find that out until much later.

Lisa: So you didn't find it out until much later, but you'd already made that decision on your own?

Graham: Yeah, because I was brought up that way. I was

brought up to explore, I was brought up to push the edges back, I was brought up to speak my mind. But I didn't find out until much later that they were thrilled that I was escaping from that mentality, that Victorian mentality of gold-watch-dying syndrome.

Lisa: So they brought you up that way, but you didn't realize that they'd brought you up like that until later. You know, what knocks me out about you, Graham . . .

Graham: Oh tell me, Lisa . . . .

Lisa: . . . is that . . .

Graham: OK, I'm listening . . .

Lisa: . . . you produced the entire Peace Sunday concert at the Rose Bowl in 1982, helped coordinate it all, plan it, then those two days at the rehearsals, and then at the end of the whole day's concert, at 12:30 in the morning, at the end, you were still up on the scaffolds with the people taking down the stage, thanking everybody.

Graham: Sure, absolutely. We couldn't do it without them. Nobody does anything alone. We've all got tremendous help, and a lot of people helped, from your level of getting Stevie Wonder for me, to being there taking the picture, helping on your end, to me doing my job. But everybody, the guys that put the scaffolding up, the lights up, the sound up, people that sold the tickets. Tremendous amount of great people worked on that thing. I was just the tip of the iceberg maybe. But I couldn't have done it without them.

CRAIG PRESTON

Craig and I met for the first time the morning I interviewed him in a small park in the Haight-Ashbury in 1989. David, a friend of his, was to meet us too, but he became shy and hid in the bushes above us. Craig was bleeding internally that morning from too much booze, but he wanted to get this message out and he put up with the pain to do it. He sat on a metal bench, holding his chubby little black Labrador puppy, stroking it as he told us his story of being a part of the Vietnam war and how he ended up homeless on the streets of San Francisco.

Lisa: How many people do you think live in this little park?

Craig: Personally, I know at least fifty people.

Lisa: In here?

Craig: Right around here, in a four-block area, and they all sleep in the park.

Lisa: Are a lot of them Vietnam vets?

Craig: I would say almost two-thirds of them. Almost every vet I know is so screwed up he can't do anything. We can't hold jobs. We can't keep relationships. We can't keep houses. We can't keep cars.

Lisa: Why do you think that is?

Craig: I don't know. It's just like the pressure gets too intense.

Lisa: What happened to you when you went to Vietnam?

Craig: I had a good job over there. Actually, I thought I was safe 'cause I was in a trailer—computers and NASA and Lancet, you know? And we were calling down fire control. They laid the napalm two grids back, right behind the trailer and lit it on fire. I had to run out the door, and this neighbor shot me right through the neck.

Lisa: You said when you went over there you immediately got into heroin.

Craig: Yeah, because you didn't want to be there. And you didn't want to know what was happening. And if you went down to Saigon on R&R, it was easy, you know? You pick up some good chevas, and God, you could get enough with just scrip money to knock your ass off every day.

Lisa: Who were you buying it from?

Craig: Just slopes.

Lisa: What are slopes?

Craig: Well, I guess what they really are is Vietnamese.

Lisa: How'd you feel about the war itself, the fact that we were over there?

Craig: Why? Why in the hell are we here? What the fuck is this about? I mean, you old men are sending us over here to die. How come? What for? I'm in somebody else's country. I can't tell one person from another. What the hell is going on? I can't even tell anybody that I was over there without them telling me I'm a baby-killer and shit. It's like, what the fuck was this all about? And then you give it all up. We could have won. We could have won easy. Why? That's what I still want to know is why?

Lisa: So you got back over here, and you weren't accepted?

Craig: No, you couldn't tell anybody you were there. If they knew you were in Vietnam, man, people wouldn't talk to you.

Lisa: So you tried to reintegrate by getting a job, right?

Craig: Yeah, I got picked up by a phone company—real easy being a Vet and being into communications already. I did that for eight years. People still didn't talk to me all that time.

Lisa: You said you were hooked on heroin.

Craig: Yeah, I've been in eight different hospitals over addiction.

Lisa: Then you gave up the job with the phone company. You said you just gave up.

Craig: Yeah, well, my old lady went south. She went to Denver. I said, "Well, fuck the job, fuck everything, what the hell, why do it? Why am I struggling still?"

Lisa: You said that they only taught you to kill.

Craig: That's easy. They didn't teach us how to love. What are we supposed to do now?

Lisa: So they don't give you much help?

Craig: The VA is a piece of shit. They just give you a hard time.

Lisa: So you're feeling real sick today?

Craig: Yeah.

Lisa: What's wrong with you now?

Craig: Well, I think I'm dying of alcoholism.

Lisa: What can you do for it?

Craig: I gotta go back to the VA Hospital. I gotta listen to their ass.

Lisa: So what do you think about those kids that were out here demonstrating against the war? How did you feel then when you were over there? Did that confuse you, or did you understand what they were trying to do?

Craig: I did understand them. I didn't want to go over there. I thought I could get out. When my draft number came up bad, they promised me I wouldn't have to go, and then they kicked me out of a plane over the fucking fire zone.

Lisa: You were eighteen?

Craig: Yeah, I was eighteen when I first went.

Lisa: What year was that?

Craig: 1972, January.

Lisa: Where were you before you were eighteen?

Craig: I was right here.

Lisa: What was the Haight like in 1967?

Craig: Yeah, I do remember. It was beautiful! You could walk up and down the street—everybody hugged you, everybody loved you.

Lisa: Like a tribe of people, huh?

Craig: Yeah.

Lisa: Do you find that today in the Haight?

Craig: I do. With the rest of the Namese and the street people.

Lisa: What's in the Haight today that's different than in 67?

Craig: A whole bunch of yuppies.

Lisa: So you've got yuppies?

Craig: Yeah, you've got yuppies, you've got the Deadheads, and you've got the street people, and the Namese are part of the street. The Deadheads—they just cruise up here because they think it's a picnic. The yuppies—they drive in from Concord or something. Some of these people won't even give you the time of day. You say, "What time is it?" And they pretend like you don't exist. And it's like, *God damn!*

Lisa: What do you think they're reacting to?

Craig: I think they're afraid. I think they're afraid to live. I've seen life. I'm not afraid to live. I'm here. They should speak to me. I'm part of their reality. I see people walking by with Sony Walkmans and sunglasses and all kinds of shit all over them, you know. It's like, god, if you wanted to go to the moon, you can get a space suit, you know?

Live right here now. That's all we got. And my friends here on the street, they're my brothers. We share everything we got with each other. Whether it's money or food or whatever we got; if somebody needs it, you got it. I just took one of my friends down the other day and bought him a pair of shoes 'cause I got my check.

Lisa: You said you get how much a month?

Craig: I get $672 a month.

Lisa: And what happens to that money when you get it?

Craig: This month I'm doing good. Most of the time I blow it all on drugs in a week.

Lisa: Where do you sleep?

Craig: In an abandoned car, and I don't know when it's going to get towed, or anything. We've been lucky, so far. But I've got two other spots. I got a bush, and I got a side of a building I can sleep on. So that's OK. The other night, two cop cars pulled up, six cops got out, and there was a guy passed out in the middle of the park. They said, "Go find someplace else to sleep."

Lisa: So you prefer to spend the money on drugs than on yourself. Why is that?

Craig: I don't know what to do with the money either.

Lisa: What do you feel the money is?

Craig: Garbage.

Lisa: So the money that comes from the government is sort of like weird money?

Craig: It's the same thing as scrip money in Nam. It's just like, throw it here, throw it there, I don't care. Once it's gone, I'll get some more somewhere. Nothing seems to matter anymore.

Lisa: Before you went into the service, things seemed to matter, right?

Craig: Yeah, well, I sure thought it was going to be a lot different than this. I thought of myself as smart, and I was going to do all these fantastic things. You know, I had a future. And now I don't know what to do anymore. I didn't know what to do for years, actually.

Lisa: Doesn't seem to be an answer?

Craig: Yeah, I still want to know why.

Lisa: What do you think the government could do for you and other people like you who are out on the street, who are all over New York and San Francisco? What do you think they should do?

Craig: The government? The hell with the government.

Lisa: They asked you to go over there. What should they do to make it better for you? What could they do?

Craig: I don't know. But they should do something. I don't know what we need. We need an answer is what we need. Why the hell did we go anyways?

Lisa: The 60s were . . . ?

Craig:
> *The 60s were the last time I was happy.*
> *The 60s were what led me into this kind of addiction.*

It took a long time to learn that. And I'm not sure if any of us are ever coming back. If I could figure out what I cared about, I wouldn't be so fucked up. That's half the problem. It's like I'm trying to figure out what the hell's going on.

Lisa: What do you think you care about?

Craig: I care about her.

Lisa: Your wife and daughter?

Craig: Yeah, I did. Kids are good. Kids work for you. The one thing about kids, they're honest. They'll tell you straight up where you're at. And they love.

Lisa: Do you love yourself?

Craig: I don't think so at the moment, 'cause I'm not taking care of myself very good. I think I hate myself.

Lisa: Why?

Craig: I'm not sure. The bottom fell out heavily.

Lisa: Well, the 60s were the love generation. For you, when you talk about that feeling, was that there in the 60s?

Craig: Oh, yeah. I mean, I was already out here in 1969. I

didn't have to go till 72. I lived right up on Masonic. It was like, no matter who you were, no matter what you looked like, no matter what you wore, people held you. And that felt good. The street was a party all the time. It was so warm, even on the coldest days, and when the Grateful Dead had their stages down the street, and they were playing and street theater was still going, everybody was happy.

Lisa: Where is all your stuff?

Craig: I threw everything away. I'm OK. I'm still alive. It's like what you own don't mean nothing. The only thing we really have is each other. That's what it's all about. Plain and simple. We're here. And then we're gone. We have to hold on to each other.

Lisa: So, tell me where and how you eat.

Craig: Well, my big meal of the day is the Haight-Ashbury Food Program—a soup kitchen. It's over at a church, and we stand around in a line, but they serve good food. And that's mostly what I eat. Other than that, sometimes I sit on the street and panhandle, and people give me food.

Lisa: What do you usually do, say, a daily routine of yours . . .

Craig: Well, I wake up. If I'm lucky I sleep late—to me, late is about 7:30. If I'm not lucky, I get up at 5 o'clock in the morning when the first birds chirp, and I gotta wait for a liquor store to open, go down there, get my wake-up, and I sit around for a while, go down the street, panhandle, get another drink, go wait in the park until the soup kitchen happens. And then after that, if I get enough money up for a drink after the soup kitchen, I can pass out for three or four hours. And then in the nighttime, I can panhandle some more money, and I get my nightcap. And that's it.

Lisa: Then you crawl into your car.

Craig: Yeah, it's like I sneak down to the car 'cause I don't want the neighbors complaining too much. But at least it's dry and warm in there.

KEITH MCHENRY

We found Keith feeding people at Golden Gate Park in 1989.
We had followed Craig there when he went for his meal.

Keith: I'm Keith McHenry, and I'm with Food-Not-Bombs, an organization started nine years ago to serve free food, and then one day this van pulled up with a group of hippies in it, and they said, "Did you ever hear of the Diggers? You're just like the Diggers!" And we had never heard of the Diggers, had no idea that they existed, and they gave us this book about the Diggers, *Ringolevio*. That's the first we'd ever heard of them, and here we'd been doing it for a year or so. We've done it in this location constantly, and it wasn't until last August that the police eventually came and arrested 92 of us for serving free food over a course of three or four weeks, and that was because the real-estate people in the area were concerned that we were attracting the homeless. But the homeless have been here forever, in this exact location. It's just a coincidence that we were here and didn't know about the Diggers.

Lisa: How many homeless are there in the area?

Keith: It's estimated that there are between 300 to 500 homeless living in Golden Gate Park, and about a quarter of the homeless are Vietnam vets. All the time we meet people who are suffering from Agent Orange or other kinds of things. A lot of the Vietnam vets live in the park because of the way society is, as far as they're concerned, from their experiences in Vietnam. It's just not worth it to go out and get a job and be mainstream. The American Dream is a farce, according to most vets' point of view.

Lisa: They just prefer to live here and not go get a job?

Keith: Yeah, it's like a certain amount of freedom. Basically, in fighting the Vietnam War, they never became heroes. Because it was a corrupt war, people were never honored. And the whole thing they were fighting for they were denied when they came back from Vietnam. So the only way to really achieve that kind of freedom is to just say, "Forget it, we're not going to participate in this society. We're going to live free and live in the park, eat for free." And so, to a certain extent, that's what Food-Not-Bombs does. We serve the Vietnam Vets and the other homeless people who have felt that they are not going to be given a fair shake in this society at all. Why bother to struggle for a minimum wage when you can't even rent an apartment at minimum wage anyway? It's just not worth it.

The really interesting thing about the 60s that's happening right now is that people, the media, and the government, and the authorities are trying to say the 60s are dead. That it's an old bad fad—why bother with it anymore, you know? Like we all sold out. And I was, like, only in eighth grade when I started going to antiwar demonstrations. I'm thirty-two now, and I never stopped being a protester the whole time. But it's like there's this group of twenty-year-olds trying to say that the 60s was a fad, and they're sick of reliving Woodstock—live now. It's just no good. Basically, I think it's a conspiracy to try to say that its passé to be a protester, it's not hip to be a protester, it's uncool to believe in freedom and free thought and any of the ideals that come from the 60s.

And, basically, it's a concern that people who have lived through the 60s twice—once in the 60s and once in the 90s—are going to be much more serious about what they had

experienced as kids in the 60s, and actually, really make a go
for making the society better this time, because we have a lot
more experience. We won't make the same mistakes. It won't
be as naïve a movement. This anti-60s thing that's happening— like, I don't know if you ever watch TV, but man it's
just horrible. Like "Thirtysomething"—they just make it look
like the people were just pathetic that were protesting in the
60s, like they were total moronic fools, and why did they ever
go out and protest, you know, how stupid it was of them to do
that. And every show is just like that: "Family Ties" was an
anti-60s show that they ran. Every one of these shows is just,
like, how idiotic and naïve and childlike we were, and now
we're grown up and we know better. And here the same exact
wars are happening, only to a much worse extent, in Latin
America and Southeast Asia and everywhere. The same things
are happening, and so the wars are no longer passé. They are a
constant thing. Genocide is a constant thing, but somehow
protesting genocide is supposed to have stopped. That's the
sick thing. It's at the worst level. So, hopefully, we'll take the
lead of the Chinese, and we'll start having massive student
demonstrations.

DENNIS HOPPER

Dennis, who I call the multi-dimensional artist, is a great friend and a supporter of the arts. He has encouraged me in every step I have taken in creating a record of the times from the 60s until now. I did this interview with him in Albuquerque, New Mexico while he was directing his movie Back Track *with Jodie Foster in 1989. In 1999 I interviewed him again at his home in Venice, California in a second-story loft filled with furniture he had brought from the famous Mabel Dodge Luhan house in Taos, New Mexico, where he edited his second film,* The Last Movie, *in 1969.*

Lisa: What were the 60s like for you?

Dennis: The 60s were an important time for me, because it was the first time I directed a film—*Easy Rider*. I was taking drugs during that whole period, drugs still seemed to be working for me at that time. I didn't seem to have a problem with them—probably did, but they seemed to work. It was a very spiritual time too, which probably saved a lot of us, the ones who didn't OD on drugs. We seemed to be looking for something, and there was a real sense of community that I don't see any more, but it was wonderful.

Lisa: I really like your civil rights photos. How did you happen to take so many photos of Martin Luther King?

Dennis: I had met Martin Luther King at the Chateau Marmont, where I was living. I was brought into a room by Sidney Poitier. Harry Belafonte was there, and they had this young guy named Martin Luther King, and Rosa Parks was there. They'd just had the incident with Rosa Parks. She had refused to sit in the back of the bus. King had just done some sit-ins and gotten arrested and was out trying to get some backing to go on with the movement. I remember I was the only white person in the room. That was the beginning of it. This was a few years before Brando asked me to go on the march. I went on the march from Selma to Montgomery, and went on the march to Washington, and got involved in the civil rights movement that way.

Lisa: How did you happen to go on the march?

Dennis: I was out one night in Hollywood with three or four people, and Brando pulled up and said, "We are going on a march from Selma to Montgomery with Martin Luther King and would any of you like to go?" I said, "I'd like to go." He said, "We're going in a couple days," and gave me a number to call.

Lisa: What did you do on the march?

Dennis: I marched with Joan Baez and Mary from Peter Paul and Mary. Mary and I walked through Bomber's Row to-gether. I took a picture of Joan Baez's feet in the mud. She was barefoot.

Lisa: It must have been exciting to go on that march.

Dennis: It was exciting, and it was scary because the people were so angry . . . I mean, the people we were walking through were so uptight.

Lisa: Right, white supremacists in a mostly black community.

Dennis: The majority of the people at that time in these counties where we were demonstrating were blacks, and whites were holding onto the power over all these blacks. Sometimes ninety percent of the populace would be black, and ten percent would be holding them in check and having all the power and keeping them out of politics. They were marching to get the vote so they could take over the state, which they did eventually.

Lisa: Did you get involved in any other civil rights movement?

Dennis: Later, when I was in Taos, I got involved with Reyes Tijerena and the Chicano group, because he wanted me to do his life story—the raid on Tierra Amarilla. He wanted to make it into a movie, so he took me through the whole Chicano scene. I got into trouble when these kids tried to beat my brother and me up. We tried to make a citizen's arrest. They said they were going to kill me, so I went to Reyes, and he sent my brother's and my pictures around and said these guys are friends, don't do anything to them.

Lisa: You lived in New Mexico in the late 60s. What was that like?

Dennis: My experience in Taos was not a pleasant one. I wasn't allowed to create anymore because of *The Last Movie*, which I edited there. I became an over-abuser. I am an over-achiever, and I was not allowed to create, so that was the end of my world as far as I was concerned. I felt used and put-upon, and everybody who came to Taos wanted to stay at Dennis Hopper's, and I finally had to move out of my own house, I felt so used. I didn't enjoy the 70s. I went off to Europe for two years, to Mexico City for two years. I didn't have a pleasant time. And coming back to Taos was not pleasant for me.

Lisa: I would like to see more of your photos of the civil rights movement.

Dennis: I gave them to the movement and I never got them back. I gave them the film to develop—over two hundred rolls of film—thinking I would get them back some day, but I never did. The civil rights movement is when I had my first sense of doing something that had some historical significance. I knew that this was an important moment and that the pictures would be valuable as history some day.

Lisa: In your book, *Out of the Sixties*, you have lots of photos of artists.

Dennis: My main concern at that time as a photographer was with taking photographs of the painters who I thought were going to be famous. Taking the first photographs of Andy Warhol and Jasper Johns and Rauschenberg and Oldenberg and Rosenquist . . . all these guys who I thought were going to rock the boat, and they did—they became very famous. I shot them when they had their first shows. I shot Andy before he had his first show. The California artists I photographed were Wallace Burman, Bruce Connor, Keinholz. You know that Bruce Connor, Michael McClure, Stan Brakhage, and Billy Al Bengston were all from Kansas? At one time we were put together as one group, and we were called the Wichita School, even though only Michael and Bruce were from Wichita. Billy Al and I were from Dodge City, and Stan might've been from Wichita. Michael and Bruce went to school together.

Lisa: So now those photos are being used a lot in books and magazines?

Dennis: Because of the time that I was taking them, they're important. There were different areas of my life—one was the music of the 60s and the other was the art of the 60s, and the people involved in the music were not involved in the art, so I had a rather dichotomized life. I was a gallery bum—I hung around the art galleries. Some people went to the beach, some people went to the mountains, I hung around art galleries. I collected art that hadn't been in galleries at that time. So I was involved in the art world as well as the music world.

I was very fortunate, because I was in Los Angeles, New York, and Europe during that whole period of time. I met the Rolling Stones before they ever came to the U.S.—with

The Animals in England. Brian Jones and I were friends. In the 50s I was friends with Phil Spector, so I met Ike and Tina Turner and the Ronettes and the Shirelles and all those people. I met Elvis when Elvis was King in California. He came to see me before he saw anyone else because he was going to make a movie with 20th-Century Fox called *Love Me Tender*. It was his first film, and he wanted to know about James Dean. So I spent a couple of weeks with him.

Lisa: You spent a lot of time in the Bay area?

Dennis: Peter Fonda was involved with the Byrds and David Crosby. I'd known David earlier—when he was much younger, a child actually. His father was Floyd Crosby, a cinematographer, and we had worked on a film in the mid-50s called *Night Tide*. I met David with Peter, who played guitar left-handed and knew a lot of musicians. I met Graham Nash, David Crosby, Stephen Stills—a lot of those people. When I was a photographer for *Vogue* magazine, they gave me an assignment to photograph groups. So I photographed the Grateful Dead, the Jefferson Airplane, and Lovin' Spoonful, the Byrds, some others. I went up to San Francisco and got involved in the whole Haight-Ashbury scene with people I knew from Kansas—Michael McClure, Bruce Connor.

I was in San Francisco almost every weekend with the free speech movement, and a lot of my activities meant going through Berkeley. Bruce was one of my favorite artists. We've had a number of shows together. He made the first really interesting experimental movies.

Lisa: So Michael McClure went to the Be-In? I was right behind you, shooting photos of the same thing you were. I got spiritually married that day to Tom Law. Reno married us.

Dennis: I remember Reno . . . Michael spoke there, and Bruce was involved. I was already a friend of Ginsberg and Leary. I knew everybody there. Bill Graham was a really good friend of mine at the Fillmore. Bruce did all the lights at the Fillmore. I would go up and hang out with a lot of the musicians. I was sort of wandering in and out of their lives. I found the Bay Area much more stimulating at that time. Berkeley was on fire. Stopping the war. Everything I was involved with at that time came out of Berkeley and San Francisco more than anywhere else. My favorite poet was Lawrence Ferlinghetti. Honestly. More than Kerouac and Ginsberg. Still. I remember one of his stanzas: "I was an American boy. I rode an American Flyer bicycle. I delivered the *Herald Trib* at four or five in the morning. I can still hear it thump on lost porches." "I stand in Joe's pool room every day, and I watch the world walk by in its curious shoes." Just his way of looking at things. He is always available. He still works at City Lights Books. To me, he is their greatest poet. He was the one who first published Ginsberg and Kerouac. He's the man. Ferlinghetti was the greatest poet, but "Howl" is the greatest poem. That just tore my head off. That was written in the 50s. I matured in the 50s.

Lisa: You were really into jazz at an early age, weren't you?

Dennis: I was involved in jazz in the 50s. Miles Davis was a friend, and he had a group with John Coltrane, Cannonball Adderly, Philly Jo Jones, Red Garland, Paul Chambers, and so on. One day I came in to Miles, and he said, "I just wrote a song for you." I said, "So what, Miles." Miles would say something, and I would say, "So what." I'd just say, "So what." "So what" was just something I would say all the time, because I had no fucking answers, so I just said, "So what." So I came in one night, and he said, "I just wrote a song, and I wrote it for you, and it's a called 'So What.' Really a good song." The album was called *Kind of Blue*, and "So What" was on it.

Lisa: The first time I ever smoked pot was with a bunch of jazz musician after a gig one night in Sausalito. I was with Jack Sheldon, Jim Marshal, and Joe Mondragon, and we were all hanging out with Count Basie. What a trip that was.

Dennis: Yeah, far out. You know in the 50s, the act of smoking marijuana became social. You smoked and went and listened to jazz. The mere act of smoking marijuana led to jazz . . . led to associating with blacks on a very friendly, equal basis. There was no prejudice at all, and nothing was felt about it. The 50s were a great melting pot for the races, coming out of the 40s and going into the 50s. I knew Miles and Count Basie and Duke Ellington, Maynard Ferguson, Ben Webster . . . and out of that I knew Lenny Bruce. Lenny and I were very good friends. I met Lenny when his mother was a stripper, and she also taught strippers. It was in a strip joint I first met Lenny. I was like eighteen or nineteen years old. One of the burlesque comics had gotten sick, and Lenny'd gone on, and he was so nasty that they pulled him out of the show. They wouldn't let him do any more. This was way before he played the Renaissance and the Hungry I and became very famous. Lenny led to the free speech movement.

Lisa: He used to get busted for using bad language, and that was it, right?

Dennis: Right. For cussing. He used profanity in front of people in a public place. He would talk about Jesus and religion and race problems and being Jewish and the politics of the day. He was very funny.

Lisa: What about the Beats?

Dennis: Bohemians were the underbelly of the culture. Usually the poets and painters and the people who create culture do not come from the upper classes. They come out of the working class. The people who weren't working and who were scuffling to have an existence . . . these were the bohemians. I think of turtleneck sweaters and beards and tights, drinking a lot of coffee and smoking a lot of cigarettes and reciting a lot of poetry. Out of that came the Beat movement and then poetry, and jazz happened out of the Beat movement and that led into the hippie thing, and everything came basically out of that. The same people who were in the Beat movement went right into the hippie movement with no problem at all. The hippie movement was their dream. It really happened. Marijuana came out of the cellar and came out of the closet and was out in the field and all was wonderful.

Lisa: And it went right into psychedelics?

Dennis: You've got to remember that a lot of us were already into psychedelics. A lot of us had already taken peyote with the Indians early in the 50s. I took acid very late because I had already done peyote, and I said what do I want to do this chemical for? One is like eating a flower, and one is like eating an IBM machine. I didn't try acid until I was going to play the dealer in *The Trip*, which Jack Nicholson had written and Peter Fonda was starring in. I played the connection he got the LSD from. Bruce Dern and Susan Strasberg were in it too, and Roger Corman directed it. I had a really great trip. Amazing.

Lisa: Then in 1968 what did you do?

Dennis: In 1967 we started writing *Easy Rider*. I was the only hippie of the group. Peter was not a hippie. Peter wanted me to have short hair in *Easy Rider*. And Steve McQueen said I should get a haircut, that long hair was over and ridiculous, it was just a fad and don't do it in the movie. Peter doesn't have long hair in the movie. The whole hippie scene and all that— Peter didn't want it in the movie. That was because of my involvement with San Francisco. All that hippie stuff had nothing to do with Peter. And [Bert] Schneider, everyone, wanted the farm sequence out of the picture. The farm is my history, my life. It's where I'm from. I'm from Dodge City, Kansas. My grandfather had farms in Garden City, Kansas. And I was the one who was involved in the political things in Berkeley, and the free speech movement, Martin Luther King, the civil rights thing.

 Easy Rider is about the political things that were going on in the country at the time. Also, the whole acid trip was out of the "Gospel According to Thomas," which is something a young prostitute gave me when I was in New York. It had been discovered in 47 because of the discovery of the Dead Seas Scrolls, and these are called the Nag Hammadi Scrolls and were discovered in Egypt. Thomas and John were the only two disciples who actually wrote, and they went into Egypt after the followers of Christ became known as the Orgiastics. "Love your brothers and sisters as you love yourself . . . share the wine and share the bread." Thomas and John said that's not all that it was about and went into Egypt and wrote what is known as the Gnostic Bible, which is not accepted by the Catholic church because it stressed personal spiritual experience. Would have put a lot of priests out of work. They accept them as minor scriptures. The Gospels of Thomas and John were put into a crypt in Egypt in 140 AD and the other Gospels weren't written till 500 or 600 AD. They were just the sayings of Christ, not the miracles. What he said was . . . he was the Lord . . . they would call him the Lord of Peace, but he'd come to cause wars and cause divisions, for he had guarded the world till the world itself was afire, for he was the fire, he was the light that was above them all, he was the all. They were just the sayings of Christ, not the miracles. They all came forth from him, and they all strove to attain him. "And if you don't love your mother and father as I love mine, and if you don't hate them in the same way that I hate them, you'll never be able to be a disciple to me." He says, don't pray or you'll be condemned, and don't give alms or you'll beget sins for yourself. He says, when you are one or two, I am with you, and when you become three or more, you become as God yourself and you should behave as gods. If you want to slay a powerful man, put the sword through the walls of your own house first to see if you have the thrust and, if you do, go and slay him. He says a lot of heavy shit, man. So that is what the acid trip in *Easy Rider* was all about. The inside and the outside. "When you know the inside is the same person who made the outside, why claim solely the inside of the cup and not the outside of the cup?" The same person. When you make the male and the female into a single one so the male is no longer male and the female is no longer female, and when you make a hand in place of a hand and a foot in place of a foot and an image in place of an image, then you'll enter the kingdom and then you'll enter the light. When you enter the light, how much will you bear? That is what the acid trip was about.

Lisa: *Easy Rider* changed moviemaking.

Dennis: *Easy Rider* was the only film made about the 60s during the 60s. Made about it in a symbolic way. Because we'd just had *Pillow Talk*. It really didn't change anything. It just showed another perspective. It was the first time "found" music was ever used. Peter had Crosby, Stills, Nash, and Young do songs, and they had a whole group of songs in the movie. When I was editing it, I put the found music that I heard coming to the studio every day into the picture. "Born to Be Wild" got down to "Pusher Man," "If Six Were Nine". . . Hendrix . . . the Byrds. They had always written a score for the movies. They had never taken songs and put them in. So, at the time, it was really easy. All I had to do was ask the artist's permission. Today try that. It costs more to get found music than to write a score. I got all the music free. Dylan wrote the last song on a piece of paper. I wanted to use "It's Alright, Ma (I'm Only Bleeding)" [Bob Dylan] at the end, and when I showed him the film to get permission, he said, "You got to have [Roger] McGuinn sing it, I can't let you use my record because of my contract. I'll give you permission to use the song, so have McGuinn do it." Then he wrote down, "Take me from this road / To some other town." He wrote down the words which became the "Ballad of Easy Rider"[Roger McGuinn]. At the end, when the camera pans up off the river, there's a song that plays. Dylan wrote down the words for it and said, "Give this to McGuinn and he'll know what to do with it." Bob just gave it to him. McGuinn got the title and got all the money for it. McGuinn made over a million dollars off the song.

Lisa: Didn't Dylan get credit for it?

Dennis: He couldn't do that because he had a contract with whoever he was with at the time. So he gave us permission to use the song . . . "The river flows, / It flows to the sea. / Wherever that river goes, / That's where I want to be. / Flow river flow . . ."

Lisa: You sat with him, and he wrote it?

Dennis: Peter and I showed him the film. and he wrote it on a piece of paper. Right there. Right after the screening. First of all, he was really angry that they got killed. He wanted to kill the guys in the pickup truck. He said, "Why can't a helicopter come down and blow those guys right off the road?" Well, Bob, where would the helicopter come from? "I don't know!!!!" He was really angry. He said, "I would rather see Peter pull out a machine gun and kill them"—because I was already shot.

Lisa: What were you doing in your younger years that got you into acting?

Dennis: After my father came back from the Second World War, when I was about nine, we moved from Dodge City to Newton, Kansas and then to Kansas City, Missouri. At all three of these places I was moved into schools that were more progressive than where I'd been. Between nine and eleven, I fell really behind. When I went from Dodge City to Newton, I was put in a corner with lima beans and a dunce cap on my head because I didn't know anything about mathematics. When we moved to Kansas City, I was really behind in reading. I think art—this is just me trying to analyze the situation—I think art and acting and those things became the way that I could express myself. I didn't have to have the technical abilities to add, subtract, multiply, read, and do the kind of things that I had gotten left out of. So my whole drive became art, and I considered acting and being in movies and theater and painting and poetry—all those things are what I was all about. The academic world and the act of actually reading a book was for people who didn't have a life. I wrote great essays about this when I got into high school in San Diego, because I moved at thirteen to San Diego, California. I was kicked out of social studies and had to take correspondence courses from Berkeley. I was kicked out of art, drama, and social studies, which were a requirement to graduate, because I'd written this thing about being amoral, not believing in society's mores, and that only people who break society's mores can make change, and that people who read and got their lines out of books and got their ideas out of books would not have any original ideas. I had built up this whole defense about the fact that I had danced through it all without having to really apply myself in any of these areas because of being backward and not wanting to feel like a fool. I excelled in these other things and left everyone in the dust and graduated "most likely to succeed" from my high school, and still the counselor was coming to me, saying, "How are things going with Berkeley? Because I can't put you in the yearbook as 'most likely to succeed' if you're not going to graduate." I had so many correspondence courses going because I had been kicked out of so many classes. I was anti-social and amoral. It was my idea of a way to go.

That's how I came to Los Angeles. I had won in Dramatic Declaration for the state of California in the National Forensic League in high school. I'd played in Shakespeare at the Old Globe Theater in San Diego and had acted there since the age of thirteen. I starred in my high school play. Then I won a contract with Warner Bros. when I was eighteen years old, and I did *Rebel without a Cause* and *Giant* when I was nineteen. Then Dean died and my life changed quite rapidly. I got in a lot of trouble, and I got blacklisted by director Henry Hathaway in *From Hell to Texas* when I was under contract with Warner Bros. I was blacklisted for eight years, so I went to New York and studied with Strasberg for five years, then came back.

Lisa: Why were you blacklisted?

Dennis: Because I was considered too difficult to work with.

Lisa: How did you feel about that? Did you think that you were too difficult to work with?

Dennis: No, I felt that they were antiquated. They had no idea what the work was about. I had seen Dean work and I'd seen Brando work, and I saw how they fought with the directors, and in my opinion, Dean and Brando were correct in what they were doing and the directors were assholes. They were old, antiquated schoolmarms who wanted you to do line readings and wanted you to do gestures that they told you and wanted you to do everything that they told you, and they didn't know what the fucking work was about. It was just a revolution and because I was not a star, I took the brunt of a lot of things and couldn't really block myself. I mean I could . . . but at the cost of a career. And so I went and studied and just did television until Hathaway rehired me for *The Sons Of Katie Elder*, and that was because I married Margaret Sullivan's daughter, and Duke said he had decided that because I had a little daughter of my own and I had married a nice Irishwoman's daughter, they had better put me back to work.

Lisa: So you still act the same way today?

Dennis: It is so much easier to work now because everybody knows better. Everybody is already hip to it and so they just get out of the way and let the wonderful things happen. Also, I don't go into a project wanting to direct. I just want to act in it.

Lisa: Tell me about *Apocalypse Now*.

Dennis: It was four and a half months of work, and there was a lot more to it than ended up in the movie. I had a great death scene that wasn't in the final cut. There was a lot of stuff that didn't make it, but I enjoyed the movie.

Lisa: What's your most vivid memory?

Dennis: My most interesting experience was that I moved in with the Ithigal, who were the headhunters who built the village around the temple. I moved in and lived with them. I lived in one of their buildings, which they built right next to the infirmary. I moved into the village that is the village that the boat comes into, where the temple is. Francis [Ford Coppola] had the Ithigal move down from their rice paddies, and they were the ones that Mao based his rice paddies on. The Ithigal were never conquered by the Japanese in the Philippines. The Japanese could have conquered them, but they decided it wasn't worth it, because all they were getting were bodies without heads, since they were headhunters. They just left them alone, finally. They're the ones who do the animal sacrifice that is depicted while Brando is slain by Martin Sheen.

Lisa: Were you on drugs?

Dennis: Yeah, I was doing a few drugs.

Lisa: Tell me about your character.

Dennis: My character meets the boat. "I am an American. You guys are Americans. Want some cigarettes? Got some cigarettes?" Francis and I wrote every morning and improvised. There was no ending to the movie, so we did it as we did it.

Lisa: What did you think of the movie?

Dennis: I enjoyed the movie. It was a great love of Francis's. He put everything on the line. He lost his house, his studio—

everything. He went on the line for the picture, and he won.

Lisa: Any other great memories?

Dennis: Anybody who was in that picture, we bonded for life. It was like fighting a war. The film took almost two and a half years to shoot. I was only there for the last four and a half months. Mike Medavoy was quoted as saying, "First came the hurricanes, and then came the tornadoes, and then came all the natural disasters, and then came Hopper—and he brought the madness."

Lisa: What did he mean by that?

Dennis: I don't know. You'll have to ask him.

Lisa: You must have been in true form.

Dennis [*laughing*]: Things livened up when I got there.

Lisa: Why?

Dennis: What do you mean, "Why"? Because I'm such a charming guy.

Lisa: Can I quote you?

Dennis: Sure.

Lisa: How do you think *Apocalypse Now* rates as a film?

Dennis: Didn't the AFI have the greatest hundred films of all time, and I was in four of them? *Apocalypse Now* was one of them. I don't know which number it was. *Giant* was one of them, *Rebel without a Cause*, and *Easy Rider*. So I am in four of the one hundred all-time great films, according to the American Film Institute. *Citizen Kane* is one of them, and I would go with that.

Lisa: Do you think that your photography is just as important as your acting?

Dennis: Probably more important. Important in different ways. First of all, I don't make a living as a photographer. I make a living as an actor. What's going to last longer in time? The photographs have a chance of outlasting the films. It's hard to know, because once you're dead it's hard to know how you're put into historical perspective. If it's all clumped together in one thing and Dennis Hopper is somebody who should be studied and looked at, then maybe the whole thing will last for some time. But the photographs are of other people who are historically important. I mean the older photographs of Andy Warhol, Rosenquist, Rauschenberg, Oldenburg—the artist group—Jasper Johns, and so on. These are important photographs. It's an important series of works that were done. The area of Man Ray, for example, is the area of photography that I'm closest to.

Lisa: So you've recognized your destiny as an artist in many ways?

Dennis: Yeah, because I've lived with artists. I've been closer to artists and closer to the art world than the film business, because I've been allowed into the inner sanctums. Leo Castelli and I are tight. I know all these people. I know Larry Gregosian really well. I know all the top dealers and all the top people. I know the art world. I have never been allowed into the movie business in that kind of sense. I've never been taken into the inner sanctums of the studios, but in the art word I have. In the art world I've also maintained an aesthetic and maintained a position that has importance. In the film business you're sort of like yesterday's newspaper whenever they want you to be.

Lisa: The film business is very fickle.

Dennis: It's full of people who are only there for business, and art is something that they don't want to know about. They may put it on the wall, but they don't really know what art is, so they don't want to know about it at all. They're really in a commercial way, and that is something that was established by Jules Stein, who was a friend of mine, when he put Lou Wasserman into position. He wanted business people. He didn't want people who loved movies. He wanted people who were taken out of business school, not art school. That caught on. I go into offices, and I meet young men who don't have a fucking clue about making a movie. You can mention a movie, and they don't know what you are taking about: "*Bicycle Thief?* . . . What did it gross?"

Lisa: Then the movie business is basically soulless unless you come across a Spielberg or an Oliver Stone?

Dennis: Once you stop making money, they don't care what you've done. They don't care. They don't know. They always think the next thing is going to be better, it's going to be a younger person who is going to do it better.

Lisa: That's why I feel that all your art—your photography, collecting, painting and collages and movies and photos of movies—keeps you more centered in your soul than if you just depended on acting.

Dennis: If I were dependent on acting, I would be living in some prison somewhere. I mean, I wouldn't know what to do. The art has kept me balanced. The photographs were at one point my only creative outlet, because there was a long period of time I couldn't get work. That's when I really got into my photographs. The main body of my work was taken between 1961 and 1967. 1961 is when I married Brooke Hayward, and I bought a camera. 1967 is when we started writing *Easy Rider*. I didn't take any after I started making *Easy Rider*. I didn't take photographs again until seven years ago. There is a whole period of time I didn't take photographs at all. That's why my 60s photographs are unique—I didn't go on taking photographs. There's just that block of work. Now I'm doing a coffeetable book of three hundred of my photographs with Tony Shafrazi.

Lisa: The 60s were . . . ?

Dennis: Free love and drugs and rock'n'roll . . . free love . . .

PETER FONDA

*Peter is a fish, a Pisces, like me, and a great, soft-spoken
storyteller. I could listen to him forever. In 1989 he came to
Santa Fe for the twentieth anniversary of* Easy Rider, *with
Dennis Hopper and Bert Schneider. I was documenting the
event with my trusty camera, and even lent my hippie bus for
one of their* Easy Rider *events. When Peter had a moment, he
gave me this interview in a hotel room in the heart of town.*

Lisa: Was the making of *Easy Rider* a form of rebellion?

Peter: The making of any film cannot be a form of rebellion.
It's a very specific art job. It's the most expensive art form
there is. You might be the world's biggest rebel, but not when
you make a movie. My character was, supposedly, a rebel, but
he was just a very pragmatic person, trying to make money
and skate, like everyone else. I have rebellion. I had rebellion
then. Certainly, rebellion against a certain atmosphere of the
establishment brought me to the sense: "This is the kind of
movie I'm going to make." But that wasn't so much rebellion
as it was just logically looking at the way the industry was
applying itself.

The afternoon before I wrote the original story line for *Easy Rider* in Toronto, Jack Valenti made a speech, and this is the quote he gave me: "We have to stop making movies about motorcycles, sex, and drugs. We have to make more movies about Doctor Doolittle for twenty-seven million." That night, I wrote the story for *Easy Rider*. The next morning, I got up at this massive exposition in Toronto for exhibitors and distributors, and I talked about how nice it was to meet the people who ran the galleries, as it were—the people who showed our paintings, the people who showed our art— because we need to know each other. Would you think how horrible it would have been if a gallery owner had said to Picasso, "Well, yeah, we like it, but my wife would like a little more red in that Blue Period." They laughed, and I said, "But really, what it all comes down to—from what we've heard for the last three days here at this symposium—is that the only time twenty-seven million dollars is to be mentioned is at the box office—never in the budget." And sixteen hundred theater owners stood up and gave me a round of applause. Of course, I already had *Easy Rider* in my pocket, so I had a little bit of a cocky attitude, knowing, I can get away with this. I just threw sevens. I made my point when all the bets are on the table. Nobody can scram. I get all the money.

Lisa: You felt it was important to make this movie. There must have been some reason that you wanted to get this out to the public.

Peter: I went into this convention, right?—this big convention of distributors and theater owners. I went in there to do the normal business of promoting a product for American International called *The Trip*, which, by the way, Jack Nicholson wrote. I was very disappointed in it. I thought producer Roger Corman had just dug a knife into my back by not taking care to understand what in fact an altered-state experience was all about. So I had a chip on my shoulder. And when Jack Valenti was saying those words, I was recording him. I was recording getting off of airplanes, crossing borders, getting into taxis, and hearing everybody say, "God, we really love your sister, man, it's incredible, you know, and your father's one of our favorite actors."

That was to be played in the background while I was

singing songs on a recording I was working on with Hugh Masekela and Bruce Langhorne. The main song was John Lennon's "Gotta Get You into My Life." And that was, if you recall, the end of the 60s. The new thing to do on an album was to have this constant kind of noise in the background. It was like a narrative thread, you know: kids laughing, people talking . . . The Beatles, Pink Floyd, everybody was out there doing it.

I realized when Jack Valenti said we have to stop making movies about sex and drugs and motorcycles that he was looking right at me, so I'm assuming it was directed to me, and I'm thinking "Well, if I've got to get anybody into my life, I've got to get him out of that kind of mind- set." So I didn't do the album—I did the movie.

The movie isn't my life, not by any chance, nor is it Hoppy's, although it did very well for our lives. The movie is me saying, you don't understand about motorcycles, sex, and drugs until you see how we can deal with it. This was not a biker film. This was not a drug film. This was not a sex film. This was a Western. This was a very moral film about America. This was a very deep moral look at our problems in America, amidst the beauty of our great country. The poverty of the people. The poverty of their lives, their politics. The poverty of their meager attitude of self, the poverty of their relationships with their fellow man, and the poverty of their relationships to the planet and its environmental demands.

Lisa: Did you personally identify with your character in *Easy Rider?*

Peter: Not at all. I talk a lot, but Captain America didn't say anything. I co-wrote that part of the script, so, obviously, I purposely said nothing. I didn't want to be saying, "Wow, that's beautiful. Far out, man"—all those simplistic things— and develop a character that everybody would feel was really saying something tremendous, giving insight to all the youth movement, giving us a voice, giving us a leader. Are you kidding? Someone says, "Wow, man, that's beautiful . . . Far out!" That's not a leader. Not that I wanted to be cynical with this, but I never wanted anyone to tell me I was the spokesman for the generation. I don't speak for anybody but me.

Lisa: Well, it seemed like you were, by not saying anything at all.

Peter: The few things that Dennis made me say, which I didn't want to say, we fortunately took out after Dennis left the editing room. Bert Schneider, Bob Rafaelson, and Jack Nicholson—all of us were in there, editing the film, and we all agreed, "That's got to go, man, you don't want to be explaining everything." See, I like to be enigmatic. In terms of being very dramatic, the more enigmatic you can get, if your drama is sincere and deep and rooted in its foundation, the enigmatics make other people see their possible failures, their possible successes, and not explain, "Well, that was his thing, that's what he did." By being enigmatic, we could make it possible for other people to think, "What does that mean to me? What are they trying to say? What am I listening to? How am I hearing that about myself? In fact, if I think these people are making a movie for me, what am I about?" If I don't explain it to them—because if I did explain everything, they'd nail me to a cross right away—then they have to find out for themselves.

Lisa: In *Easy Rider* you say the commune will make it. Did you really think that?

Peter: Not for a second.

Lisa: Why?

Peter: When Dennis goes, "Hey man, look at this, they can't grow anything here. This is sand, this is shale, nothing's going to grow in here," and I say, "They're going to make it," that was the falsest line in the screenplay. And it was written in the screenplay, and I didn't want to say it. I knew at that time, or I felt at that time, and the proof has been in the pudding, that this alternative lifestyle attitude, this dropping-out thing, this other way of dealing with yourself and being closer to the earth, was wonderful—*if* you were a Sioux Indian. But placed on the ofay populations of the world, this is like going back to the Mullahs in Iran. This is like the fundamentalist movements all over the world today, including, and very dangerously so, in our government, in our Supreme Court, in our elective branch, and in our communities. Dropping out seemed to be nice then because we didn't believe anything that was told to us, and we thought that the people who were in the position to be telling us what was happening and what we should be doing were full of shit. And in fact, they were. But to drop out and say, "We're not full of shit. We're going to go out and grow our own corn," or, "Hey man, we could do that in the bathroom with the Gro-lights that we use for growing the pot"—there's no big show of our ability to deal with the world. If we drop back to fundamental life—and understand, I'm saying that the hippie movement was the youth fundamentalist movement—then we're going back to the fundamentals: "By golly, we're not going to have flush toilets, we're going to dig holes in the ground." And, "By golly, we're not going to have running water, we'll make it distilled from the air." And all this stuff. All of these things today mean an awful lot for our ability to save our resources, but at that time we weren't even considering, we didn't know there were resources to be saved. We just wanted out of the Establishment's way of the Rock-Hudson-and-Doris-Day life. It wasn't us. And Tony Randall and Monty Clift and these guys were not the people we should have become. But these people were told that they were our role models. Our parents certainly weren't. They never spoke to us.

I believe strongly that this fundamentalist attitude is what devastated the entire movement of the 60s. Because, when you have to start dealing with the terrible carnage at the end of the Vietnam War, the incredible mishmash of politics that happened from then until 1980 and then the devastation of eight years of Teflon, the devastation of eight years of manipulation for the rich, and taking a big dump on the poor, you wouldn't be able to attack that devastation with straight vigor, foresight, insight, if we were all fundamentally out there making our own water, washing our clothes in a stream. I don't mean to be putting that way of life down, because I also had a very good time in my life enjoying that simpler thing. I live on a farm, on a ranch in Montana, and I don't do my own wash on the rocks. We put it in a washing machine. It's a lot easier. We're very careful that the products we put in that washing machine, that go into our septic tank and eventually go into the ground around us, are not toxic. But it's not "fundamental" at all. Anything "fundamental" would be totally out of my ability to follow. As a matter of fact, I will rebel immediately. If it's "fundamental," I'm not there. My name, "Fonda," is an Italian name that means the base, the foundation, the bottom. And I am opposed to that part of the name. I'm not the base, the foundation. But the best part of the name was the motto that went with the family, which was the Latin imperative of the word "persevere." It is not a suggestion. It is a command, and it means you *must* persevere. Stick to it. That's how I've made it. It's not survival. It's keeping my eyes open and knowing I can't drop into that "fundamentalist" point of view. Neither can I drop into what Nixon was up to, what Ford was up to by pardoning Nixon. I mean, where is that? I believed then, and I believe now, that the failure of our alternative life system was because we got lost, because we got lost in our own return to a better way of life. We failed to realize we were turning our clocks back in the very midst of an incredible amount of new technology that we needed to put to use in order to save the very planet we were on, to save the very natural resources that we need to exist today: clean air, clean water, good food.

Fundamentalists cannot deal with that problem, "Because that problem," they'd say, "is God's, and He'll take care of it." You bet. And there are people from Venus that Jack Nicholson talked about, who are going to come down and take care of all their stuff. You bet, I'm going back out and washing my clothes on the rocks, and I love living in a tipi. But I'm sure happy in sixty-degrees-below-zero on my ranch that I have a log cabin with heat. And with my big dish, I receive every bit of news from around the world, and that's not "fundamental" at all.

Lisa: It was a good idea, but it didn't work.

Peter: It was a good idea, but it got too "fundamentalistic."

Lisa: In the movie, you said, "We blew it." What did you mean by that?

Peter: In order to play that as an actor, in order to get up the feelings and emotions that are on my face when I say this very simple line in the fire, while Dennis is all hot that we've made it, we're rich, we can retire. Every filmmaker wants the chance to do his own movie. This was our movie, this was our chance, and we blew it—oh my God! That's how I got to say it as emotionally as I did: "No, Billy, we blew it." In real terms, it follows through with my desire to remain enigmatic when somebody wants an answer to a question.

In fact, as I said at the press conference for the end of our version of the movie—not the answer-print, but our last work-print, where we went out to get our permission from the musicians—I wanted to have all of "It's Alright, Ma (I'm Only Bleeding)" in there. But Dylan said, "That's redundant, that's redundant. You've already said it in the film." He wanted Dennis and me to reshoot the ending. He wanted me to ride my motorcycle into that pickup truck and blow it up. This is happening in a little room—I mean, as big as a closet—with Bob and Sara (his wife then), Dennis the lunatic, wonderful genius, and me in this little tiny room, trying to convince Bob to give us the song.

He said, "I don't like my harmonica . . . the scene's redundant . . . and I want you to do this to the truck."

I said, "Whoa, Bobby, you want some revenge, don't you? The whole reason it's upsetting you is you didn't get that revenge. There was nothing to take you off that hook. And you're not quite sure what we meant by 'We blew it,' and after the bike blows up we want to hear those lyrics about questions in the nerves without answers."

"No, no, I don't want you to hear that. It's redundant. What do you think, Sara?"

"It's your song, Bobby."

"I won't give it to you."

Dylan's in a chair, and he turns to me, and he turns to Dennis, and he turns to Sara, and he turns to Dennis, and he turns to me—like RoboCop. Dennis is so cool. Dennis says, "Gee, Bob, that's really great the way you do that. Keep that in the act." And, you know, Dylan's never been talked to like that.

"You see, Bobby, Dennis had me say this thing in the movie that I didn't want to do. And I didn't like the sound of my harmonica, Bobby. Dennis had me up on a statue, asking my mother why she copped out and telling my mother I hated her, and this was something that was tremendously personal to me that Dennis knew, because he was a friend of mine. My mother had committed suicide in an insane asylum by cutting her throat from ear to ear, and I need to hear those lyrics about 'suicide remarks.' Can you dig that, Bob?"

The throat thing really blew Bob away, and he was stuttering, "Ah . . . well . . . um, well, you can have that part, and have McGuinn do the singing and stuff, but I won't give you the last lyrics, the end part. What does the end mean to you?"

This was not a question I was prepared to answer at this particular time. I said, "Well, I mean, there's the end. You see the road, the road that man built, you see what happened on that road; and there is the river, you see God's road and what happens on that road. Which is the road to travel?"

Dylan picked up a piece of paper—seriously, no bigger than this [*shows small size of paper*]—and wrote down, "The river flows, / It flows to the sea. / Wherever that river goes, / That's where I want to be. / Flow river flow / . . . Past the shady tree. / Flow river flow. / Flow to the sea." McGuinn added, "All they wanted / Was to be free. / And that's the way / It turned out to be" in order to give a little more edge to the song, which was so lyrical and ballady at the end of this massive fight, where we had just decked the world.

Dylan's my favorite songwriter, singer. He plays a soulful, wonderful guitar. His harmonica is raw and beautiful, and his lyrics just touch every stone.

TONY PRICE

Tony Price is an Atomic Artist, and in 1989 he had a show in Santa Fe of his many sculptures made from parts purchased at the Zia salvage yard in Los Alamos (the home of the atomic and hydrogen bombs). Some of these sculptures are over eight feet tall, with hanging parts that clang into each other, creating a cosmic sound as they are blown by the (atomic) wind. We interviewed Tony on a bench outside the gallery next to "The Great SALT Talks."

Lisa: What do you think caused the shift of consciousness in the 60s?

Tony: The 60s had a lot to do with the 30s and 40s and 50s, actually, and you have to go back to that kind of mode the whole country was in: great world wars were being fought, and we were being born in those years. The whole world was at war. We grew up with daily advertisements for war, which ended in this great finality of a nuclear explosion. Basically, as we grew up, we saw that all our parents were traveling in patterns of fear. We were afraid of each other, and each country was afraid of each other, and there was great fear present in our lives. We grew up with this fear, and somehow we all got together as we got older, in our later teens, and we kind of fell away from these ways of our parents. We were trying to get away from the fear. And so, we collectively got together in little groups, like in Greenwich Village, and there were groups happening in Chicago and Los Angeles and San Francisco, and it seemed like when the New York group met the Chicago group—they were thinking exactly alike. It was the beginning of a movement, and it was all of these kids, who had grown up in all of this fear, deciding to drop out and find any kind of avenue that was different from what their parents were.

What each individual was looking for was the truth, about reality and about himself and about opening up a little, getting a little love going again on the planet. But we had to break down these huge barriers that were set for generations by our parents, which trained you to do what your father did, and somehow we just broke away from this. We began thinking of each other more as a family and getting support from each other for what we did. And so, as time would go by, more and more of these people would get together who had the same kind of feelings. They wanted to escape the fear. And the escapism was alcohol and drugs and things, but these were used basically as tools to unleash the consciousness of each individual. It was like a giant pyramid being set up where people were all stacking each other up, trying to push a few individuals through this great eye of the needle into the unknown, into eternity, so they could come back and give us the message that basically each one of us is the center of the universe. That's what the message was. And we weren't born into a world where you had to fight for a place. But the minute we opened our eyes as infants, in came the universe to that infant, and he was basically the center of the universe. Each person. And this was to be discovered in the 60s. We were trying to break down all these other social vices that were holding us in place as they had held our parents.

We actually found the whole world reversed in the 60s and the people pushed certain individuals to find out as much truth as they could. And people got opened to this thing we call eternity, where this lifetime is a moment in many lifetimes that we live. And our idea was to refine ourselves, to drop these social things that kept us fixed-focus on reality. Our idea was to find objective reality, to see things as they really were. And once we began seeing things as they really were, all this other stuff slid aside, and we were starting something new.

Lisa: You mentioned the bomb.

Tony: The atomic bomb had a great deal to do with it, because the minute they found this weapon to end the war of all wars, it produced total fear all over the planet, like a huge dark cloud. And then the news media picked up on it, and daily they would keep up this progression of how the bomb was doing and who had it and how many they were exploding, and it kept the public in tremendous fear. We all had become nuclear hostages. Each side was holding all of its people hostage with this nuclear weaponry. And it produced other things. Once there was no tomorrow, people began living for today. The horror of it. All of us who were growing up in those times had no idea if there was going to be a future, because they had come up with this weapon, and we all knew that, at any moment, we could be blasted off the earth. This put this huge cloud over everyone, where everybody got drunk and took drugs and just didn't care because there was no tomorrow. So the greed multiplied. The whole world got raped behind the greed of this fear that we're going to die and there's no more future for any of us, so why bother to take the nuclear waste out of the back yard? Why bother to hide it? Why bother to do anything with it? 'Cause there was no future. So the greed became really rampant. But our generation was out looking for the truth. We were out trying to find it, and it wasn't there. Our elders hadn't explained the truth to us, nor had it been explained to them. There had been hundreds of generations where the truth just wasn't here. We were going to find this truth, and we were going to activate it as best we could. And the truth became that each one of us is the center of the universe. We have to share with each of us, because it's their universe, it's my universe. We're in each other's heads.

One of the basic truths was "I am you, and you are me," and we share this common essence that we're trying to refine. This type of a movement allowed us that kind of flexibility to experiment, to find things out, and to break down all the old walls of channeling fear. It was our earth too. We were born into it. So let's change it. And the way we went about changing it was to wake people up. If you become conscious, then the natural laws will show you what to do and how to do it.

Lisa: How did the Eastern religions deal with that?

Tony: The Eastern religions had held truths through time, and it was just up to us to rediscover all these truths. They showed you that you are the center of the universe. And you shape the universe by the way you think and feel about it, and unless we can learn to pull ourselves out of matter, absolutely pull ourselves out of matter and walk upon the earth again, then we're going to be lost. The whole earth is going to swallow us up, because it's our thought-forms that shape the whole earth. Our thought-forms shape reality, and if we think and fear, then we cause great thought-forms of fantastic weapons to be placed on us and tremendous tortures to be placed on us. We've gone through all of that and found out it doesn't work. But it's right. I mean, if a system is going with absolute dictators slaying everybody and having them believing their word, then we need a revolution. We have to get rid of these people. We have to find out that it's up to the individual as a person to change the way he's thinking and thus change the world. It's up to us. The 60s were like a giant wedge of people pushing through matter, releasing some of us from this kind of matter.

I personally got involved on another level of trying to affect the weapons program. To me, way back in 1965, when I first started doing this, I found that if I could take images of all the religions on the planet and shape these icons of each religion with nuclear-weapons parts, I could affect the nuclear-weapons systems on a whole other energy level of trying to allow the light force into these dark bubbles that we were creating with our weapons. Over the years, I built a lot of these pieces—I call them Atomic Weapon Systems—from the labs of Los Alamos, where the Nuclear Age was born.

We have to break away as individuals and try to reshape the thinking of the world, try to form new patterns, where the individual becomes sacred because he is in control of the universe. We have to do this as individuals, not through giant groups, all praying to some idol and our energy reflected into some idol to the creator. We found out in the 60s that each one of us was plugged into this creator.

Lisa: Could you describe "The Great SALT Talks"?

Tony: "The Great SALT Talks" is a satirical piece. It took
about five years of collecting these metals from the laboratory
to come up with this piece—about the same time it took to
build the atomic bomb. It's a trophy for the winners of the next
nuclear war. I explain it as two super powers facing off, and
then an angelic umpire with a forked tongue overseeing this
face-off and a monitor—all surrounding a nuclear monolith
that happens to be an ICBM nose cone. It's a bleak kind of
humor—after we're all blown away, the machines get together
to decide what to do with the world. They're all musical
pieces, so that as the giant wave of hot air and energy from
hydrogen bombs crosses the planet, these things would start
singing and bouncing around. It's mostly satire.

My attitude was to try to do something on another
level: a kind of reverse voodoo system of trying to balance off
the demons out of the weapons program using the forces of
light. So I started building icons of all the world's religions—
Ganesha and Rat. Ganesha is the remover of all obstacles in
the Hindu religion and bringer of great good fortune, and
Hanuman was a monkey who heard the teachings from the
Gurus and actually surpassed the humans and ended up in
heaven, a god himself, having gone through these yogic
procedures, and Jesus and Buddha and Bodhisattvas and
masks of all the world religions, like Kachina masks, that the
Indians worship, that plug us into the vast amounts of spiritual
energy that's been dammed up in the Americas for centuries. I
found it was like trying to plug in capacitors to each other. I
saw Christianity as a giant capacitor in the fourth dimension
that would give and take energy from its devotees, and
Buddhism as a giant bubble in this other dimension that would
take on energy and give energy, and the Muslim religions and
all these Hindu religions and the great gods of the Nordics—I
made a Mercury and Thor and Odin—became like doorways
to the weapons-energy system, where this super-good energy
from these other capacitors of religions could flow in. A type
of reverse voodoo in effect.

All these things I would build out of these parts in
hopes that the energy would flow together and cause a great

demon-chase out of this weapons program.

We're the ones responsible for setting these things off. We're the ones who built this weapon. All of this madness about radiation and what it does and how we're going to get rid of this stuff all has to do with this thing. Radiation is something that God gave us. Everyday it showers us with fantastic energies. Let's harness that energy. But how are we going to get rid of this stuff? One of the greatest cosmic truths is to "flush after using." The best visual image of nuclear waste is: OK, you've got a little baby in your hands, and it's just shit in its diaper, and instead of taking the diaper off, you just put another one on; then, within a month, all you've got is a big ball of shit and diapers on the floor. That's what we're doing with this nuclear waste. It's affecting the whole world again. We're either terrified of it 'cause we don't know what it is, or it's so damn hot that we don't know how to handle it.

If we were to look at action and reaction, we would see the way man is going is the absolute wrong direction. He's going deeper and deeper into matter. The easiest, most objective example of this is to take your hand and jam it into muddy ground. You would see the mud shoot up through your fingers. The direction of your hand is down and straight into the earth, and the action/reaction shoots the mud up through your hand. Now if you're in the heart of New York City and just look up, you'll see the direction man has gone—straight into the earth. He has placed himself at the bottom of a canyon, and the harder he goes at it, the farther down he goes. What we succumb to are lower influences that are beneath the earth: metals and all of the things the earth has. We should call these "lower forces," since they're below our feet. The United States is like this beast that has driven itself up through the earth, and each city is an organ of this beast, connected by arteries of freeways and highways and airports. Technology is taking us deeper and deeper and deeper into matter. And our whole connection to the cosmos has been blown, because we're beings that were made to walk upon the earth and to be plugged in by the sun. We should plug ourselves into the sun instead of the earth itself. And we should be walking upon the earth, directing the earth and helping with its natural move-ments and correcting things where they need to be corrected. Our aboriginal culture still holds a connection to this, and we tend to want to put them into matter, as we are being put into matter.

We've got to wake up to these things that are taking us over. We're losing our connection with the cosmos. And our connection is what holds the whole earth together. If we all submit to this matter, then nobody's there to hold the earth on its axis, and it will flip on its axis. We have to see that the whole universe is in our individual heads, and the way we think about it is the way it is shaped. We have to correct our thinking and learn to think much more on a cosmic level. We have to wake up as individuals. And what "wake up" means—it's not a biblical statement or anything—is to just be exactly where you are at each minute and not to submit yourself to the past or the future. Just pretend to be right where you are, and you'll begin to wake up in the present.

Everybody's trying to be here right now, and if we can establish that, we'll replug ourselves into the cosmos, and the cosmos will tell us what to do. It knows what to do. We, as individuals, won't know what to do until we re-establish our contact with the cosmos. But in order for that to happen, we have to pull ourselves out of matter, and we have to join with each other and see that we are within the other person—the same essence trying to evolve. But we've got to come out of matter. It's a tremendously important thing right now, because we're about to be judged, and if we're not out of matter and connected with the cosmos, we're going to go under. The whole planet will go under.

Lisa: How have the American Indians influenced you?

Tony: The American Indians are very, very spiritual people. I lived with these people for a while, and they could go out with twenty-two men and two ladies and start stomping on the earth in some pattern, and within an hour the skies would cloud up, and it would begin to rain. Now what kind of contact do we have to make it rain? These Indians have been guardians of the earth for thousands of years, and in the last forty years we've totally trashed the earth with our necessities of having this type of energy and this type of technology. The whole universe is in your head, and it's the way you think about this universe that's going to cause it to reshape itself.

RICK KLEIN

*Rick is the founder of the New Buffalo Commune, which was
created in 1967. My husband, Tom, and I visited New Buffalo
that first year, set up our tipi, and lived with the members,
helping them build their main communal building. Tom and I
left New Buffalo for Santa Fe, where we gave birth to our first
child, Dhana Pilar. I interviewed Rick sitting outside in the
sun, leaning against the wall of the main house at New Buffalo
in Arroyo Hondo, New Mexico in 1989.*

Lisa: Tell me a little about New Buffalo.

Rick: New Buffalo was founded as a social, religious, scientific, and work-oriented commune. When we first came on the
land, we all lived in tipis, and it was very hard. We learned
how to make adobe bricks from some of the Hispanic people
that lived here in the valley. This is all earth [*touching the
wall*], and we laid the bricks. We lived outside, we cooked
outside, we had a communal kitchen. There was a child born
in a tipi here the first year, I remember that. There were people
who died here also. There're some friends of mine buried here
on this land. So it was real beginning, basic reality that we

209

were learning about. And I think out of that reality, we learned an earth-oriented spirituality. Again, the people from Taos Pueblo taught us these things. Our experience taught us these things. But they showed us how valuable it was.

Lisa: Where'd you come from?

Rick: Well, I was a Beatnik, and I was living in Paris, and these strange people were coming from California, talking about this new drug, and this guy gave me some LSD, and I took it in Paris. And I immediately said, "Hey, I'm going to New Mexico." I had been here before, but it just seemed like this was the place you could live out the revelations we were having. When I got here, there were a lot of other people hanging out, in El Rito.

There were people who had come to hang out with the Indians, to learn about peyote from the Indians, and Max Finstein was here—he was an old friend of mine, a Beatnik poet. It just happened that we all wanted to do something together. That's what we got from those drugs. We had been living in this terribly alienated, middle-class society full of exploitation, and this kind of opened up other possibilities. We didn't know what those were, except there was some kind of instinctive thing, I think—an instinctive truth of living closer to the planet which we're all a part of anyway. We all evolve from the planet, which is not something they told you in school in the 50s. It was real heartfelt stuff.

So we got together, and I had an inheritance. I bought this piece of land, and we moved out here. And Max came up with the name The New Buffalo as the Provider. The land was going to be the provider, as the buffalo was the provider for the plains Indians. The sacred part of nature that nurtures us all. But, of course, there were people from New York's Lower East Side, there were people from California. Nobody knew very much about living off the land, especially here in New Mexico. Teachers appeared to us, though, when we got here— the people from the Taos Pueblo. I don't know what it is about the people from Taos Pueblo, but I've been around a lot of tribes and stuff, and somehow the people from Taos Pueblo just have an incredible heart. The people told me afterwards, "Well, we saw you people, and we decided to take pity on you." We were pretty pitiful. But they took pity on us. They knew that our hearts were in the right place. And their hearts were in the right place to come and help us.

A lot of the people from California, particularly, were drawn to this area because of the Peyote Church. And to me, it's still incredible that the people from the Taos Pueblo would come over here and help us out and show us how to use this medicine in a way that was really meaningful and deeply religious and had a lot of tradition and a lot of heartfelt feeling. I mean, here they are—these guys who have years of tradition behind them—and they come over and help these hippies who were just outrageous.

It's astounding to me, but it shows me how deep these guys, characters were. People like Little Joe Gomez and John Gomez and Henry Gomez, Joe Sun Hawk and Tellus Goodmorning and Frank Zamora. These were guys who go back and tie into the really old ways, the ways of the plains Indians. We're not going to see their kind again.

So we were just incredibly lucky to have people like that. With their sense of humor, they could come and laugh at us and still be our friends. And joke with us. They showed us ways of building these buildings and growing corn—things like that. I mean, we were so naïve! I remember we were going to get chickens. We said, "Why don't we buy some chickens, and we'll have eggs here at New Buffalo." One of our guys said, "If we eat eggs, we should gather them from the wild birds' nests." The absurdity of it. We muddled along somehow. It was real hard, but when I look back at it, some-how we had a spirit that carried us. They were real exciting times.

I remember sitting here and watching people come up the road. We'd say, "Well, are those people from California or from the East Coast?" And somehow you could always tell they were either the blonde space cadets from California or the speed freaks—the pale speed freaks—from the Lower East Side. But, you know, for a while there, everyone was wel-come. It was an incredible time of people coming together. You could see someone and realize that we had the same secret or something, we had the same revelations.

Timothy Leary came here, you know, playing with one of those millionaires, who was his patron. We felt that we were the vanguard of civilization here. Civilization was going to end with us, or we were going to change civilization.

Civilization as we had known it was going to come to an end because of these incredible revelations that were coming to us. But, see, these guys at Taos Pueblo, they knew all that stuff anyway. I was thinking the other night about how the biggest revelation when I took acid was that everything is connected, that nothing is separate. That was the revelation of the 60s. The same thing came down in science at that time, but somehow it entered us instinctively like a divine light. And we knew it, and we said it, and then the scientists starting talking about it. Ecology in the 60s: I bet it was 1969 the first time I ever even heard that word. But the first time I heard that word as an intellectual concept, I knew it. I knew all about that stuff. I knew it in my heart. These guys out here knew it too. But middle America didn't know it. We weren't brought up that way. We were brought up to be separate and not together and to be in a civilization that exploited the earth. So we were very extreme, but it was real pure too. It was a real brave and honest and heartfelt attempt at doing something new.

Timothy Leary came all in white in a private plane, and he wanted to eat some peyote. And he was told, "No, we only use that for ceremonial purposes." Dennis Hopper came to shoot *Easy Rider*, and he wanted to shoot the scenes that are in the actual movie, he wanted to shoot them here. And he said, "Well, we're going to come in, and we'll cater. We'll feed everybody. We'll bring in really good food, and we'll feed you all when we shoot." And that was how we would get paid. But we said, "No, we only eat brown rice, Dennis. We're growing our own food." Besides, we didn't want the publicity. He shot over here at the Hot Springs, and the commune scenes look a lot like this room in here. They're sort of a plywood reconstruction of this scene.

This is an ancient valley of Hispanic agriculture. Getting up every morning and looking at the mountains, there's a sense of reality here, of spirituality. One of these old men at the Pueblo told me one time, "This doctor came." He was going to take him to one of their ceremonials—a peyote meeting. And the doctor kept saying to my friend, "Well, when I go in there, you Indians, you say that you don't talk about Jesus, you say you talk to Jesus." He says, "When I go in there, will I see God?" And my friend said, "I see God right now. He's that tree right there."

There was this incredible spirituality in the air at that

time. Probably all over the country. I was mostly here, but I
feel very fortunate to have been here, and I think there was a
lot of confusion in other places. Here it was real centered. I
mean, we were going through our changes. We all got hepatitis
'cause we didn't know a lot about sanitation at that time. But it
was real pure here. It was good.

Lisa: Why were people dropping out and going back to the
land?

Rick: Well, people were dropping out and going back to the
land because there was no reality in that world, in that middle-
class world at that time. People can talk about taking these
psychedelic drugs and going way out, but actually there was
another process happening there, where you're coming back to
the planet here and the earth and to a truth, which is that we're
all part of this planet, that we're all evolved on this planet, and
that we're all humans together. I think that kind of spirituality
really came to earth here at New Buffalo. It's like I said:
we've got these incredible teachers here. It's not like somebody came and said some very profound thing to us, but just
seeing the way they lived and the way they conduct their lives
and the way they are as people, I think it influenced an
incredible amount of people who came through here.

Lisa: Do you think New Buffalo worked?

Rick: The initial idea, of course, didn't work. But in terms of
influencing a lot of people, it sure worked. I think the original
idea of dropping out and forming an alternative society was
very naïve. But in terms of a place that influenced a lot of
lives and had a long-lasting influence on, let's say, the culture
at large, I think it was very, very successful. There was an
amazing number of people who came here and spent a couple
of years and left, and people who were really lost—people
from the city who were into drugs or something—would come
here and find some values that had to do with the earth and
work and other people. Simplifying their lives, getting their
ideas clarified. It's very confusing out there, especially if
you're taking drugs. I think that, for me, the drugs, in a way,
saved my life, because I was very confused when I was a
young man, and they gave me some values and some revela-

tions and some truth. But I don't need them now, and I think in fact that, before, my spiritual path was taking drugs, and, now, the basis of my spiritual practice is not to take drugs, or anything. It's almost as if those things we were shown in the 60s, they're in the culture now. When I really look at it, the main truth that came out of the 60s is that we're all one. Nothing is separate. And now everyone talks about that. It hasn't quite reached the White House yet, but I think that it certainly has reached the schools, and I think it's reaching more and more people. Scientists are talking about it, and if the scientists talk about it, they can teach it in the schools.

STEVE GASKIN & INA MAE GASKIN

We were visiting the Whole Earth Festival at the University of California, Davis in 1989, filming the event and getting interviews. Steve Gaskin was one of the invited speakers, and even though I hadn't interviewed him for my documentary, I wanted to get an oral history from him and his wife, Ina Mae, while I had them in sight. We sat in their VW bug one evening on the grounds of the festival, smoked some grass, and had this conversation.

Lisa: It is so great to see Pilar co-producing this festival.

Steve: It's funny, you and kids. Like, I had a nice thing with a kid a couple of years ago, and then his family moved off The Farm, and he had problems with the other kids—being a bully to the smaller kids—but he and I had a very good intellectual relationship. And I just saw him, and he's got a big old curly mop of hair hanging down, and he's big and maybe gonna shave pretty soon and remembers me good and is still my friend and outgrew the bully part, coming out of childhood, but he didn't outgrow being my friend, and it's real nice.

There's a lot of beautiful kids that are grownups that I have to look at for a moment and say, "Who are you?" From rug rat to some ravishingly beautiful woman in a matter of years.

Lisa: I heard through the years that a lot of people had come through The Farm and left their kids and went off to do something else, because you really liked having a lot of kids around.

Steve: It wasn't because we liked having a lot of kids around. I do, but it was because a couple of kids were given to us by some people who said these kids were on an ego trip and they were spoiled, and we don't want them anymore and just left them and split, and we never heard from them again. I had both those kids at my house, and they had been tied up and left standing in their high chairs while their mother went to the store, and they're grown up and out in the world doing their thing now, but they call up and tell me they love me now and then, almost like some of my kids that way.

Lisa: Were there a lot of kids like that who you took care of?

Steve: We took in a lot of kids over the years. We had four thousand people who signed on The Farm as complete residents at one time or another. We had at least two hundred thousand people come through as visitors, and we never charged a penny for visitors' food or board or anything. So we had a lot of action like that, and for some people we were just as happy to take the kids, because the folks were so obviously unhealthy, the kids were unsafe. There were other times where you'd say, "Hey, you and this kid could make up and be friends."

Lisa: I remember back when you had your Monday Night Class. At what point did you decide to go and do The Farm?

Steve: It wasn't really anything I decided. I was just so thick in the hippie dream that I went out and got a thousand acres and a few 4WD vehicles and started digging in there some-where, making a hippie civilization, and it was always the dream. Everybody's dreamed that—throughout our culture. Guys would come up to me and say, "I got a little money put aside, and you're going to have to go to the land some day, so you let me know when you go, and I'll go with you and help out."

We paid $70,000 for our first thousand acres, and we paid half of that down, and we paid it off in two years. Then we bought the seven hundred acres next door, and we never intentionally encumbered the thousand acres after that. If we borrowed money, we'd do it on the seven-hundred-acre piece. The local bankers came to consider our thousand acres to be a real plum—they'd love to get their fingers into it.

Lisa: What year was it that you first moved to The Farm?:

Steve: We left San Francisco on Columbus Day in 1970, October 12, and we were on the road in the caravan for five months, and then getting back to Tennessee a couple more months, and finally on May 9th, we stopped and parked in Tennessee, about a quarter of a mile from where we now live, and in September we moved onto our land.

Lisa: So 1970 is when you decided to do it and take this caravan?

Steve: I didn't know I was going to the land when I took the caravan, I was just going in the caravan. But in the caravan, we became a community. The Hog Farm should understand that. When we left San Francisco, we had twenty-five school buses. By the time the caravan was out on the road, we had sixty great buses, some smaller buses, campers, cars, and pickups. We had one hundred vehicles. We stretched twenty miles on the freeway. We were outrageous. It was fun. One time I'll never forget: we hit this little mom-and-pop gas station down in the south somewhere, and we sucked up all their gas, bought all their pop, bought all their candy, bought all their crackers, and left them standing there with a handful of money and this amazed expression on their faces. We drove away and left them sucked dry! They had nothing to do but wait for the gas man to come and fill them up again.

Lisa: We thought that was going to happen at the Harmonic Convergence in Chaco Canyon, but we only got a thousand people instead of twenty thousand. So where did you travel on this caravan?

Steve: We circumnavigated the United States. I had speaking engagements in forty-two states, up the coast to Bellingham, Washington before we turned right, and then to Spokane and right across the northern part of the U.S. during the winter. We went through Yellowstone, and the park ranger said that the last long-hair who had come through there was a guy who had eaten somebody, and he kinda didn't want to put it on us, but he wanted people to know that some of your longer-haired folk down the road actually ate somebody. We had folks who were hypoglycemic when we weren't doing sugar at all, who would just get off on a joint and a little candy.

Lisa: So then you went all the way around the U.S.?

Steve: I talked in what they call the Chapel at Princeton, which is about like a cathedral, and we did Sunday services in Union Square in New York City, and we did services at the Washington Monument, and it was seventeen degrees. By the time we got down to Atlanta, we were very well known. The wire services had had us on their 'scope for months.

Lisa: You traveled around the country with how many people?

Steve: Well, there were about four hundred people, I guess, when it was really big. By the time we got back to San Francisco, we stayed there one week, and we said, "This not being a community-on-the-road is no fun at all. Let's continue to be a community." So we turned around the next Sunday and pulled right back out and went to Tennessee, and it took us months, because we had breakdowns, hard times, winter times—froze up in Rock Springs, Wyoming, had to drive across a couple of states to find a rear end for the bus so we could get out. Ended up, these guys were trying to fix my bus, and they were two strong dudes, and I weighed one hundred twenty pounds and had a blown back, and these guys were down there—they couldn't get this bolt undone to try and get me out of the garage. And I said, "Let me get down there." And I went down and crawled under the bus and picked up a sledge hammer and bashed that sucker a couple of times and put a wrench on it and broke it loose and pulled it out. Both of those guys weighed one hundred pounds more than I did, but they didn't want out of that garage as bad as I did.

Ina Mae: And we had one three-day labor there. That's how I got interested in being a midwife. I'd never seen birth before and never knew what a midwife was. Suddenly I felt drawn to something. Before that I'd never had any idea what I might want to do as a grown-up. I was thirty when we were on the bus. I was twenty-eight when we got together.

Steve: We've been together over twenty years now. That's good.

Lisa: So you went to Tennessee. What was the philosophy of The Farm?

Steve: I liked the hippie philosophy, so when we went in, we were going to show Tennessee and the world at large that hippies were not only OK, they were even good. We wanted to show the world the generosity of the hippies' hearts.

Ina Mae: It was not only that you could take care of yourself, but you could pull some other weight besides.

Steve: You could take care of yourself, and you didn't have to wait until you were a millionaire to be a philanthropist.

Ina Mae: I think there was something implied in there that you had to have a land base to do it. He would say at the end of the caravan talks that we're going to get some land, take care of ourselves, grow our own food, and grow healthy babies.

Steve: And prove that our philosophy is functional and that any gathering of hippies won't just degenerate into going home to their mothers.

Lisa: You built businesses?

Steve: Everything. We have a motor pool. When we were still a collective, we owned a lot of businesses together. Even now, people who started businesses either inherited them or bought them from The Farm, and we still have about forty owned businesses on The Farm right now. There's the tie-dyes and the book-publishing company and the tempe spores and soy dairy—tempe is an Indonesian soy dish, and it's grown from spores, and we at one time were the only distributor in the U.S. We still distribute it heavily, internationally. We have two construction companies, The Farm Construction Company and Fred Harrison & Sons Construction Company, and we have several independent small contractors and plumbing contractors, and we have the Farm Foods Dry Branch—split and whole soy beans and good-tasting nutritional yeast. We still have the private school and the clinic. The private school will take anybody, some on scholarship and some pay. But we hosted the alternative schools conference last month on The Farm. It was great. We really enjoyed it, and it was nice to have the party. We have a catalogue store, and we're thinking of becoming a shipping/distribution center for a large cooperative warehousing and shipping company that's a co-op, and they're thinking of us, because Tennessee happens to be pretty centrally located for shipping lanes and stuff.

Ina Mae: Where people work at the clinic, we have our primary health care, which we can do by agreement with a local family-practice doctor, so that one of the midwives works as a clinician. She doesn't have a nursing degree or anything like that, but real experience and training by a doctor for fifteen years or so, so she does all the primary care.

Steve: She's good at looking in ears and down throats and listening to chests, and she can prescribe with phone counsel with a doctor. So it means that we can cover our community—mostly people that don't have health insurance—and provide safe and legal and economical health care, doing our own lab work—very economical. Lab tests are seven bucks instead of seventy-five, stitches for fifteen bucks instead of one hundred fifty. Anytime you go to an emergency room, you pay through the nose.

Lisa: So you're originally from San Francisco too?

Steve: Neither of us are from San Francisco. I'm from Colorado, and she's from Iowa.

Lisa: But you met up here.

Ina Mae: Yes, we met in San Francisco in 67, and got together in 68.

Lisa: You think that The Farm worked then? And it's still working? A lot of communities fell apart.

Steve: I think it's still working. I'll tell you what some of my philosophy was, going in: I thought that doing calisthenics was silly if you needed an outhouse dug, and that you could dig an outhouse and exercise the muscles and have an outhouse at the end of the exercise. And that we should channel these things and not just do silly exercises, but we should channel the energies into accomplishments. Then I thought that, rather than put yourself into untenable situations deliberately to find out where you're at, like having Dr. Warwick hang you over the cliff by the ankles, you could start on some great huge projects that were going to be hard to finish and maybe even fail, and that's how you would learn how to function in heavy situations. I always believed that trippers who learn to trip generically would know how to handle trips. And we proved it, because we came in, and we took care of a multitude of different kinds of stuff for people, just working from tripping principles, like keep your nose in the wind and keep flying and keep at it and don't lose heart, and keep the faith and don't drop your whole card and all that. And so we became a lot of different things, but starting out of that basic hippie philosophy. I love that basic hippie philosophy, and to me, when people talk about the hippies being dirty and silly and superstitious, and being all strung out on addictive drugs and stuff like that, that's not hippies to me at all. Hippies to me were brave, incredible young people with the courage to step into the face of their entire culture to try something out—an incredible courage—and they have proved out. Our music is the music of the world, you know. I'm real gung-ho.

Lisa: It's what came after that that gave it a bad name.

Steve: They didn't know what we were doing. I defended the Straight Theater from the Motherfuckers, a group of heavies that came in from New York. I went to the Straight Theater and said, "Can we meet at the Straight Theater?" And they said, "We're afraid we're going to lose the theater to the Motherfuckers this weekend, and if you will stay here and help us defend the theater, you can meet in it." So I did defend the theater from the Motherfuckers that weekend, and we found out that we had to hold the control room and stuff. We had to physically hold the control room while they gigged in our hall. And we did.

Lisa: Well, I had in Truchas, New Mexico a little health-food store and a toy shop, and I was the only health-food distributor in that area. I'd go to Santa Fe and buy everything in bulk and bring it up there, and the people from Ojo Sarco and La Joya and everybody would buy from me, and twice I went into my store and there was nothing left. I went down to Ojo Sarco, and those guys had just ripped me off. I went directly to their house, and there it was. And I said, "Why did you steal from me? I'm on food stamps and welfare too. I'm providing this for you as a service." And he said, "Well, we went in there to get some nuts and raisins for our trip into the mountains, and we decided we better just liberate it all."

Steve: Liberate what? I know there was that kind of thing, and I had no patience with it. This rip-off was walking around the Whole Earth Festival, the guy with the stocking cap; he picks off small women and comes on smiling and clowning and a little intimidating behind it.

Ina Mae: He has his nose painted red, and he's wearing one of their official shirts, so you take him to be a help, but he's a problem.

Steve: He's a stone-ass rip-off, you know. And I used to see guys like him—you know, there are people like him who are very weak and who will do anything for the energy, and you feel sorry for them, but you've got to protect other people from being ripped off, because they leave you weak and trembling when they have a successful raid. And that's a lot of what Monday Night Class was about: the people who wanted to get high and not be ripped off, and be able to relax and express themselves and not be afraid some guy's going to come and jump in their stuff. So the Monday Night Class parties up on Mt. Tam were pretty stoned affairs, because the people who went there weren't into being ripped off by the meth freak of the week.

Ina Mae: It was about recognizing another grown-up and cooperating with them to keep someone who was a rip-off small and unimportant.

Steve: And don't let them grow huge and take over.

Lisa: So the people who were part of your trip were all eager to do something and create something, rather than just lay back, smoke dope, and hang out.

Steve: That was not our trip. We were all really idealistic. That's what kept us going at such an incredible level of collectivity for so long.

Lisa: There has to be some reason why you carried on for so long.

Steve: Yeah, well, we were very idealistic, and we did not start off with any prior ideas. We were not macrobioticists, we were not Marxists, and we weren't the liberation theology and we weren't Buddhists. We weren't anything. We were hippies, and we wanted to live together, and we would assume what level of discipline we had to in order to successfully live together. It was a voluntary discipline we would assume that way. And when we got to fifteen hundred people, I couldn't be personal with everybody. Just no time. I had six telephones at the head of my bed. And like when we were smaller, I probably had taken acid with most of them, you know. We were really tight. And then there were people who'd live on The Farm for years without really knowing who we were.

Lisa: But basically it was your leadership that kept it all together.

Steve: To a point, but it couldn't have been done if that wasn't the direction everybody was going. I was merely facilitating a commonly shared vision, and I wasn't afraid to take on a scary rip-off.

Ina Mae: It very well might not have come together if he hadn't been there to provide that and been somewhat of a focus.

Steve: No, there would be no Farm.

Ina Mae: He was forever giving away power, and there'd be people that would try to put him on a pedestal, and, you know, he would get off of it. Then the problem would be how to keep a balance. It's hard to find the middle way there.

Lisa: I'm doing lectures at the University of New Mexico on communes and alternative societies, and I have documentation of the Hog Farm from the beginning until now, and Yogi Bhajan from the beginning to now, and the New Buffalo Commune, because I've kept documenting them all along. And I've showed what happened to Yogi Bhajan because he took the power personally.

Steve: I had this vision at Boulder, where we were all laying down and doing some breath-of-fire and going through the thing, and then the guys that were directing the breath of fire got a little nasty, and when you get a little nasty, you scare the energy off the folks, and it flows to you a little, and then somebody would come along and be nasty to him, and I felt like there was a rip-off chain that ran right up hill to Yogi B., and it was vacuumed, juiced to Yogi B. And I felt like, compared to that, taking acid for your juice was positively honorable.

Lisa: He would talk about treating women right, and yet he transgressed. Now did that happen at all on The Farm? Did you get into that kind of thing?

Steve: Well, we had a lot of experimental group marriages when we came out of San Francisco, and it took a few years for that to wind down, just under the pressures of being hard to stay together.

Ina Mae: But it was always equal. It wasn't like men had more privileges than women.

Steve: The midwives had so much juice.

Ina Mae: There were a lot of four-marriages, but it wasn't
dominant that the men necessarily engineered them. It wasn't
an agreement between two males. Many times it was an
agreement between two women.

Lisa: So that was normal in society?

Ina Mae: Yeah, and there wasn't a situation where he got
special privileges, sexually, because I wouldn't have been into
it. I wasn't into that. It was a before-the-pill sort of morality
thing, so the hippie thing was very different for me.

Lisa: A lot of charismatic gurus tended to abuse their power ...

Ina Mae: But that wasn't how it was on The Farm. I used to
bring Steven to births, and he knew about Tantric energy and
could help me with a couple of hard births, because he would
feel sexy with the woman, and I would feel fine about it, if
that's what it took to get the baby born and be alive and well
and all. And I knew that getting that one eight-pounder born
over an intact perineum, when I had hepatitis, had involved
feeling good together. You can vibe and relax, and I have to
say that our relationship that way has made me a better
midwife, because just to have another person to be able to feel
sexual energy in a way that doesn't exploit somebody but
helps relax the situation is to me sane and healthy, and at the
same time it's very unusual in our culture. But he told me that
he didn't want to come to any more births. If I had a scary one,
I'd call him as my backup. And so that was maybe five more
births, because the second birth we had, I would have lost the
baby if he hadn't been called in by somebody.

Steve: The lady walked up to me and said, "The baby's born,
it's so beautiful," and I looked at her face, and I knew the baby
was either dead or not breathing.

Ina Mae: And the baby was not breathing.

Steve: What she said to me was, "Oh, it's so beautiful; the
baby's born." And I just read her face the opposite, and I ran

over to that bus, and that baby was gray, and I said, "In cases
like this, you start them like this," and I started that baby up.
That mother sends me a card on that child's birthday every
year and tells me that she's 99% in her reading group and that
she came out with all her marbles and all that.

Ina Mae: He gave her mouth-to mouth-resuscitation, gave her
breath, turned her pink.

Steve: But you can't be afraid to get snot in your mouth—it's a
life at stake, you know.

Lisa: I've also worked with three dying people. Three births
and three dying people. Almost the same.

Steve: In ways, yes it is.

Ina Mae: So we weren't like that. The type of thing that he
was always stepping away from was the tendency of the
people in those times to say, "OK, we'll give you the best . . ."

Lisa: Idolizing

Ina Mae: Yeah, and so they made us this house, with this
beautiful stone fireplace, and we moved out of it into a tent,
because he didn't like the direction it was going.

Steve: You guys moved out while I was living in the penitentiary.

Lisa: What were you doing in the penitentiary?

Steve: Well, I took the rap when a bunch of folks grew grass. I
mean, I didn't want to grow grass, because I knew we weren't
out in the boondocks; we were not that far away from the
other farmers. But some people thought we were way out in
the boondocks, and I said, "If anybody's going to grow grass,
you just throw a handful of seeds somewhere and come back
in three months and see what God gave you." But they were
out sitting, playing flutes to the plants, and fertilizing and
leaving the fertilizer bags in the fields with them, visible from
the train that went by, and they didn't think the guys on the

train would care. I didn't know how crazy it was, and then we got popped. They took me. And people said, "This is collective grass, this is just as much my grass as it is his." And the cops didn't act like they had spoken. They wanted me. So they got me, and they put me up for a year, and we appealed our butt off for three years before they put me up. They thought they would take the head off The Farm, and The Farm would die. But The Farm was a different kind of animal, because by the time three years were up, I was not necessary for them to survive, and I left. I always said that people try to make you be a leader, and leadership is something that you extrude or something. It doesn't have anything to do with anything except itself. But being a teacher, if you lose your leader, you're lost; if you lose your teacher, maybe you already knew that and learned it and aren't hampered by it, perhaps.

Lisa: Do you find that the Age of Pisces was that of gurus, whereas the Age of Aquarius is more direct learning? That's why so many channelers and crystal healers are around.

Steve: That's what I liked about acid. Acid to me was the next step from open Bible. You know, Martin Luther and those guys fought for open Bible. Let the poor people read the Bible and find out what it really says. I say, "Let the poor people have the experiences and make up their own mind." I can't really advocate mass acid-taking or anything 'cause there's a lot of crazy people out there who are just trying to maintain, and they would be attracted to it and get knocked off their centers, and you would have more crazy people out there than you could handle.

Lisa: So there were fifteen hundred people on The Farm at one point?

Steve: Yeah, and three hundred of them were visitors.

Lisa: And then it just organically changed, and finally something new happened?

Steve: No, four years ago we realized that we had been doing a two-and-a-half-million-dollar budget a year and not building any new houses.

Lisa: You were spending it on all the people visiting?

Steve: And just spinning wheels. People making lots of money, but we weren't all business majors. We had a few MBAs.

Lisa: If you could change anything, what would you do?

Steve: People ask Ina Mae what she would do if she could do it over again, and she says she wouldn't be in a position where she made money and didn't get to see how it was spent.

Ina Mae: We made a lot of money, and we don't get royalties.

Steve: We don't get royalties from any of our books. No royalties. We've sold well over a million copies between us.

Lisa: It was all going back into The Farm?

Ina Mae: It still is, and it still sells.

Steve: It still supports the book company. *Spiritual Midwifery*, the tofu cookbooks, and *This Seasons People—A Book of Spiritual Teachings* are what sell right now, and we still get no money from it.

Lisa: So there was a change.

Ina Mae: Yeah, so we weren't on a pedestal; we were on the bottom of the pile.

Steve: It's not like we were on the pedestal. It's more like we were more hooked into the harness to keep it rolling.

Lisa: You didn't need anything, right?

Ina Mae: When people think that about you, it's not quite human.

Steve: When The Farm did its economic changes, I had to borrow money from my father to buy a car, 'cause I had no money. I carried no money.

Lisa: But what happened? What was the change that happened? All of sudden you had to make a change?

Steve: No, instead of the store having free food in it, you bought your own food. Instead of free medical care, you had to pay something for it. Instead of midwifery being free, you had to pay something for it. You had to pay for everything, on two weeks' notice, on the decision of the Board of Directors, an elected Board.

Lisa: So a lot of people moved?

Steve: Oh shit, they felt, why should they do that?

Ina Mae: If you were pregnant, you didn't have to pay for the midwives, because the midwives knew that you can't squeeze blood out of a turnip.

Steve: But after the changes were complete . . .

Ina Mae: After the changes, right, but we had to do the first nine months where we put out the money and the time and the energy and got nothing back. So that was just one of the things—that we had to keep our own integrity that way.

Steve: Out of this huge pile of people I've been intimate with over these two decades, I winnowed out quite a large number of really good friends. They're all over the world, and I feel very well-connected, and I like this festival a lot because it is pretty pure. The kids are pretty idealistic, they keep it pretty clean.

Lisa: This Whole Earth Festival reminds me of the old days. I look at the kids and I watch them dance and I listen to the drumming, and I'm looking and taking pictures, and I think, "This is just like back then."

Steve: That's the thing. The first time I walked into a Grateful Dead Concert, there was some kid, seventeen years old, Jewish, fresh from New York, hadn't started a beard yet, had a huge pile of natural hair . . . the next time I went to a Grateful Dead Concert, he was there again. But the first one I'd seen was now thirty-five years old and probably a stockbroker. This ws another one just like him.

Lisa: It's so interesting how kids are doing it.

Steve: I think it's great.

Lisa: At the end, you decided that it wasn't working anymore financially?

Steve: I didn't decide that. What happened was, we had tried a lot of forms of government. We'd had a council of elders and various boards and committees to try to run it. At one point, I don't know who got it, I thought it was me, some other people thought it was them, but we got the idea that there was one board we'd never used and that was the Legal Board that the state of Tennessee requires that our corporation have. So, we said, "OK, we want to make people accountable. Let's make that our Board, our real Board, let them run us, and they're accountable to the state." So we did, and I feel like they got scared and dropped their whole card. We weren't in any trouble. We were sluggish and slow, but we were not in trouble. Nobody was mad at us, nobody was out to get us. In my heart I think it was a paranoid move. But I ain't attached to socialism as a political philosophy. I do think it's the only right way to divide stuff up in the world, but, you know, I'm not a political socialist. That party ain't big enough in this country to do anything. So I'm not attached to us being little families with checkbooks instead of being one collective thing. That doesn't make any difference to me. We used to stop them all at the gate—FBI, DDI, all of them stopped at the gate and said who they wanted to see. They did not come into The Farm. And I liked it that way. They came in one time and said, "Look, if you open up The Farm's roads as public roads we'll come through, and the county will build them all for you." And I said, "I appreciate your offer, but we like it the way it is now, where it takes a search warrant to get in the gate." And I was sitting in the car with the county judge and the sheriff. I liked that sovereignty, and that's the only part of the old thing that I want back. And we're getting that back as more people become braver and relax from their cringe and straighten up and get courageous again. 'Cause it takes a certain amount of courage to do it this way. If you let yourself get scared back out of your courage, it's hard to do it.

Lisa: So everybody had to start buying their own stuff?

Steve: Well, some people figured, "If I gotta work this hard, I might as well go somewhere else." A lot of people felt like that. Some guys felt like we'd blown it, so they just split. But when all that was past, it came down to that there was a bunch of us who moved to The Farm because we wanted to live in community with other people and because we felt that we would derive a strength from that, and it's still true, and we're still doing it, and right now the most exciting thing on The Farm is the big kids. The big kids are outrageous. They're going to take it over.

Lisa: They are?

Steve: They're beginning to think so, you know, each Ragweed Day. Ragweed Day is our National Holiday. Some people came to The Farm, didn't like us, went away and told the cops that we had force-labored them to work in the marijuana fields, and the cops believed them and came back with fifty carloads of cops and four-wheel-drive vehicles and helicopters, and the Attorney General parked outside our gate from midnight to eight in the morning. And in the morning, when the sun came up, they saw the field they had staked out was ragweed. The press went for them hammer and tongs, and the Democrats went for them in the State Legislature, and the press had a cartoon of the Attorney General jerking up a plant, smelling it, and sneezing. They had another one that was for the Highway Patrol: how to tell the different varieties of marijuana. There's *Marijuana ragweedias*, and there happened to be a watermelon field under the ragweed, and they said that there were watermelons which you could tell by the distinctive sound they made when you landed your helicopter on them. And then we began to ask the press to back off a little bit; we've got to keep living here. But that became our National Holiday, and it happened to be seventh month, eleventh day— seven/eleven, shooting craps—so we called it Seven Eleven Day. And on the weekend closest to Seven Eleven, we have a family party for The Farm. And the kids come back and old

Farmies, and we have a nice big swimming hole 'dozed out by a pretty cliff down in a hollow, and we've got a little stage built down there, and we're far enough back in from our gate, you can hardly hear the rock'n'roll from the gate. We get back in there and just boogie our butts off and nobody knows.

Lisa: What are you planning now?

Steve: I want to go on being an activist in whatever way I can. I got specific things I want to do. I'm trying to get a grant to go down through Central America to get well enough educated on it to hit the college circuit up here and start hipping these young kids to what we're doing to Central America. I'd like to try to diffuse Vietnam, if I could. The Right Livelihood Foundation has a slush fund for the winners for projects, so I put in what I had in mind, and they said it sounded pretty good, that I should make a formal application. So I'm going to make a formal application and see if they'll give me a grant too.

Lisa: So now you're educating yourself and then helping to educate others, rather than sitting on The Farm?

Steve: I haven't been to Guatemala in a couple of years, and I need to have fresh stuff. I understand the history of it very well, but I just want to go down there and taste it and feel it and get fresh-charged-up with it again. There's stuff I know that went on, that I know the Army's done to the Indians, but it's long ago, although it outrages me now.

Lisa: Killing all those different tribes off?

Steve: Killing some guy and leaving his body in the town square, forbidding the townspeople from picking him up, and leaving him there until the dogs eat him.

Lisa: And bashing babies against trees and cutting throats of the old people.

Steve: Yeah, stuff like that.

Lisa: What do you think happened in the 70s? Everybody says

the 70s were lost, and I don't think so.

Steve: Well, the 70s weren't lost for me, because the 70s were the first ten years on The Farm, and we were really hauling.

Lisa: I think that's when a lot of stuff was growing. The seeds were planted in the 60s, the stuff was growing in the 70s, blooming in the 80s. Don't you feel that?

Steve: In the 70s, our realization was trivialized and commercialized. This lady from Canada, who was very good, said, "Here's the thing about the counterculture—getting up behind the counter and selling the culture." I had a master's degree and was a combat veteran and a father before I ever took acid. I didn't get it through the chain-link fence around the high school. I had seen a lot of heavy people and a lot of heavy action, and it was heavy. It was not trivial, and the realization that we had was very heavy, and one of the reasons I love Wavy so much is because he's faithful to that. Probably why he loves me. Probably the same thing. And the other role-trippers were still out doing it. Love 'em. Hang right in there.

I had a realization about that. I was gigging at Purdue, Bloomington, Indiana, and they put up a little potluck for me and Ina Mae at somebody's house, and we got to meet a couple of local guys from the school before our gig, and I suddenly déjà-vu'd that I had been at somebody's potluck when Pete Seeger was coming through. And I realized I was about as old now as Pete Seeger was when he came through some time back, and we're faith-keepers. We're supposed to keep the faith and travel around and help people and remind them to keep the faith. And so I'm a traveling faith-keeper. There's a bunch of us. I burned karma, I had read enough of the old books to know how to hang motionless on the thermal and not do anything, but there was all this shit needed doing, and nobody else would do it, and I knew I was accruing bulk karma to take it on, and I just thought, "I will survive this somehow, I don't care." It was like I had a karmic credit card, and I just plunged to the hilt with it

TAJ MAHAL

*Every time Taj Mahal came to Santa Fe to play, either with his
band or solo, I was there. He played the blues to world music
and back again, picking his guitar and banging out a tune on
the piano. He had been in L.A. at the same time I was there in
the 60s and then moved to the country (Topanga Canyon) and
painted his mailbox blue. His roots are firmly planted in
traditional music, which is reflected in the songs he writes and
sings, and he has never been influenced by fads in the music
scene. He is constantly touring and recording new albums. He
was just finishing a sound check in Santa Fe for a gig at Club
West in 1989 when we did this interview.*

Lisa: Can you give me some examples of what impact the 60s
had on the young people in that era?

Taj: For me, the 60s represented an incredible opening of the
conscious mind, and it seems like, for one time, a whole bunch
of us had arrived at a point where there were some direct
issues which were necessary for us to confront. One was man
and woman's inhumanity to man and woman—that we were
our brother and sister's keeper—and environmental issues,

personal growth issues.

People were really experimenting on a lot of different levels, and not only, as oftentimes it's focused, on drugs. People were experiencing different types of metaphysical levels, spiritual levels, and cultural levels, and exchange was intense, and almost no group was excluded from the situation. You could go to a Love-In and everybody in the world was represented there, and in large quantities. Particularly on the West Coast—the L.A. and San Francisco areas. There was a lot going on there, and the issues were hot and there was communication between the establishment and the young people at the time, who were anywhere between youngsters to people in their teens, twenties, thirties, forties.

And you saw adult people who chose to take a livelihood such as a baker who would drop out and start going to Love-Ins and start listening to music and stop worrying about a lot of things. People were growing their beards and their hair, and paying more attention to what was the real lay of the land and what were we doing? what was our purpose? and politically where did we stand? and morally where did we stand? and financially how do we deal with wealth and ego and the haves and the have-nots? and I'm black and you're white and what can we do about our differences? and we know we have them, which is fine, but how do we get together to have something going? People were sharing on a very intense level.

As a black youth growing up with a pretty progressive family—not even middle class by the standards we're talking about today, you know—things were pretty much taken care of, and we had to work if we wanted to amount to anything. I was thoroughly disappointed with what the European/Americans had done to the Native Americans, Afro-Americans, and the general ethnic population of the U.S., and I didn't really see that there was ever going to be anything different or they were going to do anything different about it. But the 60s seemed to bring a lot of hope to that situation. where these people were really genuine—the hippies, even the people who came out only on the weekend to groove. At least they were trying to open themselves up to more positive relations with their fellow human beings, and I never really wanted anyone to carry me or carry the weight or my weight. I don't believe in that, but I do believe that if I walk into a space, I'm innocent until I'm proven guilty about something, and I didn't like to be pre-judged any more than anyone else likes to be pre-judged. Of course, when people don't really know what the score is, oftentimes they revert to the regular human behavior, which sometimes is not the greatest way that humans can really represent themselves.

But there were a lot of things that were really positive. People with long hair and beads and bells and skirts and whatnot and jeans—you could walk up to these people and start talking, and they'd have something nice to say, and you'd get invited to go hang out and have dinner. People really opened themselves up. and that was really thrilling to me. But I was involved with the business thing, and also, up until that point, I began to see politically what was happening—like civil rights. I think an unfortunate part of the whole civil rights movement was that it was always preaching to the converted and not at all to the people who didn't know. So, consequently, we have a new generation who don't realize—black and white kids—how much everybody put into making things the way they are presently. It didn't come about by nothing short of hard work.

And oftentimes young black people are unaware of how many white people in America really stuck their necks on the line—from the beginning, when slavery was involved, and all along—all the questions about whether black people were really human beings, couldn't even have a vote. There were people who seriously thought they were intelligent enough to tell the masses that these darkies over here weren't even human: "We can do anything we want—buy them, sell them, rape them, burn them, hang them—do anything we want." By doing that, they thoroughly convinced themselves. What if you were from the former Yugoslavia, and you couldn't speak your tongue, and you couldn't talk to anyone you knew, or anybody around you—even though they were white and came from a different tribe—and I tell you what you had to be. You spend three or four hundred years doing that, you'd probably be pretty dumb and pretty stupid and pretty ignorant and pretty scared and pretty weird yourself. And no one thinks of it that way.

But fortunately, there were a lot of people, and there still are a lot of people of high consciousness, who are conscious about human beings, which is what we're dealing with, and that is one of the things that was really exciting about the 60s. People were very aware, sensitive with each other, and sometimes I think they went a little overboard, like towards the Native American thing. Everybody was really trying to be an Indian. Well, it just doesn't work that way. You can live the life, but it isn't like you can just live the life and jump in and out of it. It's really a big commitment. It's like committing to another person or higher order. But I fully enjoyed what was going on in the 60s, because I got a chance to travel around, meet a lot of people—people really opened their houses up to me, their farms, their states, their sleeping bags, their tents, their buses. During that time, the women were absolutely wonderful. I befriended lots of people, and they befriended me, and to this day I hold some of the greatest friendships I have made in my life from the 60s.

It was also when I got my own career off the ground, and it was also when a lot of music, which up until that point had been pretty much connected to the black masses, became even more popular, and people became more aware of music by so-called ethnic minorities of America. That was really important. I think, unfortunately, money got involved in it to the extent that it started to become this one, that one, the other one, and all of a sudden people were worried about competition as opposed to constant creativity, and eventually that shut down the whole movement.

But before that happened, people who were stars for a long time in the black community, like Otis Redding, came to the forefront and created such incredible energy amongst the large group of people moving around at that time, that I was really shocked. I never thought that the masses would be able to hear Otis Redding—they just wouldn't understand what the music was about. That was a real lucky thing.

I came all the way, three thousand miles from the East Coast to L.A., not knowing anyone out there except this one person, another musician, and we were going to play together out there. He talked about Ry Cooder as someone we ought to get together with, and we eventually did, but I had to find my way in a real strange land. It was like coming from an area where I knew everyone and landing in the middle of the desert where I didn't know anyone. It was a different lifestyle and everything like that. On the East Coast, black music was really underground. There wasn't a station that played solidly black music or rhythm and blues, like there was in the south and, as I'm told to understand, like places in Chicago or Cincinnati or other places like that that have a large black population.

Even though the East Coast has large black populations in general, the music was played at another level. I remember occasionally we'd be able to hear some of these artists on the air, but not very often. But when I came out to California, twenty-four hours a day there was a rhythm-and-blues station I could listen to. So when I came out, Otis Redding's "Tenderly" was playing, and I absolutely adored Otis Redding, because I had heard a lot of these other guys play, and they were real nice and good, but there was something that Otis gave to me personally. It was, like, everybody played good music, but Otis gave a whole person with his music. It was the most amazing thing in the world. If there's anybody that I could think of—actually, several people: Ray Charles, Otis Redding, to a certain extent Wilson Pickett—I mean, when they opened their mouths to sing, it was like there was no place I wanted to be except where that music was happening. Of course, there were the older musicians and the country musicians like Howlin' Wolf and Muddy Waters and Elmo James, and the farther-out guys, like Sleepy John Estes and those kind of characters. They were really exciting to me and other African instrument players and Latin players, but at the forefront was Otis.

And we were lucky. This group I played with, called the Rising Sons, had a lot of different people: Jesse Lee Kincaid, Ry Cooder, Ed Cassidy, who eventually went to play with Spirit, and Gary Marker, and a few other different guys at different times. We got a chance to open for a week for Otis during the time that he was recording *Otis Live at the Whiskey*. Those guys were so nice. The band was there earlier in the day when we came in for our sound check. We walked in, and these guys were sitting there, and normally the rhythm-and-blues crowd was like a hard-edged crowd—they were somebody, and we were nobodies, so they didn't talk to us, and we basically had to go through those kind of changes with most of the other bands. But Otis's people were so friendly and so nice, and they came over and introduced themselves and introduced us to Otis, and he was real friendly.

We had dressing rooms upstairs, and he was next

door, and we were playing, and he'd come in and listen to what we were playing, and he'd sit down and talk, and he really was just a marvelous person. That's why everybody loved working with him. He wasn't an unfriendly man, like a lot of other guys, like hard drinkers and really bitter guys, gambling all the time and losing their money and unfriendly and a bit dangerous. Otis was a very nice man, and he just loosened up a lot of stuff. A lot of people try to. They talk about "the blues does this and the blues does that." For me, for a certain kind of emoting and opening myself up to the world, Otis really had that feeling. Sometimes I can't listen to him for a long time, because it's just too easy to find myself wanting to re-create that sound. I spent a lot of time wanting to sing like different people and eventually finding my own voice. And after my experience with Ray Charles, I decided that I could enjoy these things. Today, if I wanted to do that, I could certainly do that, and every now and then I say I'm going to do an album dedicated to Otis Redding, and I really scare myself.

Paul Rothchild was trying to put a band together one time, and I was living in L.A. and got called up to Berkeley to be involved with this band—and it was like a crazy scene to be flying to San Francisco airport, and then the helicopter and then flying me to Emery to the heliport and then rush me to somewhere in Berkeley where Janis Joplin, Stefan Grossman, Steve Mann, and somebody else, maybe Barry Melton from Country Joe, were—and they had an idea to put this band together. We spent the afternoon playing and just had a great time, but at this time Janis had just begun to work with Big Brother and the Holding Company, and she had given them her word that she was going to be with them. So even though this was a good thing and she was having fun with it, she had already committed to these other guys. And I was always sorry we couldn't get involved in it. I felt that the band that was playing behind her was really not solid enough for the type of music she wanted to play, because you can't be a folkie and try to play Stax-Volt, Memphis hard-line rhythm-and-blues unless you really go for it. You can't take the folkie concept and apply it to that kind of music. It's hard-edged, it doesn't have a lot of chords, and these guys just didn't do anything to me for her, except frustrate her and her effort to try to get out there, because she was ready to go. And they were concerned with a lot of other things, because they were getting a lot of popularity. They were more concerned with how they looked on stage as opposed to really playing. And that type of music is a black art form, which has now been absorbed into a major art form of American music. But as a black art form it is designed for the person who is the singer to be the person you're focusing all your attention and energy and music on. You do not focus your attention on yourself. Now you may dress sharp enough to be recognized, and you might have some hip steps, but don't you ever drop the music behind the person that is being focused on.

That was my opinion, and I really felt sorry for her, because I thought she had a lot of talent, and she just didn't have the band that could focus behind her. But eventually it did come to pass where she needed a band that represented that kind of music, and Snooky Flowers and a whole bunch of other guys put together this real hard-edged r&b band which was the Full Tilt Boogie Band. I'd heard about them, but I'd never seen them.

I was in LAX once, and I was putting my guitar and bags on the counter, and I looked down the line 'cause I hear all this noise, and here comes Janis, just sashaying. She must have lost I don't know how many pounds. She was just looking as cute as she could possibly look in all the days I'd seen her, and she had this band of musicians. She was so excited. She reminded me of Bette Midler, she was so excited, and she introduced me to all these musicians, and they were the wildest-looking cats I'd ever seen. And I said, "It's about time," but then I figured that it wasn't going to happen for her, because of the fact that there were too many black musicians in the band. Not that I thought there was anything wrong with that, but I knew being just a sole black musician in a band, that the climate in American music still was not able to accept interracial bands with any degree of seriousness, in terms of making it in the big time. There were all these little rules you found out, and ultimately they finally took that band away from Janis. From that point she went downhill, because she had no support from the music. She was just an entity with a name. All these people would say, "Go out and give it to them," and she'd go out and try to give it, and the bands were never behind it. The only time that the band was really fully behind her was when she had that Full Tilt Boogie Band, and the type of music she was playing was connected with the type of musicians who were playing the music for her. They knew how to dress sharp, look tough, catch, pull, but when it came time to play the music, they all played as a unit, as opposed to five separate things going away from the center, and then leaving her out there to scream in front of the stage.

Lisa: The 60s in general?

Taj: It's really simple. It was a great era of expansion. Up until the 60s, there was nothing happening. The 60s opened up, and it was like serious. You could really, seriously express yourself on every possible level. You felt really elated as a person that you could fully realize things long before you got to be forty years old.

 People were relating to one another. It wasn't so much the "I" generation, it was the "we" generation—we did this, we, etc. People were going places in groups, in droves, and trying to be a part of a group of people, tribes, which had been missing in America. The 60s brought back the tribal feeling, and it was very important. This was what the music is all about right now. Why do you think all these kids like to gather in these arenas and go crazy? 'Cause they need tribe, and that gives them some kind of feeling of connection to a whole tribe of people who have similar ideas, similar feelings, similar aspirations. And the 60s were that, but they were also politically based, culturally based, and never before or since has there been a time like that, where young people had the freedom to move around as much as they could—and did. It was very exciting to be there. The exchange between musician and musician, painter and painter, dancer and dancer, dancer and musicians, painter and poets—I mean, the exchange was tremendous in all the types of things that people tried. Spirituality from the East came very much into focus. And people challenged the thoughts of Christianity, dealt with Zen Buddhism, dealt with Taoism and all these other things. The premise that people could make some kind of difference in how the world was, and what people sought after, and thought about—they really personified that.

 The Grateful Dead connected with the people. They did not connect with the record companies. They connected with the people. And the people were Deadheads—are still

Deadheads—and their kids are Deadheads, and they don't feel
bad about being Deadheads. The Dead are what they are and
who they are.

I've worked everywhere else—South Pacific, Austria,
Australia, New Zealand, Fiji Islands, all across Canada,
Alaska, every state except North and South Dakota, and the
Caribbean, South America, Africa, and Europe—and this is on
the strength of the music and some of the projects I've been
involved in. In the early 70s, I was involved with the motion
picture *Sounder*. I was an actor in that movie and did the
soundtrack, and in the sequel, that was supposed to be a TV
movie but never was. And then I got involved with Billy Dee
Williams and some other people in a movie called *Scott
Joplin: Ragtimer*—I was an actor and a piano player—and
then a William Faulkner story and some things with Levar
Burton. And then, a lot of the scripts were garbage. They
wanted me to play pimps and confidence men and stupid
people.

We're all survivors from that particular era. We're all
guys in our forties, and some of the guys are fifty, man. It's
been the music that's kept us alive from then until now, and it
hasn't changed. For us, it's a great honor that we maintained
whatever it was we were, and that we're in it now. I like to
work with musicians who are independent on their own. I
don't like characters that can only function when there's a
group and a leader. Every one of these musicians who works
for me has his own space and his own things that he's doing
and moving down the line with. The bass player is working
with different groups here and there, producing other people.
Leon, the guitar player, is also a painter and interior decorator
and designer. The drummer raises grapes in the Napa Valley
and is involved with the wineries. Myself, I'm doing movie
scores, a children's album, a project with Dylan, [John]
Cougar Mellencamp, U2, Springsteen, Emilylou Harris, Little
Richard—we're all putting out an album of songs from
Leadbelly and Woody Guthrie to pay for the acquisition of
Folkways Records by the Smithsonian Institution—and
projects here and there. Last year I did a project called *The
Man Who Broke a Thousand Chains*, and I'm available for
different types of political support. So that's where I'm
at: maintaining myself, continuing to put out real positive
music, seeing that folks have a good time, and putting myself

wherever I can do the best that I can do.

Lisa: Do you have a message for the youth of today?

Taj: My basic message for young people today is that you have to get involved with whatever your roots are. I don't care if you come from Timbuktu or Nairobi or Scotland or South America—wherever—get an understanding of your culture together, your education, learn to talk, to count, get some sort of business education behind you, and get out there. Opportunities in the music business are available if you want to go for it. As time goes on, it gets harder, but that is not the problem. The problem is being motivated. If you're standing still, you're not going forward. You say OK, that sounds real good, but that's what a lot of people do: they stand around and banter this stuff around and become more and more intellectual, and they don't put themselves into the action of it.

It's like a lot of people are really looking for love, but they don't really love themselves, so how can you expect anybody to give you something if you don't have anything to offer? You have to know how to give and to receive. These are very important things, and whatever it is you go into, try to be the best at it. Just go for it. And in doing that, you don't realize how many people are paying attention to your movement— you'll never know. As my friend Howard Johnson, the tuba player, says, "You just never know who's in the kitchen watching."

MICKEY HART

Mickey has always been there for Wavy Gravy whenever Wavy asks for musicians to help with his benefits, and this SEVA concert for the homeless at St. John the Divine in New York in 1989 was no exception. I was in one of the side rooms, watching a group of Tibetan monks create a mandala sand painting, when I ran across Mickey and did this interview.

Lisa: What were you doing in the 60s besides making music?

Mickey: I was discovering myself in the 60s and discovering everything around me. I was learning how to feel, how to touch, learning how to think, learning how to be myself and finding out who I was, and then it takes the rest of your life to find out who you will be and how to manifest what you learn, how to go through everyday life with all the things you've learned and make it work for you—that's the struggle. And that's also the impermanence of life. That's what you learn. That's what I learned then. That's what I learn now. I'm learning the same things, basically. I'm a learner.

In the 60s, everyone was sharing and everybody was learning for the first time, and it was a collective thing, and we were all in one place and getting high on each other. You can do the same thing now—it's just a lot harder. There're a lot more of rules and regulations and a lot more authority, but it can be done. You have to be ingenious. You can get high, and that's what it's all about: making do and getting high. Getting high on life. That's what it was, that's what it is.

Lisa: Define the 60s in one sentence.

Mickey: I can't really give you a sentence for the 60s. One word will do, you know—it was *fun*, and I learned a lot. It felt good, and it was fun, and it was the Grateful Dead, and that's what the 60s were for me. They also taught me how to learn, to find out who I was. You have to learn how to learn, and that's what it was. The 60s were happening on all levels.

Lisa: Who do you learn from now?

Mickey: The Guyuto Monks are very great people—very humble, very small. They understand about the impermanence of life. They're the teeth of Tibetan Buddhism. They re-create a new world every day. That's what their chants are about. They recite the Sanskrit text. They empty their bodies and re-fill them with positive thoughts, so they're really into transformation, into making a better world. That's my connection to them. We're friends, and I love their chanting, and I love the range in which they chant. They chant around seventy cycles. Each monk holds three notes simultaneously. They're reciting the Sanskrit text—450-500 years unchanged. So we have a unique chance and a rare glimpse at a 500-year-old ritual right before our very eyes, and they have it. They know what's it all about.

JOHNNY RIVERS

Johnny told me he never gives interviews, but for me he'd make an exception. In 1989, we sat outside his Beverly Hills home overlooking the Valley, and he reflected on those wild and crazy days of the 60s as his three young children watched from inside the house.

Johnny: In the early 60s, rock'n'roll was taking a snooze. It was asleep. I'm talking about 61, 62, and 63. There was not much happening. Patti Page and Andy Williams and guys like that were having hit records. And just about the end of 63 and 64, when the Beatles hit and Bob Dylan came on the scene, all of a sudden rock'n'roll woke up again. It didn't just wake up, it was woke up with a whole new energy. But basically it came from the 50s. Rhythm-and-blues and I grew up in south Louisiana, and my influences were B. B. King and Fats Domino and Jimmy Reed and a lot of local groups that most people never heard of. But when I started playing out here in L.A. in the early 60s, I was just playing songs that I played in my old junior high school and high school band back home. All the old Chuck Berry tunes and some of the Motown songs and stuff like that. A lot of people had not even heard them.

They sort of forgot about them in the early 60s. And then of course, when the Beatles hit, that changed everything, and it was a whole new consciousness that had a look. Everybody changed their hairstyle, starting wearing different clothes, but originally everybody started off sort of conservatively. You remember the early pictures? I know when I was playing at the Whiskey, we opened in early 64, and I was wearing a suit and tie, really straight, and everybody says that was really straight. But when the Beatles began, they were wearing suits and ties and real short hair. And I think the folk influence, which then became the hippie movement, had a lot to do with loosening up, taking off the suits and ties, and starting to wear wild clothes and beads, and it was sort of a natural evolution. Everyone started to let their hair grow longer, started growing beards, and I got caught up in that as well. One of the main influences for me from the folk thing—I never was that much into folk music—was actually when I met John Phillips. We had the same producer as the Mamas and Papas, and John had come from that whole folk world, you know. I really got to a lot of that music from him, other than, you know Bob Dylan and the Byrds and whatever. We eventually got around to the Monterey Pop Festival in 67, which is where it really hit its peak.

Lisa: What was so different about Monterey Pop that hadn't happened up to that point?

Johnny: Well, Monterey Pop was the first time that everybody really came together, and the groups all played together. Before that, it was everyone doing their own thing. You didn't hear so much of so'n'so's doing a show with so'n'so and so'n'so together. After that it became a whole new thing: "Let's have a concert with five or six acts instead of just one or two." It brought a lot of diverse kinds of music together as well. Monterey Pop did especially, because Ravi Shankar was there, jazz players, rhythm-and-blues guys, Otis Redding, Janis Joplin, Simon and Garfunkel. I introduced Jimmy Webb there. There was something that happened at Monterey that I don't think was ever duplicated again. And I don't think it ever will be. It was just one of those times, and everyone was ready for this thing to happen. It was the birth of something.

Lisa: A magic moment.

Johnny: And after that, it was all, "Let's try to do it again, but bigger," and it never—as far as I'm concerned—never really happened the same way again. Yeah, there was bigger, and Woodstock was important, but Monterey Pop was it.

Lisa: Also Vietnam was really heavy at that moment. And it was like a statement. Victor Maymudes told me, "It was the musical statement against what was happening in Vietnam." All the artists had come together.

Johnny: Yeah, for peace and for a voice in government and all of that stuff, and also the thing I remember about Monterey Pop was it showed that the authorities, the police, the promoters, and the concertgoers could get along. It was a nice feeling there, a really friendly feeling. People were really helping each other. I think the spirit of love was really there.

Lisa: The chief of police, I understand, was wearing flowers.

Johnny: Everybody got into it. The whole Monterey community. It was really commendable. And there weren't any wild incidents there.

Lisa: Who wrote that song "Down in Monterey Bay"?

Johnny: Eric Burdon, the Animals, yeah.

Lisa: What about Elvis's influence on music? That broke something loose.

Johnny: Well, his was in the 50s.

Lisa: What happened with Elvis?

Johnny: He got on right at the beginning of it. He brought sex into music, and also a flash and dancing and all that. Before that, it was Fats Domino and Little Richard, but Elvis was probably the first white artist that really grabbed ahold of that rhythm-and-blues and really took it on a grand scale. And then Jerry Lee Lewis came along, and there were several of them,

but Elvis had a tremendous influence on me and on everyone.
Chuck Berry, as well.

Lisa: Who's Johnny Rivers right now?

Johnny: I still work all the time and still play music. I enjoy
doing the same kind of music I did in the 60s. Basically, it's
just straight-ahead rock'n'roll, and people still love it. I've
been very fortunate to keep my following and be able to work.
And one of the things I'm very grateful for is that I'm able to
make a living at something I really want to do. So, you know,
we've come through a lot. We were all looking for God in the
60s and trying to find some kind of meaning to life, and
people had talked about dropping out and doing this or that,
but I think right now we're all involved in just life and
families and children.

Lisa: Do you think that the use of drugs helped what was
happening musically?

Johnny: Greatness is in the person and their spirit and in their
being. Jimi Hendrix was great when he was born, before he
took any drugs. He was destined to be great and had he not
taken drugs at all, he would still have made it and been a big
star because he was a great innovative musician and, unfortunately, because of the drugs, he's not here anymore, and he
might still have been with us. His greatness doesn't have to be
just a flash. There are a lot of great old jazz players who are
incredibly innovative and creative, and they're in their
seventies and eighties, still creating. It's a shame, you know, in
a way, but it was part of everyone really trying to reach out,
looking for short cuts, looking for some kind of tool. Everyone
was experimenting, looking for tools, searching for God,
searching for the meaning of life, in a big way, and wanting it
all at once. I remember in the 60s people would go, "Well, if
you don't know God, just take this little pill, you'll find him."
Well, I don't know about that.

Lisa: The 60s were . . .

Johnny: In the early 60s my parents moved out to California
from Louisiana. We bought a house together, and I got to

relive my childhood with them, which was kinda neat. That was a very good time for me.

Lisa: For a generation of people, what do you think the 60s were?

Johnny: I think the 60s really expressed the feeling of what the United States was founded on—the voice of the people being the government, not the government dictating to the people. I think, through music and film and whatever else, the powers-that-be were finally persuaded that, "Hey, we're on the wrong track here, we really can't just do what we want to do. We have to go along with what the people want." It proved that the system really works.

SIMONE ELLIS

Simone lives in Missoula, Montana, writing and constructing hyperspace environments until the wee hours. She is the author of Santa Fe Art *as well as the collection of poems,* Rosy Belligerents. *She has done theater, film, and newspaper criticism. I got to know and love Simone in the 90s, yet since her viewpoint on the 60s was so multidimensional, I wanted to include her here. We used e-mail to do this interview in 1998.*

Lisa: What were the 60s all about?

Simone: They were the years of a global awakening. I was in sixth grade when Kennedy got shot, and when that happened it was as if someone had hit a very loud gong that reverberated through everyone, shaking the whole world to its very foundations. For me, oddly enough, that day was an awakening to the structure of power that was firmly established in our minds. I was in the middle of the daily lunch routine, which entailed standing in line at the junior high while all the older kids and the teachers ate their lunches. We elementary school kids had to wait until they were finished to get ours, and I was always inordinately hungry by the time I finally got my tray. But on that day, the junior-high principal's voice came over the loudspeaker system and announced, simply, that President Kennedy had been shot in Dallas, Texas. From where I was standing, I could see the faces of a couple hundred kids and teachers, and the reactions were chaotic. Some grimaced, some cried, and some laughed. No two people responded the same. All I could think was, "Who did it?"

The teachers all got up and ran out of the cafeteria, a major break in the power structure. A food fight ensued, and I don't remember if we ever got our trays. One brave male teacher with red-rimmed eyes (another break in the structure of what held things together—men didn't cry) got stuck with walking us back to our school a couple of blocks away. For some reason, that day our line was perfect: the exact two-by-two we'd been trained to assume for the daily lunch commute. It was as if the kids were toeing the line, hoping to bring order back into the world after such disastrous news. But all the way, for some reason, everyone was asking me who shot Kennedy. I often was placed in this position of explaining the world, and attributed this to the fact that I was inches taller than most of my peers, including the boys. But then it could have been my willingness to guess. I always came up with an answer to their questions, no matter how far-fetched. I've often wondered if some of them realized I was just making it up! Anyway, I answered without hesitation that it must have been the Russians, and that we were probably going to be in a war and get bombed, like at Pearl Harbor, any minute now. This was taken with grim acceptance, and a few looked up into the sunny, blue Colorado sky like little brave soldiers.

When we got back to the grade school, we sat around while the red-eyed teachers tried to get a picture on the twelve-inch TV sets hanging from the corners of the class-rooms. For once, no one cared if I left the room and went to see what was happening in the room next door. In fact, I was encouraged to go scouting for more information. I was in the hall when a teacher's voice came across the intercom an-nouncing that President Kennedy was dead, that there would be no more school that day, and that we were to go home and be with our families.

I remember being strangely excited, possibly at the prospect of getting out of school. But since my mother hated

Kennedy, I didn't really want to go home, because I'd miss all the rest of the action. For that, I'd have to go over to my friend Lanny's house, because her mother loved John Kennedy, and I loved hanging out at Lanny's house. It was always so noisy and colorful and dramatic. And now that something really big was happening, it would be especially exciting over there. With an inappropriate smile on my face, I re-entered my classroom, looking for Lanny, and saw pale fear on my classmates' faces. One of them asked me if we were going to get killed going home, if the Russians were here yet. I assured him that he might get killed going home, but to walk a different route and maybe then he'd be safe.

Within record time, the whole school poured out onto the adjacent football field, heading in all four directions to their homes. Many were carrying whatever they could from their desks, convinced that they would never be back in school again, now that the war was here. Just at that moment, a noisy crop duster pulled up on the horizon. Probably the hardworking pilot was completely unaware of the nation's disaster, having been up at dawn, doing the dusty, dirty work of a farmer's pilot for hours. Who knows why, but as fate would have it, he decided to give the kids a thrill by flying low over the field. All it took was one word—the word we'd been trained to respond to for our entire school careers—firmly and audibly yelled out, like a football player's hutt-hutt-hutt— "Duck!"—and the entire population of the school hit the November cold grass. I was the only one left standing as the plane tilted its wings and flew on over the trees at the edge of the field. I knew from that point on that in the world that we'd created, the only ones left standing would be the ones who barked out the orders. And that didn't seem right. The rest of the 60s, and in fact all the way through to this day, my life has been about challenging and playing with that power structure.

Lisa: What was so special about the 60s?

Simone: It was the adolescence of a generation who'd grown up with the threat of total annihilation via the atomic bomb. I call us the Bomb Babies, rather than the Baby Boomers. Sure, during Genghis Khan's time the "end of the world" was a possibility to the villagers on the steppes, but that would have meant the end to the world of those one knew personally. With the atomic bomb, it was the end of the world—the people, the plants, the animals, even the air and water would be transformed. We were drilled almost weekly with "duck-and-cover" routines, which were supposed to protect us from nuclear destruction, so this annihilation was very present in our minds, growing up. I think that thousands of us came to the conclusion that if we were inevitably faced with a giant transformation—either on a molecular level via atomic fission or through a spiritual awakening—we would go for the spiritual awakening. It was a desperate time, a magical, wonderful, cosmic, and a desperate time to be growing into adulthood.

Lisa: What did you enjoy the most about the 60s?

Simone: The play. I loved the way we played! Any time you met another tie-dyed, full-skirted, bell-bottomed long-hair, it was time to play. The whole world would just have to wait until our game was through. And the game was spontaneous. Maybe someone would start playing a harmonica and the rest would start dancing in circles on the street corner, or maybe it would be more elaborate play, like a theatrical performance in a tent in the park. I was in a summer-stock theater company in Telluride, Colorado when I was sixteen, and that was one of the very best times of my life. The oldest person in the troupe had just turned twenty-one, so we were all very young. And we were on our own, most of us, for the first time in our lives. We took acid every Monday and after the first few weeks threw all structure out the window, used Viola Spolin's techniques, and improvised our performances for the rest of the season. We played in front of people and got paid for it! That was grand.

Lisa: What influenced the music so much?

Simone: Cosmic energy, primal survival urges, and LSD.

Lisa: How did psychedelic drugs influence the youth? What did they get from it?

Simone: Psychedelic drugs worked on the youth culture of the 60s much in the same way that they worked on tribal people for centuries before the 60s. As Huxley said, they "opened the doors of perception," or as William Blake, whom Huxley was quoting, said, "If the doors of perception were cleansed, everything would appear as it is, infinite." That's what happened to us. We had our perceptions cleansed, and what we saw was a universe of infinite possibilities. In fact, I think the Internet and global communication is an outgrowth of this awareness. But one reason the experience was so different then was the atmosphere in which we took psychedelics. We knew to ritualize it, to prepare ourselves, and to give ourselves over to the influence of the drug entirely. Today, the kids don't have Leary to tell them the proper setting for taking acid. I mean, you don't see medicine men and women taking peyote and going to a movie or driving around in their cars. They sweat and fast and prepare to take peyote. That's what our founding hippie fathers and mothers knew, and that's what we understood as well. Take acid on a bad vibe, and you were bound to have a bad trip. Take it when you're cleansed and in a good place, and you'll probably have a great trip. Or at least a trip that teaches you something. See, that's what the native peoples know about psychedelics: they are to teach you something. They are medicine. And just like any medicine, they are not to be taken for entertainment, though I have to admit I've had some pretty entertaining times on acid!

Lisa: How did the Native Americans influence the youth in the 60s, and do they still?

Simone: I think the tribal societies were very appealing to us, because in rejecting the status quo we ended up forming a tribal society of our own. I don't think that at first this tribal consciousness was intentional. It was almost as if our tribe was created by default. It was what was left when we dropped out and rejected the nuclear family model. Then we became aware of the tribal nature of our bonds. In the same way, we turned to the Native American cultures. It wasn't that we rejected middle America for Native America, but one thing that was left that made sense to us after rejecting middle America was the native tribal societies. And fortunately for us, the tribes opened their arms to us and were willing, in most parts of the country, to teach us. They taught us about making harmony with nature, about living communally, and about taking psychedelics, among other things. And though we learned from them, we also realized that we were not Indian, and most attempts to live communally, and to live the Indian way were abandoned by the mid-70s.

But I do think the sense of being a tribe of sorts is still very much in place. I mean, this book is a tribal affair, and every time something happens to one of the tribe we learn about it within hours. I knew William [Burroughs] died within hours of his death. Even though I wasn't at home or easy to reach, a tribal member and friend of twenty years tracked me down and called me so I wouldn't have to hear about it on the news. I'd dreaded his death for years. He was a dear friend to me, but having an old friend go to that much trouble to find me and tell me he was gone helped immensely. When one of us gets sick or is in trouble, we still alert everyone who is in the tribe, and that's much like Native American societies. Personally, I believe that Native American societies are influencing the world more today than ever before.

This time around, in the 90s, our turning to Native America is much more conscious. We are very consciously looking for something that the native people have been keeping intact for eons. We are intellectually more aware of what it is that Native America holds sacred, and we want to connect with that. Our connection is mostly about spirituality, environment, and art today. Taking peyote with a medicine person is definitely a spiritual ritual and not just getting high today. Sweating in the lodge is also sacred, rather than just a time to get naked and party. We've finally learned some of the precepts that they were trying to teach us thirty years ago. Or, for that matter, since our ancestors arrived hundreds of years ago.

Lisa: Did free love work?

Simone: In a way, yes. For a while, yes. But that was mostly because the physical dangers of sex were at an all-time low. It was pre-AIDS, the pill had just come out, and penicillin had pretty much wiped out VD—for the time being. I think, emotionally speaking, the free-love movement worked to teach us our limits, and we often learned those the hard way. I mean, I claimed to not be at all jealous, only to find out that I was really very jealous, given the right situation. I think that we reached past the limits we would have inherited, though, by trying free love. Most people from the tribe that I keep in touch with still try to be generous with their friendships, their affections. But we have certainly drawn the line in the sand when it comes to "free sex." It's just too dangerous to even contemplate these days.

Lisa: Why did so many people drop out and rebel against the establishment?

Simone: Well, the establishment was lying. We'd grown up with what I used to call "peachy-keen reality," which was phony and full of holes. Parents were getting divorced, moms strung out on pills and booze, dads having affairs, big brothers beating the crap out of you, whatever, and still the front was always to act as if nothing was wrong. Beaver Cleaver reality. And we got sick of lying. In my case, I started rebelling long before I was an adult. I was out on the street protesting the war as soon as I was old enough to get away from home. Probably, without the divisiveness of the Vietnam war, we wouldn't have pursued the drop-out route so wholeheartedly. But with the war and with the threat of atomic destruction, we had little to lose dropping out. Or so we thought. Actually, today, I see a lot of aging hippies really getting into the money thing, and I wonder if it's because they are making up for lost time. Making up for all the time they spent as dropouts. We were so sure of ourselves back then, that money and establishment values were not what it took to be happy. I really wonder what happened to some of us who are now pursuing those very things with vigor. It's mysterious.

CARL GOTTLIEB

In 1989, Carl lived in Hollywood, just off the Sunset Strip, where he has held court ever since writing the screen plays for Jaws—1, 2, and 3D. His house is filled with movie posters and books, and although he never used to own cats, he now has three, and they are his family.

Lisa: You were involved with improvisational theater and The Committee in the mid-60s, weren't you?

Carl: Improvisational theater became the mode, became the norm, became to the 70s and 80s what the Actors Studio was to the acting styles of the 40s and 50s, the way Lee Strasberg and those guys created the Method School of acting that survives through today.

      In the 60s we had improvisation—Second City, The Committee in San Francisco, where I worked—and that formed a style and approach to performing comedy that changed the world. It was the ancestor of "Saturday Night Live," and an entire generation of comedians and actors and improvisation, which began in the 60s with Viola Spolin, who wrote

261

the book. What Viola created as a game theory for underprivileged kids in Chicago became a theory of comedy and comic performing for a generation of performers in the 60s and 70s. And the rules of improvisation are the rules for life. You listen, you deal with what is, you say what's necessary, and you don't try to write ahead. You live an existential moment—that's the same on stage as it is in life.

That was a lesson that was relatively new. And out of that came comedy that spoke to political issues, comedy that spoke to social issues, and comedy that was rooted in the consciousness of the population, comedy that spoke about things that were of concern to everyone. We were funny about stuff that mattered. We were funny about the war, we were funny about General Westmoreland, we were funny about Nixon and Johnson, and the draft. We were funny about dope, and we were funny about sex. And to be funny about all those things makes me laugh now. It was a time when there wasn't a lot of fun being poked at the major institutions. There was Lenny Bruce, who died for his sins, there was Mort Sahl, who got old and bitter, and then there were all of us and Second City in Chicago, which has to this day spawned an empire of improvisation.

The Committee ran ten or eleven years and then folded. But along the way, we produced the people who became the writers and the producers and the directors of the new comedy. The stars of this generation—the Bill Murrays, the Robin Williamses, the late great John Belushi—all those people came out of improvisation, and it's reflected in what they do, and it's reflected in how they think about things. And that's what was important.

Lisa: What were the guts of the 60s?

Carl: The core of the 60s was a sense of community, a sense that we were all in it together, whatever it was. It was a sense of identification with your peers, with your fellows, people your own age—all over, not just nationally, globally. It was an international movement that came to a head, I guess, in 68 with the riots in Paris. But before the riots in Paris, there were riots in Berkeley, and before the riots in Berkeley, there were riots elsewhere, and they weren't all bad riots. A lot of times, they were demonstrations for peace and justice, and they were peaceful. The March on Washington was just a sense of doing things for the common good and doing things in common with everyone else, and these were the things that made us sense each other's presence in a very real way.

Lisa: You said that you could trust anybody with long hair.

Carl: In one sub-sector of the society, if somebody had long hair and smoked dope, you could trust them with your life. I had a friend—actually, he wasn't a friend, I'd just met him. We met twice—once at a party, and a second time at a restaurant on the Sunset Strip. I was having breakfast, saw him walking down the street, I said, "Hi," he joined me. Over the course of breakfast it turned out that he was living in San Francisco, had to leave his apartment, needed a place to stay. We were in Los Angeles. I gave him the keys to my apartment in San Francisco, because I was in L.A. making a movie, so I stayed here, and gave the guy my keys, and he moved into my place in San Francisco.

   He called up, said, "I have a few pieces of furniture, can I move them into your place?" And I said, "Yeah," because my place was a loft apartment and it was kind of barren. When I got back to San Francisco about six weeks later, he had built shelves, put in a TV, stereo, chandelier, and we turned out to be roommates and partners for two or three years, and were in business after that, and are friends to this day, and it's more than twenty-five years later. And this guy, at the time, had long hair, smoked dope, and I met him on the street.

Lisa: What created the explosion of consciousness? You were talking about Vietnam?

Carl: One of the things that created the community of spirit was that there were shared concerns that were real concerns that affected everyone. Everyone was affected by the draft. Young men were affected, because they were directly liable. Eventually there was a lottery system, and they drew your number out of a hat, and you could go to Vietnam, go to war, get killed. For everyone else, it was friends and family who they were going to lose. The war affected everyone; it was a national effort. We heard about it on television, we heard the

President speak about it. It was something that made us all realize we all had something in common. We could get killed for a nebulous political purpose or perhaps a spurious political reason. To enforce somebody's domino theory, we were going to go and get shot at and shoot other people. A great description of the Vietnam war is "black man shooting yellow man to protect the white man and the land he stole from the red man."

There was a tremendous consciousness to all that. People were affected by those things, and they reacted to it, and I don't think we'll have that community of effort again. I don't think we'll get out of a yuppie-consumer mentality now until everyone is directly affected by something. That might be a recession, it might be inflation, it might be something that we don't know about. But when everyone's going to be affected, then we will all react again in concert.

Lisa: The youth are trying to do something.

Carl: The youth are always a community; the teenagers are always a foreign nation. They set it up that way. If their music offends you, it's achieved its purpose. It's supposed to make the parents angry. I mean, if I listen to heavy metal, I go, "Jesus, what is that shit?" Then it's done what it's supposed to do: it's divided them from me; it's established them in their world. Music plays an enormous role in that. In the 60s, the music was happening for the first time. Before that, outside of Elvis and a few others, there had been no rock'n'roll.The late 50s gave teenagers their own music. Before that they had to listen to adult music—Frank Sinatra, Bing Crosby, Rosemary Clooney—everybody listened to the same pop music. All of a sudden there was a dividing line. There was pop music for the older people, and then there was rock'n'roll for the younger people, and the new music, as it got more and more intense and the language of drugs and sex seeped into the lyrics and into the expression, then everybody felt the same urges, the same relationships, and those were based on music and out of the common peril that we faced, and out of the shared joy of the dancing, and the rock'n'roll, and the demonstrations, and everything we did together . . . it all blended together. It was sex, drugs, and rock'n'roll for the first time all coming together. That's a powerful prescription.

Lisa: You said that we have an addictive society today because we've been lied to about what marijuana and LSD do to you.

Carl: Yeah, there was all that reefer madness. Like David Crosby says, "They told us if we smoked dope and had acid we'd go blind staring at the sun and have bad babies and become immediately addicted to hard drugs." Well, they were wrong about the acid—it seemed like a lie at the time—and if that was a lie, then everything else was a lie. Cocaine was going to be OK too, and maybe even heroin and speed, because the official line had been so demonstrably false that you could not rely on it. You had to find out for yourself. And the minute you started experimenting with drugs, you found out, "Ah-hah, this is OK!" And then you related to the popular press and to popular commercials where the patented, legitimate drug companies spent billions, selling us aspirin and stomach remedies and foot powder.

There was always something being advertised on radio and television and in the press that would cure what ailed you. You could take Anacin—fights headaches three ways—Bayer, I mean, drugs were being sold. You could always take something that would make you feel better. Well, when the something that made you feel better came in a white powder from South America and was on a mirror and you went sniff and you felt better, you said, "Ah-hah, this ties in with my life experience: there's a drug that makes you feel better." If you smoked dope and went to a concert or took acid and watched a light show, that was all right, it didn't seem so bad at the time, and it related to everything you'd been told: that there are things that you can take—substances—that will change your life in a positive way.

Lisa: Why is David Crosby such a hero today?

Carl: Crosby is a hero because he went through it and came out the other end. He was an advocate of a lifestyle, and the lifestyle nearly killed him. It put him in jail. He came out of jail and admitted how wrong he had been. And he admitted it about his personal lifestyle, he admitted it about the drug experience, and he was able to relate his old destructive habits to a new, sober, abstinent lifestyle.

And he's a hero because he went back to creating,

after having played and sung for twenty years stoned. He started to write music straight, and wrote good music and had an album that came out that was a success. We wrote a book together that was a success. He was able to do things success-fully without drugs and was able to admit to that. And by admitting to that, he was admitting the failure or the futility or the destructiveness of his past lifestyle. He was able to say, "I was wrong," and for David Crosby, with an enormous ego, to admit that he was wrong about anything is a major achieve-ment.

Lisa: So he's a good role model for kids who might be addicted today.

Carl: Except for food, yes.

Lisa: What happened from the 50s into the 60s?

Carl: The 60s were the exuberant adolescence of the nation. The 50s were a repressed childhood. We had a father figure—Eisenhower—we lived under codes of conduct that were handed to us from the 30s and 40s, from the Depression Era and a wartime consciousness. The civic virtues were thrift and industry and obedience to authority. And then came the 60s. And, like adolescents everywhere, we pierced our ears, dyed our hair, and made our parents crazy. That was what the 60s were, certainly for me, 'cause I was a child of the 50s, and I had a second adolescence in the 60s. I don't know if it was sex, drugs, and rock'n'roll that caused it, or some other proven combinations of medical ingredients, but what happened was that I got to do all the things that I should have done when I was seventeen or eighteen under Eisenhower, I got to do them when I was twenty-five and twenty-six in San Francisco, having served my time in the army, having migrated west to the coast, and having abused as many substances as I thought I could prudently abuse. Then I got to do all the stuff I had never done before, all the stuff I had read about, all the things that the artists and novelists and poets and painters and musicians throughout history had done before. Here was our chance to do all of that or something that approximated it. So it was our time to rebel, to throw off the shackles of our parents and authority. It was an adolescent rebellion, I must say. It wasn't an adult rebellion, it wasn't a considered rebellion, it wasn't a thoughtful rebellion, it was an adolescent rebellion. And I think it led to, if not adulthood, some adult behavior on the part of the more thoughtful of us, and it led to reaction and repression in the 70s amongst the people who voted for an administration that was a lot less kinder and gentler than it would have us believe.

Lisa: What role did LSD play in the 60s?

Carl: LSD was the ultimate break-out experience. LSD was the thing that made you realize that everything you knew was wrong. LSD was the thing that made you realize that you were connected to a universe that was much larger than your skin or your eyes or your ears or the world that you could see immediately around you. It opened doors, like Huxley said: the doors of perception. All of a sudden, the doors of perception were open and you could perceive, or think you could perceive, a lot more. And whether it was a true opening up or just a figurative opening up, in either case, it was a way in which you could see more. And the minute you could see more, you realized that there was more to know, more to learn, more to experience.

Lisa: The 60s were . . . ?

Carl:

> *The 60s were adolescence dragged out for a decade.*
> *The 60s were more fun than I can remember.*
> *The 60s were, more than anything, a time that I*
>   *became myself.*

I don't know who I was before that, and I'm not sure who I am now. But during the 60s I became who I am, whoever that is.

Nostalgia is probably the most poignant and least accurate emotion, because it makes you think about the past and select portions of it. It's a selective memory. Nostalgia is what you think about when you think about what you liked and sometimes what you didn't like. And what happened to all that enthusiasm and all that passion and all that energy from the 60s is that, like all adolescents, everybody grew up, and the novelty of it disappeared. The people who cared in the 60s, who were truly passionate in their beliefs, stayed that way—

the activists and the leaders and the Tom Haydens of today. Those to whom it was a part of their growing up became adults and put it behind them in their past. When I was a child, I played with child's toys, now I'm an adult, I play with adults' toys. Adult's toys today are less caring and less involved, perhaps, than the kids' toys of the 60s were. Adult passions are security, an income in your old age, medical care, dental care, money for your kids for college. Those are adult cares, and they are not cares that require the world to change. If anything, they are cares that require the world to stay the same, so you can make plans. Someone defined life as something that happens to you while you're making other plans. But what happened to us in the 60s? Wavy once said, "The 90s are the 60s, only thirty years later." God knows what it's all going to be like in the future. You finish a decade and start labeling another one, and then you realize that the decade labels are not really accurate, because the 60s were not really the 60s. What the 60s were was from Dylan and the Beatles through the fall of Saigon, which was basically 1963 to 1975. That twelve-year period is the decade we think of as the 60s. But that, for better or worse, is the label that we're stuck with for the generation. The 70s were just a time of consolidation and the 80s a decade of hunkering down. The baby boom gets older. Everybody who was born after World War II is now trying to buy a house or security for their old age, and the new generation has yet to find its heroes.

I think we're going to find that in the next decade and 2000, it's going to be a real interesting time. The significance of all those zeros at the end of the year isn't going to be lost on anyone. Everyone will understand: "Ah-hah, it's the millennium." And we're going to be faced with all kinds of craziness, right and left.

Lisa: Well, kids have a lot of hope.

Carl: Yeah, kids think, *a)* they're never going to die, and *b)* that adults are fucked. That's the way people think when they're young, and I think they should. That's probably the way the world works.

Lisa: What do you think about children of the 60s who have now grown up?

Carl: Like most of our kids, you wish that they would remember the lessons of their childhood, and you can't pick and choose for them which lessons they will remember. You hope that they'll remember the unique and good part of the 60s: the caring, the altruism, the affection, the commonality of interest. That's what you hope they'll remember. But, at the same time, they're going to remember rip-offs and drug deals and I'm-for-me-first, and whoever had the high ground at Woodstock didn't get dirty. You hope for the good lessons. Kids always make up their own minds anyway.

PILAR LAW

Pilar is the oldest of my four children. I took her with me
everywhere when she was young because I didn't believe in
baby-sitters. We went to concerts, demonstrations, and to
Native American, Tibetan, Hindu, and Jewish ceremonies and
also traveled in the U.S. from coast to coast and to Guatemala
and back. She soaked it all in and then took off like a whirling
Dervish on her own. Pilar has become a master of many
trades in her own right. We interviewed her twice in 1989:
first, when we were shooting concertgoers and the backstage
child care by the Hog Farm at the Grateful Dead's Stanford
show in the South Bay of San Francisco, and again at the
Whole Earth Festival, which she co-directed at the University
of California Davis campus.

Lisa: Were you a Deadhead before you starting working for
them, or are you just doing it for a job?

Pilar: No, I started as a runner and I did it as a job, and then I
became a Deadhead. It took me fifteen, twenty concerts to

finally get the idea, but I got it.

Lisa: What's the idea?

Pilar: Oh, just how fun it is.

Lisa: So you only became a Deadhead afterward?

Pilar: Yeah, after listening to the songs and getting into the music. I like it.

Lisa: I guess you are used to big concerts and music.

Pilar: When I was two years old I was at Woodstock, and that has a lot to do with what I'm doing now. That was the beginning of an era of music production and big-scale concerts, and I was participating in that, my parents were participating in that, and now here I am, doing pretty much what they were doing at that time. I cover almost every aspect of a show—backstage ambiance, crowd control, the works.

Lisa: Tom and I were part of the 60s, and we were at Woodstock, and here you are at the Grateful Dead concert. What's the relationship?

Pilar: Well, you and dad were doing a lot of things during Woodstock: running backstage, running kitchens, dealing with freak-outs, teaching yoga, working in the stage crew—doing all sorts of things. And what I do is, I am the production secretary, and I coordinate all these things. I am in charge of the crews' hours, their payrolls, equipment that's needed during the shows, catering. I'm kind of like the central area where everybody feeds in information, and I kind of keep track of it all and distribute it out to the appropriate people. And I'm in charge of taking care of guest laminate passes, and workers and their laminates, and accommodations for the crew and for my bosses, and making sure that there is a volleyball for the volleyball games during the Dead shows—I mean, everything. Every little detail.

Lisa: Tom and I were into production, and now you find yourself sort of following in our footsteps?

Pilar: Well, it's not that I've consciously chosen to follow in your footsteps. It's sort of ironic that I wound up with this job. I mean, I was in college, and I was asked to go do security for a show one summer, and I went and wound up as a runner. And then, there I was, plopped in the middle of Bill Graham Presents, and I was amazed, 'cause in high school, that's all I ever heard: Bill Graham presents this, Bill Graham presents that, and here I was in it, having the opportunity to pursue it, so that's what I did. And so now it's come full circle. Now I realize I'm doing exactly what my father and mother were doing at my age, which is really interesting, you know? And it's encouraging for me, because I know that people my age have the potential to take a job like this and really expand on it and be able to do something with it in their lives.

Lisa: Has the way that you were raised in any way seemed to give you a different perspective from those of your peers, the kids you go to college with?

Pilar: Yeah, I think the way that I was raised definitely had a large influence on my life, in respect to a lot of the other people I'm around. I seem to have a more open view to all cultures, and all types of relationships, and ideas and foods, and all sorts of things around me. It's also given me a better understanding of my relationship to this earth and the people around me. I'm really open to a lot of things, because I wasn't raised in a strict religious environment, and I wasn't raised in one city, in one community. I've traveled around, I've seen a lot of people, met a lot of people, seen different lifestyles, and so now I feel I have a larger smorgasbord to choose from as far as my life style goes.

Lisa: Why do so many kids come to the Dead concerts? What's so popular about a Dead concert, do you think?

Pilar: Well, I have acquired the feeling for that, after listening to them for so long, because it's something that happens in the music. It's unlike any other kind of music that I've ever heard—ever. And there's something that happens in your body when you start listening to it, and you just start moving and you can move very freely, and that is then translated into this different kind of consciousness, this free consciousness, and people really like the show, and they really enjoy it—you can hear them.

Lisa: In the 60s, music became sort of a religion for the people. In other words, for people who couldn't handle didactic sorts of "you shalt this," and "you shalt not that," music offered a spiritual feeling as well. Is that what the Grateful Dead offer their audience?

Pilar: Yeah, I definitely think that a Grateful Dead show is really just experience. You come into this congregation of really psychedelic and colorful people, and you start moving with the music and you start having this experience that everybody who's at a Dead show can relate to, you know? Because they wouldn't be there if they couldn't participate in this full experience of the Grateful Dead and music. It's not just the music, it's the people, and it's the whole interaction and the movement within the whole place.

Lisa: Earlier you were speaking of the perspective you have obtained from moving around a lot, encountering a lot of different ethnic groups, many different types of people. Do you think that type of eclecticism or sense of community is something that the Dead also offer?

Pilar: Definitely. The Dead offer a sense of community, because the people who follow the Dead have a society within itself. It really is. And it's got its own religion—the music. And it's got its economy with the vendors, and it's got the families and the family feeling, and wherever you go you can find people you know because you've seen them for twenty years traveling around with the Dead. It's really an amazing society that travels all over the United States, all together, and the people have kids, and the kids grow up and they travel with them, and they've got their buses and . . .

Lisa: Does this sense of community lead to a happiness that can maybe spread out and become a model for others? Are you kind of reaching for . . .

Pilar: I don't think that it can. I don't think that it necessarily works. Because I think there's only so long that you can support yourself from hand to mouth every day and have kids and be able to support them. And then, what happens when, for instance in the Bay Area, they start shutting down the vending scene because it's getting out of hand, you know? Then what happens? There goes the economy.

Lisa: Do the Dead have an agenda—to bring people together, to make people aware?

Pilar: More and more, the Dead are emphasizing ecological-humanitarian awareness. For instance, the Frost shows they're donating for the Rex Foundation. They're becoming a focus to provide information for the followers, and they put the money that the followers pay towards good causes. During the shows now, they have the SEVA Foundation, Camp Winnarainbow, and Creating Our Futures, and all these booths that they allow within the shows that can hand out literature to the people. And when the Dead are announced on stage, there are little blurbs about what is going on, why they're having a benefit, who it's going to. The Grateful Dead care for their patrons, you know? They've got to take care of them, because they know their situation, and what is really wonderful—what I've been thinking a lot about lately—is that Bill Graham also has this bluecoat security who are trained especially for Grateful Dead, or they've trained themselves for Grateful Dead, for the Deadheads. They know how to take care of them. And it's not the scene where this is the band and these are the people, and you have to keep them separated, and you can't interact. They do interact—a lot. And they allow them to camp, and they do as much as they can for them within the limits of the city or state regulations—those sorts of things.

Lisa: Do you feel that you were sort of drafted into the army and then, as an adult, you've made this conscious choice yourself to maintain a commitment to that ideal?

Pilar: I don't see myself as being drafted into it, because I've always felt myself able to choose exactly what I wanted to do. And yes, it influenced the way I thought, and it has steered me in a lot of directions, but I haven't been coerced or forced into this situation. I don't feel that I have been put into this situation without really having a choice. To be a production secretary, especially at this age, is amazing to me. I do see myself sticking with it and building on it—to learn as much as I can from this kind of production experience. I'm interested in producing benefit concerts as a focus. Not only just as a music producer but as a benefit producer, let's say. So I'm learning all the skills that I can for that. I'm very aware of what I'm doing. And I'm very thankful.

* * *

Lisa: Your festival seems like a real success. What was your theme?

Pilar: The logo this year was inspired by our theme, "gaia"— the Greek word for Earth Goddess. We wanted to find a theme that was all-encompassing, that included the whole earth and all its people. All races, all genders. The person who designed the logo was one of our longtime performers, Carl Dyken from Clan Dyken. He painted an image of the earth with the swirls of the sky, as seen from space, forming the shape of an androgynous face. The image is encircled with hands both black and white representing the interconnectedness of all people. It contains the four directions and the female symbol, which is appropriate for the earth goddess and the theme.

Lisa: For you to be co-director of the Whole Earth Festival you must really feel strongly about what it means. Could you tell us what the event means to you?

Pilar: I feel very strongly about what it means because it has given me an amazing extended family. When I became involved in the festival, I found a home. I found people to be with all the time who understood the things I have been exposed to and learned growing up. The entire experience has been a growing one. It has taught me how to work with and manage people for a large-scale event.

Lisa: What was the basic concept of the original festival?

Pilar: The original concept was to create an art happening by and for the students. As students, we can educate each other and share our learning with the rest of the world. The festival is host to ideas that are brought in from everywhere. The Whole Earth Festival attracts amazing talent and beauty of spirit, and we work together to create a forum for more people to come and learn.

Lisa: What values that you learned as a child do you take with you today and use and apply?

Pilar: Having been raised on a farm with organic food, grown that food myself, picked it out of the garden, made my own salads—all that gives me a deep appreciation for life, for the earth, for what it can produce, and how important it is to be in tune with that in order to receive its benefits, to give back, and to receive. I have carried this theme with me throughout my life. I do not like polluting, wasting anything, or destroying the environment in any way. These days it's getting increasingly difficult not to have a negative impact on the environment. I do whatever I can to preserve as much as I can. I make it a conscious effort every day. I'm able to do that through school in getting involved in student groups that are ecologically aware and promoting those ideas. I've been involved in several things on campus—sustainable research, experimental college gardens, the Whole Earth Festival—and all these things have provided an opportunity for me to express myself just exactly as I feel and to perpetuate that within the schooling, within the people. And so I am forever grateful for the way I was raised, because I feel that I have an understanding of what needs to be done.

Lisa: What is it that you're attempting to change?

Pilar: Worldwide hunger, homelessness, apartheid, injustice, discrimination, ecological destruction. It's essential now that we move on, that we understand our influences and take action to improve. There are those children of the 60s who have been raised with an awareness and consciousness that they received from their parents and extended families. So the new generation of the children of the children of the 60s are becoming increasingly aware, and they are working within the system, pursuing careers in international relations, ecology, natural resources, environmental policy and planning —all positive and empowering. And they're using their education to go out

there and work with the politicians, work with the forerunners—they're becoming forerunners and working with
everybody to expand this awareness. And it's not by protest.
It's working throughout every aspect of the society in order to
get the message across.

Lisa: In the 60s we dropped out and started a new alternative
society. In the 80s and 90s, you are including yourself—
inclusion rather than exclusion.

Pilar: Yes, I think it's very important that we include ourselves
within the society, because we learned that no one will listen
to you unless you're trying to communicate with them. Instead
of trying to protest against them, saying, "No, you're wrong,
this is where it's at," we are saying, "OK, we understand
where you're coming from, but do you understand where
we're coming from? And do you understand that we need to
work together if we are all to win?" That's the important thing.
It can't just be a small section of society that goes around
saying, "We're going to help here, we're going to help there,
we're going to go here in the world and fix that or the other,"
because as soon as you fix it, it's destroyed again, you know?
It's going to take more than a small amount of people to teach
this entire world what needs to be done. So, if we can just
make everybody understand just a little bit, we've made a lot
of progress.

Lisa: Do you find that the generation of your parents is a
generation you can relate to more than, let's say, your parents'
generation related to their parents?

Pilar: I think that our generation can relate to our parents a lot
more easily. They were rebels, you know. I feel my parents
were rebels, and I feel a lot of my friends' parents were rebels.
And so, having been rebels, if we are now rebels, they can
understand where we're coming from; our need to have
understanding of ourselves and our future and do something
about it. Our parents set the precedent. They showed something had to be done about our situation, and they did something about it. Now we're carrying on that legacy. Other
generations were more interested in progress, industrialization,
in wealth, because there had been so much poverty before.

More materialistic views. We're becoming more holistic in our views.

Lisa: Here at the festival, the younger people and the older people are talking, and the younger people are listening. Old folks and new folks, Wavy Gravy and Paul Krassner, Timothy Leary, etc. Why did you do that?

Pilar: I brought these elders here because they have a message. They are the forerunners of a movement. They were of the generation that had to jump into the cold water and try to learn how to swim in it. We are a step ahead because of what they learned. Because we had someone to follow, some ideas to inspire us and some encouragement along the way, we are better off. We are more confident with our purpose, and it is because of people like Wavy Gravy, Paul Krassner, and Timothy Leary. That is why I have invited them here. They can continue to encourage us, and we can learn more from them. They have been through things we have yet to experience. And so it's good to listen to these people.

Lisa: What's the drug of the 90s?

Pilar: The drug of the 90s? Clean air! Oxygen. Breathe deeply. Relax. Do what you know is right and don't feel that you have to do what everybody expects you to do. You do what you know is right for being here now, for the future, for creating a better world to live in. That is my drug. I mean, there is nothing that makes me feel better than knowing that I have done something to help this planet and to help the people on it.

Lisa: I recently talked to a kid who said, "I'm jealous of the 60s because I want to make a statement." How would you make a statement today?

Pilar: I think the best way to make a statement is by example. Be the best person you can be and show others that kindness gets you what you need and is more effective than cruelty or judgment. "Basic human needs, basic human deeds . . . doing what comes naturally, down in the garden, deep down in the garden, the garden of your heart." Wavy Gravy writes the formula for my life. I was raised knowing the earth as my source, my teacher, and my companion. From the time I was a little girl learning how to plant my own vegetables, to being a woman participating in a visionary spirit that will help us survive the next millennium, I have received invaluable lessons through the wisdom of my parents and siblings and the simple philosophies of the 60s. Good food, clean water, shelter, love, family, children—the soul's fulfillment—these are the gifts we deserve to inherit and to pass on to future generations. The 60s taught us that we can reinvent community; they laid the foundation for designing a life that exists and is sustained by cooperating with nature. If we emulate nature, we experience interdependence with every participant. In my perfect world a child would be raised by a village of extended family and friends, and we would redirect the energy now being put into the quest for success and accumulation toward our families and backyards. We would grow our own food again and get to know our neighbors. With a strong center, we can all be ripples emanating confidence, security, love and happiness into the world around us. I find myself among people from all backgrounds, not only children of the 60s, working toward creating intentional, sustainable communities. This time around it's not about dropping out and rebelling against the establishment, it's about finding new and creative answers to old questions about survival: can we find arable land, pool our resources to create a sustainable living with the land, and can we help each other grow spiritually, emotionally, mentally and physically toward a future we all can enjoy. How can we foster foresight to treat the symptomatic strife of single parenting, disenfranchised youth, racism, homelessness, and war? My generation has learned, by inheriting the world we live in today, that we can't afford to make mistakes and clean up our mess later. If we are to be true to our love of life, then we need to be very creative and continue to use the tools forged in the 60s to expand our minds and learn to live.

VIOLA SPOLIN

Viola: We cannot approach the intuition until we are free of opinions, attitudes, prejudices, and judgments. The very act of seeking the moment, of being open to fellow players, produces a life-force, a flow, a regeneration for all who participate.

THANK YOU

I am grateful to be surrounded by people who are willing to indulge my fantasies and share with me their time and energy and good humor. This includes everyone on the crew who filmed the documentary with me and those who gave great advice and support along the way, including my four wonderful children: Pilar, Solar, Sunday, and Jesse Lee Law.

I want to thank all the people who are quoted in this book for allowing me to document their special memories, their wit, and their wisdom. You are all soldiers in the war of the liberation of consciousness.

Thank you, Tom Pope, for your unfaltering willingness to edit everything I write, no matter how large or small the project and no matter what time of day or night. Without you, this book might never have been finished.

Thank you, Paul Krassner, Dennis Hopper, and Graham Nash, for allowing me to add depth to your segments of the book by asking still more questions.

Thank you, Simone Ellis, for helping to write the jacket notes and for supporting my struggle to become a self-realized human being. You are one of the most inspiring souls I have ever met.

Thank you, Liz Rymland, for introducing me to Lumen, Inc. and Ronald Christ.

And many thanks to Ronald Christ and Dennis Dollens for realizing the timeliness of this project.

In memory of my dear and wonderfully
funny aunt, Annette Snodgrass, Viola
Spolin, Allen Ginsberg, Timothy Leary,
Jerry Garcia, Ron Thelin, Bill
Graham,William Burroughs, Del Close,
Jon Rothschild, Owen Orr, and all the
soldiers who fought and died in the
Vietnam War.

LISA LAW

Lisa Law is the 60s' quintessential photographer, with iconic photographs of Janis Joplin, Big Brother, Bob Dylan, Andy Warhol, Dennis Hopper, Allen Ginsberg, The Beatles, The Byrds, The Velvet Underground, Nico, and many more. She has also documented children of all races and indigenous people from New Mexico to Arizona, from Mexico and Guatemala to Peru.

Lisa's documentary, *Flashing on the Sixties*, won four major awards in film festivals and has since pleased millions of viewers on Cinemax The Discovery Channel, and PBS. Actor-director Dennis Hopper called *Flashing on the Sixties* "the most compelling, moving documentary of the 60s."

Lisa's film documentation of Woodstock has appeared in more than fifteen news programs and documentaries, and she's been in dozens of group and one-woman shows. Her photographs are now part of the permanent collection of the Smithsonian, and her one-woman show, "A Visual Journey, Photographs by Lisa Law 1964-1971," was seen at the Museum of American History, Washington, D.C. from October 1998 through March 1999.

Lisa lives and works in the house she built on a mesa in Northern New Mexico—whenever she isn't traveling and capturing images and words essential to the growth of the human spirit.

JACK-O-LANTERN

SUOP JACK .

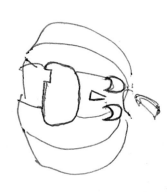